Blackstone's
Policing for the Special Constable

D1428743

Blackstone's Policing for the Special Constable

Second Edition

Edited by
Dr Bryn Caless

Contributors
Trish McCormack,
Barry Spruce and Robert Underwood

OXFORD
UNIVERSITY PRESS

OXFORD

UNIVERSITY PRESS

Great Clarendon Street, Oxford, OX2 6DP,
United Kingdom

Oxford University Press is a department of the University of Oxford.
It furthers the University's objective of excellence in research, scholarship,
and education by publishing worldwide. Oxford is a registered trade mark of
Oxford University Press in the UK and in certain other countries

© Oxford University Press 2013

The moral rights of the authors have been asserted

First Edition published in 2010
Second Edition published in 2013

Impression: 1

British Library Cataloguing in Publication Data

Data available

ISBN 978-0-19-967169-4

Printed in Great Britain by
CPI Group (UK) Ltd, Croydon, CR0 4YY

Foreword

The Special Constabulary continues to grow from strength to strength both in terms of the number of officers and the quality of the service they deliver to the public. This is a unique form of voluntary effort. Special Constables have the same powers as full time regular officers and have the same expectations from the public. As with all police officers their standards of integrity, honesty and professionalism must be beyond question. Policing is ever more complex due to the changing nature of crime and criminality and the expertise required to protect the public and provide the best possible service. It is crucial that Special Constables understand their powers and the ways they can work with local people and other agencies to make areas safer. They need to appreciate the fundamental ethos of British policing as laid down by Sir Robert Peel: policing by consent using the minimum of force. Peel also famously said 'the police are the people and the people are the police'. The fact that ordinary members of the public can step forward to become volunteer Special Constables is a powerful reinforcement of that basic ethos. There are always ideas on how Special Constables can be used in specialist areas, but the core role of Specials in local neighbourhood policing will always be getting to know local people and crucially local criminals, dealing with local issues of crime and anti-social behaviour and solving problems rather than just reacting to them. Policing will continue to adopt new methods, new equipment and new technology but the most important support to any police officer is their mouth, their power of communication, their ability to calm down situations and to calm down people, their restraint, their patience and their good humour. There is much good advice, information and knowledge in this second edition but this has to be built on a foundation of a commitment to the core values of policing and the dedication to protect and serve the public.

Sir Peter Fahy
Chief Constable
Greater Manchester Police

Acknowledgements

The Editor wishes particularly to thank:

Robin and **Sarah Bryant** for permission to adapt material from their definitive *Blackstone's Handbook for Policing Students* (2013, Oxford: Oxford University Press), and for friendship over many years;

Peter Daniell, Law Commissioning Editor of Oxford University Press—always encouraging, always cheerful, always ready with difficult deadlines; **Lucy Alexander** for chasing me to complete on time and for her help with reformatting; **Sally Pelling-Deeves**, Production Editor, for her professional approach and for keeping me focused, and **Joy Ruskin-Tompkins** for her excellent work in editing the material;

The National Archives, incorporating the Open Government Licence, for permission to quote extensively from government documents under C2007000322;

Barry Spruce, Trish McCormack and **Bob Underwood** for all their hard work in meeting deadlines (and not sighing too audibly when my emails had no attachments ...) and for being a knowledgeable and productive writing team;

Love and huge thanks to **Clare**, my forbearing wife, and **Maddy**, my youngest daughter, for all they had to put up with when deadlines loomed and tempers shortened, and to the rest of the family too: **Helen** and **Wez**, **Sally** and **Johnny**, and **Kit** and **Meghna**.

Robert (Bob) Underwood: My thanks go to **Robin** and **Sarah Bryant** and fellow contributors to the *Blackstone's Handbook for Policing Students* for permitting me to adapt material from that publication. Without their support, my contribution to this book would have been so much more difficult. I would also like to thank my family for their ongoing and continued support for this and other writing projects and for remaining so incredibly patient whilst I hide away from them to work endlessly on my beleaguered laptop.

Barry Spruce would like to thank all his colleagues in the **Partnerships & Communities** department at Kent Police, including those within the Special Constabulary. Special thanks must go to **Emma, Phoebe, Joseph,** and **Ethan**.

Trish McCormack thanks husband **Andy** for his patience during time spent on the book.

Chapter 3:
Some of the elements of Chapter 3 are adapted and updated from the chapter (4) on 'National Occupational Standards and Behavioural Competences' in Caless, B. (ed.), Bryant, R., Spruce, B. and Underwood, R., *Blackstone's PCSO Handbook,* 2nd edn. (2010, Oxford: Oxford University Press), and reproduced with the Editor's kind permission.

Contents

Contents

List of Abbreviations

ABH	actual bodily harm
ACPO	Association of Chief Police Officers
AOBH	assault occasioning bodily harm
ASB	anti-social behaviour
ASCC	Area Special Constabulary Coordinator
ASP	Armament Systems and Procedures (manufacturer's name for police extendable baton)
BCS	British Crime Surveys
BCU	Basic Command Unit
CAP	common approach path (to crime scene)
CBL	computer-based learning
CBT	Compulsory Basic Training
CDRP	Crime and Disorder Reduction Partnership (*see* CSP)
CHIS	Covert Human Intelligence Source
CJS	criminal justice system
CJU	Criminal Justice Unit
CPR	cardio-pulmonary resuscitation
CPS	*see* PPS
CSAS	Community Safety Accreditation Scheme
CSI	crime scene investigator
CSP	Community Safety Partnership; new name for CDRP (*see* earlier)
CT	counter-terrorism
DNA	deoxyribonucleic acid
DPP	Director of Public Prosecutions
EFPN	endorsable fixed-penalty notice
EVA	Environmental Visual Audit
FOA	first officer attending (scene of possible crime)
FPN	Fixed Penalty Notice
GBH	grievous bodily harm
HMIC	Her Majesty's Inspectorate of Constabulary
IDENT-1	UK-wide automated fingerprint analysis system
IL4SC	Initial Learning for the Special Constabulary, the syllabus outline for the national learning programme on entry
IPCC	Independent Police Complaints Commission

JP	Justice of the Peace, lay magistrate
LCN	Low Copy Number DNA analysis
LPG	Laws, Policies and Guidance
MAPPA	Multi-Agency Public Protection Arrangements
NABIS	National Ballistics Intelligence Service
NCALT	National Centre for Applied Learning Technologies
NDNAD	National DNA Database
NEFPN	non-endorsable fixed-penalty notice
NIM	National Intelligence Model
NIP	Notice of Intended Prosecution
NOS	National Occupational Standards
NPIA	former National Policing Improvement Agency quango
NPT	Neighbourhood Policing Team
OST/PST	Officer/Personal Safety Training
PAC	Police Action Checklist
PACE Act 1984	Police and Criminal Evidence Act 1984
PACT	Partners and Communities Together
PAVA	synthetic pepper spray
PCC	Police and Crime Commissioner, the single elected individual who replaced police authorities in late 2012 and who can 'hire and fire' Chief Constables
PCSO	Police Community Support Officer
PDP	Personal Development Profile
PIP	Professionalising the Investigative Process
PIR	Police Initial Recruitment
PNB	pocket notebook
PNC	Police National Computer
PND	Penalty Notice for Disorder
PNLD	Police National Legal Database
PPE	personal protective equipment
PPS	Public Prosecution Service (formerly CPS, Crown Prosecution Service)
PR	personal radio
PSNI	Police Service of Northern Ireland
PSV	Police Support Volunteer
QC	Queen's Counsel, a senior barrister
RV	rendezvous point (outside crime scene)

SC	Special Constable
SOCA	Serious and Organised Crime Agency now subsumed into National Crime Agency (NCA)
STR	Short Tandem Repeat DNA profiling
TWOC	taking [a conveyance] without the owner's consent
URN	Unique Reference Number
VDRS	Vehicle Defect Rectification Scheme
VOSA	Vehicle & Operator Services Agency

Special Features

The book has been written from a Special's point of view in order to help you access more easily the information contained within it. Each chapter is laid out in broadly the same manner and contains all or some of the following features:

Key point box

Where it has been felt appropriate to reinforce an important or pertinent point which has been covered within the text of the chapters, a key point box has been included to reinforce the information.

Flow charts

Several chapters include flow charts to support points made within the text. Flow charts often make the interpretation of sometimes-complicated information much easier to understand.

Case study box

Included in relevant chapters are scenario boxes that highlight the provision of good practice in certain areas. Readers are asked to consider how these scenarios compare with activities that occur within their own areas.

Further Reading

At the conclusion of each chapter, other available publications have been listed. Readers are encouraged to explore these publications in order to reinforce the information and knowledge already laid out in the work.

Test boxes

Short tests are presented at the end of each substantive section, reflecting standard police training practice in a 'knowledge-check'. A self-test should be carried out honestly, checking your answers against those provided at the end of the book. Completing these will show you how much you have absorbed and understood.

Introduction

This book is designed primarily for the Special Constable and nearly all the case studies, tasks and examples used in it are related to or drawn from the experiences of being a volunteer police officer. That is not to say that it cannot be read with profit by others in the policing family such as Police Community Support Officers (PCSOs), parish wardens and community officers and other members of local partnerships, neighbourhood policing teams and regular police officers. Indeed, the book has much to offer the student of policing whether or not s/he is actually engaged in the practice. It aspires to be as up to date as possible, subject to the continuous flux and change that surrounds modern policing in England and Wales. Actually, it is the peripheries that change; policing itself changes very little.

Sir Richard Mayne, the first Commissioner of the 'New Police' for the metropolis of London wrote this in 1829:

> The primary object of an efficient police is the prevention of crime: the next that of detection and punishment of offenders if crime is committed. To these ends all the efforts of police must be directed. The protection of life and property, the preservation of public tranquillity, and the absence of crime, will alone prove whether those efforts have been successful and whether the objects for which the police were appointed have been attained.

'The prevention of crime', the 'detection and punishment of offenders', 'protection of life and property', 'the preservation of public tranquillity' (keeping the peace) 'and the absence of crime' are all things that are as resonant now as when Mayne wrote them more than 180 years ago. We might omit the *'punishment of offenders'* as this is more to do with the courts than with the police, and substitute *'bringing to justice'* to capture a more modern role and meaning. The essential point is that Mayne's list of police objectives preoccupies the Special Constable on duty today every bit as much as it occupied the first 'blue locusts' to patrol in London in 1830.

What is a Special Constable?

Task

Make a list of the characteristics of a Special Constable.

Ours is not meant to be a model answer, but we shall assume that your list was something like this:

KEY POINT

Characteristics of a Special Constable:

- Volunteer
- Unpaid (though some forces do pay a retainer or 'bounty' and it is a subject of continuing debate whether or not Specials should be paid a form of salary based on hours worked)
- Part time
- Is a warrant-holder under the Crown
- Has the same powers as a regular police officer
- Undergoes a comprehensive training programme

- Does many of the things that a regular police officer would do
- May have held other full- or part-time employment, or another full- or part-time occupation (such as student)
- Agrees to minimum of four hours a week or 16 hours a month of unpaid duty
- Is drawn from the community
- Understands local issues
- Can identify the local leaders
- Knows what concerns local people
- Is enthusiastic, willing, committed and possessed of a strong sense of public duty and obligation

You might not have included that last bullet point. We have highlighted this because, throughout our work for this book, we have been continually impressed by how much Special Constables actually *do* in service across England and Wales, and how their enthusiasm for duty, their pleasure in serving as police officers and their sense of social obligation, of 'putting something back', is immense. It is impressive to note that Special Constables volunteer for roads traffic policing in Devon and Cornwall, for example, or that they are engaged closely in changing the attitudes of bored youths in Cheshire or that they created (for a limited period because of costs) a 'Task Force' that intervened in local instances of anti-social behaviour in Kent.

Successive governments have encouraged increases in the numbers of Special Constables from about 15,000 five years ago to a target of 25,000 for 2015. The police service can see a percentage in having more police officers available whose costs are minimal. It evidently thinks that Special Constables are worth it. So do we.

The National Strategy for the Special Constabulary

The National Strategy for the Special Constabulary is a high-level plan for where the Special Constabulary is going from 2011 to 2016. Its 'vision' is expressed like this:

KEY POINT

The Special Constabulary is embedded within the police service providing efficient and effective policing to support achievement of force priorities. It is seen as an attractive volunteering opportunity for members of the public to contribute to policing and community safety.

(*Special Constabulary National Strategy 2011–2016*, ACPO, 2011)

The twin elements of 'embedding' the Special Constabulary within the police service and the nature of volunteering are expressed clearly here, with the usual formulaic phrase of 'effective and efficient policing' (on which HM Inspectorate has always assessed forces), allied to support for force priorities. The 'vision' is as interesting in what it leaves out as much as in what it expresses. Of particular interest is the assumption that police volunteers are very much part of the police service's own vision of the future and that it is implicit that the Special Constabulary should be an integrated component of that service delivery. It is quite a journey from parking cars at village fetes.

> ### DISCUSSION POINT
>
> What do you think of the 'vision'? Does it express what you do and what you feel about what you do? If it does not, what else should the 'vision' include? Do you find such statements useful as a focus?

The other element of note is the reference to 'members of the public' taking up 'an attractive volunteering opportunity', which sits with the Big Society preoccupations of the current government and also echoes the Peelian principle that *the public are the police and the police are the public*. In other words, policing is what communities ought to do for themselves. The strategic 'vision' for the Special Constabulary produces three 'core deliverables', which are:

1. The Special Constabulary delivers policing in support of force priorities
2. Delivery of policing and community safety is enhanced by the active citizenship nature of the Special Constabulary
3. The Special Constabulary is effectively led

These are further expanded to encompass the skills and knowledge brought to bear on policing by the Special Constabulary (often enhancing those of the regular force, for example in business and commerce, or IT), the 'active citizenship nature' found in the Specials and continuous improvement in what is delivered to communities, through good practice and 'encouraging innovation'. These are dynamic and progressive factors, underlining the integration of the Special Constabulary within policing—particularly in neighbourhood policing—and the value which the volunteers add to policing as a whole. All this is designed to produce Special Constables who are '*forward looking, engaged, empowered, capable, accountable, understand their contribution and that of others.*'

It is worth noting that individual police forces are quite often at minor variance from the norm in the police service (for example, in the matter of what make of vehicles or computer equipment a force uses), so it is not a surprise that the Special Constabulary should also show variation or individuality from force to force. The point is that, on all key *strategic* issues, there is national agreement. People often say that they join the Special Constabulary intending to apply to be a regular police officer in time: during the 12 months to 31 March 2012, **16.1** per cent of police officer joiners were previously Special Constables. This suggests that, for a substantial minority, the Specials serve as a way into the regular force. Of course, to the force itself, taking on a fully trained, warrant-holding officer is preferable to a raw recruit who still requires training and experience. When we examine how Special Constables can be analysed in terms of gender and ethnic minority status, we find that the often-quoted adage that *Special Constables are drawn directly from the communities they serve*, is true.

The upshot of the numbers game is that there must now be a determined campaign to attract new people to join the Special Constabulary. Regional Leads for the Special Constabulary have been appointed to help to coordinate recruitment drives. We support any attempt to increase Special Constabulary numbers, provided there is no dilution of skills or enthusiasm for the role. Special Constables have told us that they volunteer in order to be stretched and tested, not to be bored and resentful in 'nothing jobs'.

Gender and Minority Ethnic Proportions

There were 20,343 Special Constables on 31 March 2012, 10.4 per cent or 1,922 more than the previous year. This follows an 18.8 per cent increase in the year to March 2011. Females accounted for 31.0 per cent of Special Constables, a higher proportion than for regular police officers. The 11.3 per cent of Special Constables who were 'Minority Ethnic' was also higher than the proportion among regular police officers. The Metropolitan Police had the highest proportion of Minority Ethnic Special Constables (27.9 per cent), followed by West Midlands (19.7 per cent) and Leicestershire (13.7 per cent).

In the year to 31 March 2012, 6,263 Special Constables joined the Special Constabulary and 3,983 left. The wastage rate increased to 19.6 per cent in the year to 31 March 2012, from 16.6 per cent in the year to 31 March 2011 (see Dhani, A. (2012), *Police Service Strength England and Wales, 31 March 2012*, HOSB 09/12; available at <http://www.homeoffice.gov.uk/publications/science-research-statistics/research-statistics/police-research/hosb0912/hosb0912?view=Binary>; accessed 20 August 2012).

What we may conclude from this is that more people are becoming Special Constables (up from about 15,000 five years ago when we researched the data for our first edition), but that more numerically are leaving too (nearly half of those who join). This represents a net increase, of course, and some departures from the Special Constabulary are accounted for in joining the police as regular officers, but more needs to be done to retain Special Constables generally and it is incumbent on managers, supervisors and forces to ensure that the Special experience is a rewarding one.

How to Use This Book

We don't expect you to read this book as you would a novel, starting at the beginning and reading in sequence through to the end. Riveting though our prose style is, we think you are more likely to dip into sections as you need them or as you want to remind yourself about the components of a law, or a power or a procedure. To help you to do this, we have created within each chapter a series of stand-alone sections distinguished by numbered headings. Each of the major headings is glossed in the Index, so you can look up 'Neighbourhood Policing', for example, in a number of ways: as related to a neighbourhood or community (3.4), as part of a Special Constable's deployment (1.4, 2.9, 3.3) or as a Neighbourhood Policing Team (3.8). Additionally, other references to neighbourhood policing are located under this generic heading in the Index.

A new feature for this second edition of the book is that we test you at the end of each substantive section. This is not for our benefit, but for yours. It reflects standard police training practice in the 'knowledge-check'. An honest self-test, checking your answers against those we provide at the end of the book, will show you how much you have absorbed and understood. Throughout the book, we highlight important things in shaded boxes, we pick out and display important definitions and we ask you to think for yourself at certain key 'Task' or 'Discussion' points, mindful that our readers could equally be (1) someone thinking about joining the Special Constabulary, (2) someone who has just joined or (3) a seasoned and experienced Special Constable who nonetheless wants to brush up his/her knowledge or recall of some aspect of policing. We cater for all.

However, it is worth noting that this is not just a reference book, nor a compendium of Special Constables' duties; it is much more than that. The book gives **a context to policing** as a concept as well as to what is involved in being a police officer in the 21st century. It introduces discussions, research, controversies and disagreements which may not always be evident to those outside policing, as well as looking at matters which dominate (and divide) criminal justice thinking.

Further Reading and helpful sources of information

Although this book is comprehensive and provides a full briefing and detailed information about initial learning for Special Constables, we understand that it cannot do absolutely everything, given the publishing constraints on us. There are more specialist publications about specific aspects of policing or the law. What we want to do here is suggest some which might be useful to you and which you could consult with profit:

Blackstone's Handbook for Policing Students (2013, Oxford: Oxford University Press), edited by Robin Bryant and Sarah Bryant, with Sofia Graça, Kevin Lawton-Barrett, Martin O'Neill, Stephen Tong, Robert Underwood and Dominic Wood.

Now in its seventh edition, this is edited by Robin and Sarah Bryant, and has a changing posse of contributing authors. The *BHPS* is a comprehensive introduction to policing in all its variety. However, it is designed primarily for the regular student police officer. It does not cater specifically for the Special Constable, but we make extensive reference to it throughout this book and, along with many others, we are indebted to its huge spread and detail.

Other useful reference and 'context' books include:

ACPO/NPIA, *Practice Advice on Professionalising the Business of Neighbourhood Policing* (2006, Wyboston: National Centre for Policing Excellence, part of NPIA), available from: <http://cfnp.npia.police.uk/files/np_neighbourhoodpolicin.pdf>.

This covers most of the aspects of neighbourhood policing in which most Special Constables (but not all) will find themselves working at some point in their careers. It is well worth dipping into to refresh your recall of the aims and components of neighbourhood policing.

Blackstone's Police Operational Handbook: Law (2013, Oxford: Oxford University Press) edited by Ian Bridges and Fraser Sampson (Police National Legal Database).

This detailed reference book is intended for those in the criminal justice system (but particularly police officers, Special Constables and PCSOs) who have *to interpret and apply* the criminal law. The Police National Legal Database (PNLD) is an ACPO-managed (not-for-profit) organisation which is subscribed to by all police forces, the Public Prosecution Service (previously the Crown Prosecution Service, or CPS), and others in the criminal justice system. We strongly recommend that Special Constables refer to this excellent book for detail on the criminal law.

Blackstone's PCSO Handbook, 2nd edn. (2010, Oxford: Oxford University Press), edited by Bryn Caless, with Robin Bryant, Barry Spruce and Robert Underwood.

Designed primarily for PCSOs and members of neighbourhood policing teams, this Handbook deals comprehensively with communities, neighbourhoods, engagement with citizens and dealing with minor crimes, nuisance, infringement of by-laws, anti-social behaviour, vandalism and criminal damage as well as giving a valuable context to policing for the newest member of the extended policing family. It is helpful to the Special Constable too, particularly in relation to engagement with communities, local nuisance and anti-social behaviour.

Going to Court (2006, Oxford: Oxford University Press), Brian Fitzpatrick, with Christopher Menzies and Rob Hunter.

This is a very good review or introduction—depending on whether you are experienced or a new joiner—for Special Constables who are to attend court. It gives considerable detail on how courts are organised and how evidence is given.

Blackstone's Police Operational Handbook: Practice and Procedure, 2nd edn. (2013, Oxford: Oxford University Press), edited by Clive Harfield.

This has a complete eight-chapter section—Part 3, *Neighbourhood Policing*—which was written by Bryn Caless and Barry Spruce to give a context for neighbourhood policing, and additionally 'considers its principles, parts and practices'. It is the most comprehensive published treatment of neighbourhood policing available anywhere at the moment.

A National Strategy for the Special Constabulary, 2011–2016 (London: ACPO), available as a PDF.

As we note earlier and throughout this book, this is a seminal document for the Special Constabulary, since it sets out directions and deployments which can support regular policing activities. It is very much the Special Constabulary's own document, but it is of general interest too.

Handbook of Crime Prevention and Community Safety (2005, Cullompton: Willan Publishing), edited by Nick Tilley.

Nick Tilley is a prominent academic commentator on the police and here he edits a range of contributions from different writers, on the themes of crime prevention, crime reduction and a community's sense of safety. It has some excellent ideas for initiatives in local crime prevention, not least in 'designing-out crime' as long-term solutions to blighted urban areas.

It is worth noting who the major stakeholders in the Special Constabulary are:

The Home Office
The Justice Ministry
The Association of Chief Police Officers (ACPO)
HM Inspectorate of Constabulary (HMIC)
The Police Federation
Police Crime Commissioners

There are others, as well as interested parties from volunteering organisations and individual police forces, many of whom we shall refer to or cite in the rest of the book. What may be concluded from the list shown here is that the leading police organisations and the principal Departments of State support and endorse the work done for and through the Special Constabulary.

Being Special

1.1 Introduction: 'A Manifest Sign'

The Special Constabulary is a volunteer body designed to assist the regular police, drawn mainly from the communities served by each force. Special Constables perform constabulary duties and exercise constabulary powers under the supervision of, and supported by, regular officers. They are expected to achieve and maintain a level of proficiency which will enable them to assist regular officers in solving local policing problems, and thereby to enhance the overall contribution and effectiveness of their local police force. *They are a manifest sign of partnership between the police and the public.* [Emphasis added]

(*Report of the Working Group on the Special Constabulary in England and Wales 1995–96*)

Some of the descriptions of the Special Constabulary in the extract quoted no longer apply or are slightly misleading. For example, the idea of Special Constables being always 'under the supervision of . . . regular officers' is only true some of the time in some forces. It does not hold in all circumstances; and we are aware of many forces whose response/patrol function at weekends is made credible only by Special Constables working alone or in teams. What is demonstrably still true, however, is that the 'volunteer body' supports the regular police and is 'drawn . . . from the communities'. Above all, that is the primary characteristic of Special Constables expressed in the sentence we have highlighted:

They are a manifest sign of partnership between the police and the public

and this has never been more important than it is now. It has almost become a cliché to say that, pre-eminently, the Special Constable is a **citizen police officer**. Of course, so is the regular officer, but payment to a police officer for policing and security is relatively new (from 1830 or thereabouts), whilst *citizen police service from the community for the community, freely offered*, is ages old.

The salient characteristic of the Special Constabulary is precisely that it does its policing from a sense of community; it is policing by *volunteers* who want to perform a duty as citizens for the greater good. No one coerced them into deciding that this was what they wanted to do for society.

KEY POINT

Someone becomes a Special Constable as a result of: a personal decision, voluntarily arrived at, in full recognition of the obligations that such office carries and the restriction which will be placed upon individual freedom, [which] has, as its outcome, service to the people.

This is a selfless and sociable act, but all such acts need a context if we are to understand them properly. The uniqueness of the Special Constabulary, and its place in the context of criminal justice, is what this chapter (and, indeed, this book) is about.

1.2 **On Volunteers and Volunteering**

In February 2008, the Special Constabulary took part in the first ever national Police Support Volunteers (PSV) Conference, under the auspices of the NPIA. One of the guest speakers was Baroness Julia Neuberger, who had overseen a 2008 review of volunteering in the criminal justice system. She said this at the conference, when referring to police volunteering:

> Community ownership of policing services is absolutely critical and I don't think you can do it without volunteers.
>
> (*Specials*, March 2008: 3)

It is necessary, of course, to note that PSVs include more groups than solely the Special Constabulary, but the principle addressed by Baroness Neuberger applies precisely to the processes that we have been examining here. In a real sense, the 'citizen police force' envisaged by Sir Robert Peel is exemplified in the Special Constabulary. Or, as the Chief Constable of Greater Manchester Police (and writer of our Foreword), Sir Peter Fahy, ACPO Lead for the Special Constabulary, remarked:

> You are [in the Special Constabulary] because of the personal right of every local citizen to exercise powers as a constable.
>
> (*Specials*, May 2008: 9)

1.3 **The Employer**

The other side of the volunteering equation for the Special Constable is the role of the employer. The use of the term 'equation' suggests a mathematical dimension, but actually, the relationship is more triangular than linear, as shown in Figure 1.1:

Figure 1.1 Relationship between employer, Special Constable and police force

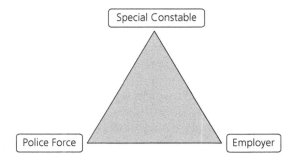

The Special Constable volunteer is usually employed at something else, and his/her commitment to the police impinges in some ways on that normal, full-time, paid employment, and upon the employer. It is therefore preferable always to engage the Special Constable's employer in the process of volunteering: at the very least the employer should be aware of activities which might affect the employee's activities at work. Normally, though, both the police force and the Special Constable would seek ways in which the employer can be more actively involved.

1.4 The Extended Police Family

Consider Figure 1.2:

Figure 1.2: The 'Mixed Economy' model of the extended police family

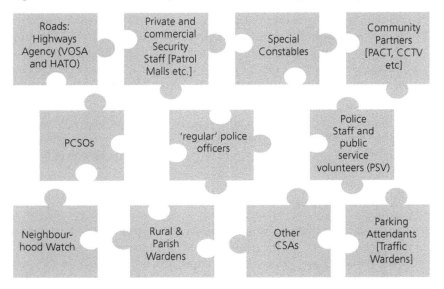

Source: adapted from model in Caless (ed.), 2010: 553

This jigsaw diagram represents the relationship between the various organisations that make up the '**Extended Policing Family**'. However, Figure 1.2 is not definitive because each police force will have other organisations that they bring into this 'family' to deal with specific and localised problems. Furthermore, the flexibility of these relationships will mean that some agencies move in and out of this arrangement in an informal and fluid way. Do not confuse this concept with 'partnership'. Although many of the Extended Policing Family operate within partnerships, the term as used by the police tends to indicate a more formalised arrangement, usually with organisations outside the law-enforcement family such as the Fire and Rescue Service or local authority departments. We're sorry if all this sounds convoluted: practice varies widely between police forces and we are merely trying to describe a relationship that may have infinite tiny variables.

1.4.1 **Extended Policing Family—three elements**

We will look at three members of the Extended Policing Family to demonstrate the relationship they have with the Special Constabulary, and suggest to you that Neighbourhood Watch is another example of the growing Extended Policing Family.

1.4.1.1 **Police Community Support Officer (PCSO)**

One significant development within the Extended Policing Family was the introduction of the PCSO by the Police Reform Act 2002. In much the same way that auxiliary nurses and teaching assistants were seen as somehow subversive of the natural order in the NHS and schools, so the PCSO proved to be a contentious political issue at first. Opposition to the PCSO came principally from the Police Federation which described them and their role in the pejorative phrase 'numties in yellow jackets' (see Caless, 2007; Caless (ed.), 2010). However in many communities, particularly those in rural locations, or those where the police presence had previously been sporadic, *the PCSO was welcomed as the visible personification of reassurance patrolling.* Most of the 16,000 PCSOs currently employed have become a very public representation of the police's commitment to Neighbourhood Policing and in many cases PCSOs have been the first police to respond to low-level incidents and anti-social behaviour.

1.4.1.2 **PCSO role definition**

It was not until 2008, six years after their introduction, that there was an attempt to define what PCSOs do. Because there are many regional and force 'variants' in both deployment and function, the PCSO role is not easy to pin down. NPIA's definition, which expressed some of this elasticity, depicted a PCSO who is integrated into a Neighbourhood Policing Team (normally geographic but could be for a defined community of interest, for example Safer Transport teams) or deployed directly to support Neighbourhood Policing Teams in their neighbourhoods. In both these cases, the PCSOs should spend the majority of their time within neighbourhoods and not be office/police station-based and/or undertaking administrative roles.

PCSOs should:

- Undertake public facing non-confrontational duties in uniform
- Be visible in the communities on foot or cycle patrol (vehicle if rural community)
- Deal with anti-social behaviour (ASB), low-level crime and incidents, local problems/priorities and quality of life issues
- Support and improve service to victims and vulnerable people
- Conduct engagement and problem-solving activity.

(Adapted from NPIA, 2008)

5

DISCUSSION POINT

Where a Special Constable works with a PCSO, in what ways can you see that this will ensure adherence to this role specification?

1.4.1.3 **PCSO powers**

To further complicate the PCSOs' position, their powers are divided between standard and non-standard (or 'discretionary'). The first are powers that all PCSOs across England and Wales have, although some will seldom be used, whilst the second are those that can be 'designated' (applied or granted) at the discretion of each Chief Constable. This has created a contradictory and inconsistent system under which a PCSO in Manchester may function in a very different way from, and even make use of different sets of powers to, a PCSO in Norwich. There has been some recent movement within the Home Office to standardise PCSO powers but this will require legislative change and therefore may take some time, and will entail the novel prospect of all Chief Constables agreeing to lose their discretionary input to the powers a PCSO has and therefore what a PCSO does or does not do. In the context of austerity in police budgets, there have been suggestions, notably from the Police Federation, that PCSOs be abolished. Given their continued popularity with the public, it is unlikely that the role will completely disappear, though, like regular policing itself, recruitment may stall. That in its turn will place even greater emphasis on the need to recruit more Special Constables to fill the inevitable Neighbourhood Policing team gaps.

1.4.1.4 **Police Service Volunteers (PSVs)**

More recent additions to the Extended Policing Family are PSVs, which we must note are *distinct in kind and degree from the more specialist and professional volunteering that the Special Constabulary does*. PSVs provide a 'gift' of time and commitment to the police in their community. A survey by the then NPIA revealed that 32 of the 43 'home' police forces have volunteer programmes with over 10,000 people actively volunteering. Most volunteers, particularly those working in police stations, are vetted and undergo an interview and/or training process. Often the force will have a Volunteer Coordinator to oversee the programme and, in particular, to work closely with the unions and staff associations to ensure that the volunteers are not taking the place of paid employees.

1.4.1.5 **PSV roles**

These are some of the roles that PSVs perform across police forces in England and Wales:

- Administrative help in Neighbourhood Policing Teams
- Mystery shoppers

- Puppy walkers
- Maintaining memorial gardens
- Opening 'satellite' front counters in small towns and villages
- Organising public meetings such as PACT (Partners And Communities Together)
- Data input, for example survey responses
- Washing police cars
- Emergency exercise role-players
- Search and rescue teams
- Role-players for training purposes
- Assisting at events.

The demographic profile of the PSV is different from those of both the regular police and the Special Constabulary, and brings considerable diversity to the policing family: 57 per cent are female, 25 per cent are over the age of 65 and nearly 8 per cent are from minority ethnic communities, whilst 1.5 per cent describe themselves as having a disability (see <http://www.npia.police.uk/en/docs/police_support_volunteer_business_plan.pdf>; accessed 3 October 2012).

DISCUSSION POINT

Where a Special Constable works with a PSV, in what ways can you see that this will enhance the work of volunteers?

1.4.1.6 Community Safety Accreditation Scheme (CSAS)

The CSAS derives from the Police Reform Act 2002 and allows Chief Constables to 'accredit' employees of many organisations, both public and private, who work in the field of community safety. Such employees are known, rather stodgily, as 'Accredited Persons' and must display a standard 'accreditation badge' as part of any uniform. In practice, a Chief Constable will accredit employees only with those powers that help community safety; it is not a 'pick and mix' menu. A Home Office audit in 2010 showed that 26 forces had accreditation schemes in place, involving 95 approved organisations and 2,229 accredited persons (<http://www.npia.police.uk/en/docs/police_support_volunteer_business_plan.pdf>; accessed 13 November 2012).

1.4.1.7 CSAS example

In 33 police forces in England and Wales the Vehicle & Operator Services Agency (VOSA) has been accredited with the power to stop vehicles for the purpose of conducting on-the-spot checks, such as those to ascertain vehicle roadworthiness. Previously the police actually had to stop vehicles with VOSA personnel doing the subsequent checks, so by accrediting and training VOSA to do the stopping as well as the checks, the police have freed up resources to concentrate on other targets.

1.4.1.8 **Advantages of CSAS**

For the police, the CSAS allows an innovative extension of community safety through partnerships with the public and private sectors. All 'accredited persons' are vetted and trained in their new powers by the police themselves, so some control is maintained, and when 'accredited persons' are on the streets, there is enhanced coverage at a time of scant resources. It is not surprising that the police find advantage in deploying others in non-confrontational, but visible (and therefore reassuring) roles. One commentator noted that

> Accreditation represents a form of arm's length governance through which the police aim to govern at a distance... It potentially allows a response to public demand for high-visibility reassurance policing without the cost.
>
> (Crawford, 2006: 159)

1.4.1.9 **Disadvantages of CSAS**

While the benefits to the police of extending their community safety remit through partnership with well-placed organisations are evident, there is a concomitant risk in managing those involved in policing who are not the police, do not have police powers and have not had the benefit of extensive police training. Furthermore, some sections in the national press have highlighted what they see as an increase in 'irregulars', whom they caricature as nosy vigilantes, extending state control into all areas of life. Typical would be this headline: 'State recruits an army of snoopers with police-style powers' (*Daily Mail*, 26 May 2009).

DISCUSSION POINT

Check what accredited persons are working with your force and what roles they occupy. (Note that from 2010, the Home Office no longer supplies national data on CSAS ('to reduce the bureaucratic burden').) Where a Special Constable works with 'accredited persons', in what ways can you see that this will enhance the Special Constable's job role?

1.4.2 **The Special Constabulary and the Extended Policing Family**

In many publications, the Special Constabulary is cited separately in a diagram or description of the Extended Policing Family. However, the Special Constabulary could argue that it is part of the 'inner family circle' by virtue of length of service. Such arguments, whilst semantically correct, fail to understand the concept of the Extended Policing Family, which is not about past history but about present-day pluralisation of policing. 'Policing' is no longer the sole preserve of paid, regular, warranted officers. The systematic development of auxiliary civilian officers with limited powers (PCSOs) and volunteers (SC and PSV) has altered the internal composition of many forces, at a time when many traditional polic-ing roles are being 'civilianised', such as 'crime scene investigators' (CSIs), nearly all of whom are now police staff rather than police officers. The fiscal constraints on the police mean that many desk functions previously the sole preserve of police officers can be covered more prudently, even expertly, by police staff. The development of CSAS, for example, has seen powers, previously jealously guarded as the prerogative of the police, being accredited to 'unwarranted persons' who are involved in community safety. Whatever resistance is offered by the Police Federation, it is behind the curve—not for the first time—because the Extended Policing Family is likely to remain. It is popular with public and police managers alike, and offers flexibilities and partnerships of a sophisticated kind which did not previously exist.

DISCUSSION POINT

Does this come at a price? Does the Extended Policing Family suggest that some tasks traditionally assigned to the police can be done just as well (or better) at a lower price by others? Is the Extended Policing Family the thin end of a wedge that is subversive of the 'public' police?

The jury is perhaps still out on these questions, which nonetheless need answers. More research needs to be undertaken to ascertain the true value and effective-ness of this 'pluralisation' of policing.

1.5 **Ranks and Command**

In 2005 an ACPO report on the Special Constabulary by Chief Constable (Sir) Peter Fahy recommended that forces adopt a national Special Constabulary rank structure using the same designations as regulars but without the regular insig-nia. It was felt that this structure would ensure greater consistency and would create an incentive for those Specials who would welcome greater responsibility. The Special Constabulary National Strategy Implementation Advice in 2008 reit-erated this suggestion, indicating that a national rank structure offers a standard. The Implementation Advice Document issued by ACPO and NPIA includes the following:

> It is suggested that forces implement a rank structure for the Special Constabu-lary in accordance with the ACPO Guidance of 2005.

There is no compulsion on forces to do this, but it makes sense that a rank struc-ture and command chain should parallel that of the regular force (Table 1.1):

Table 1.1: Rank structure and command chain

Existing	Proposed	Regular equivalent
Special Constable	*Special Constable*	Police Constable
Section Officer	*Special Sergeant*	Police Sergeant
Area Officer	*Special Inspector*	Police Inspector
No existing rank	*Special Chief Inspector*	Chief inspector
Commandant	*Special Superintendent*	Superintendent
Commandant	*Assistant Chief Officer*	Chief Superintendent
Commandant	*Deputy Chief Officer*	Assistant Chief Constable
Chief Commandant	*Chief Officer*	Deputy Chief Constable

Police forces across England and Wales differ in number (that is, the actual headcount) and in relative percentages of Special Constables measured against the regular police establishment. This means that, organisationally, command structures can vary from force to force. Depending on their local requirements, forces have either adopted this structure more or less as given or have made a slight variation to it; for example, Kent Police has no Special Chief Inspectors because their structure has no requirement for the rank. At the other end of the scale, Sussex Police has one rank only: Special Constable; while Essex Police has the full range of equivalent ranks. Typically, the Special Constabulary ranks broadly correspond with regular ranks. A **Special Sergeant** has supervisory responsibility for seven or so Special Constables. A **Special Inspector** has responsibility for a district. A **Special Chief Inspector** or **Special Superintendent** has responsibility for a basic SC command unit. A **Special Constabulary Chief Officer team** has responsibility for strategic matters through liaison with the ACPO senior management team in the regular police. Special Chief Officers also represent their respective Special Constabulary force contingent at regional and national level.

Figure 1.3 provides an indication of what the Special Constabulary rank designation may look like in a typical police force (given the variations we noted earlier).

1.6 The Structures and Remits of a Typical Police Force

There are 43 'home' police forces and a number of other specialist police forces, such as British Transport Police and the Civil Nuclear Constabulary, in England and Wales. Scotland has eight separate forces but is actively planning to move

Figure 1.3: Rank insignia of the Special Constabulary for England and Wales

| Special Constable | Special Sergeant | Special Inspector | Special Chief Inspector | Special Superintendent | Assistant Chief Officer | Deputy Chief Officer | Chief Officer |

(Hats and epaulettes constructed and adapted from a variety of sources (including *The International Encyclopaedia of Uniform Insignia*)) to a single force, and Northern Ireland has its own unified force, the Police Service of Northern Ireland (PSNI), which replaced the Royal Ulster Constabulary, GC, in November 2001. Forces in England and Wales vary in size from about 1,500 police officers in a small rural force to 31,478 in the Metropolitan Police (excluding its 5,479 Special Constables) (Home Office figures for October 2011). Correspondingly, the ways in which these police forces are structured vary a good deal, even among similarly sized forces, and there is no template which all forces fit exactly. What we suggest in the following may vary in some details from your own force; this is not a concern. The principles of the 'hub and spokes' arrangement are common to most police forces, as is the distinction between crime investigation, on the one hand, and territorial, or area, or neighbourhood policing, on the other. One deals with criminality, the other with community; but the distinctions blur constantly. Terminology varies too; we have used the most common terms and descriptors, but your force may have its own.

1.6.1 'Hub and spokes'

It is common to think of the relationship between a police headquarters and its outstations as being like the structure of a wheel, with the HQ at the hub or centre, and the outstations (BCUs or Basic Command Units) controlled and radiating out from the HQ. At its simplest, it would look like this:

Figure 1.4: Simplified 'hub and spokes' structure

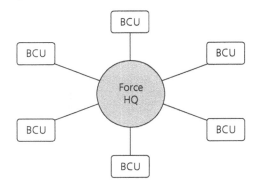

Figure 1.4 if anything is *over*-simplified because, in terms of autonomy of operation, some finance, and budgeting, as well as in many aspects of organisation, Basic Command Units (led by a Superintendent or Chief Superintendent) are often virtually independent of Police Headquarters (led by the Chief Constable and a 'top team' of chief officers), other than for performance and allied matters.

To get an idea of the complex structure of a police force we may need a more linear depiction, as shown in Figure 1.5:

Figure 1.5 Typical force structures and remits

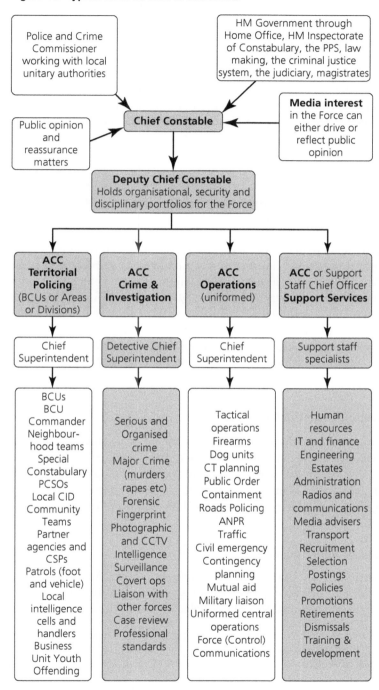

Source: figure adapted from Caless (ed.), *PCSO Handbook* (2010, Oxford: Oxford University Press)(NB: shading denotes normally located at force headquarters)

The point of showing you all this is not just to examine the context within which you function as a police officer, although that is very important, but to show that the police structure is directly relevant to you because your individual duties, such as your work in a Neighbourhood Policing Team, may have a direct impact upon the force itself, in areas such as performance, reassurance, community engagement, detection, prevention and reduction of crime, clear-up rates, 'sanction detection' rates, 'brought-to-justice' data and many other less measurable and tangible areas such as reduction in anti-social behaviour and arrests for criminal damage.

1.7 Recruitment, Retention and Resilience: Becoming a Special Constable

The recruitment process will have little interest for you if you are already a serving Special Constable. However, if you are intending to become one, the areas outlined in this section will be of real importance and will help you with your application process. One caution though: we cannot provide local and precise details of how each of the 43 police forces in England and Wales recruits and organises its Special Constabulary (nor other forces, such as British Transport Police) so we have provided a generic explanation. Please make sure that you look at the website for the police force you want to join, so that you have the most current information available.

1.7.1 Recruiting a Special Constable

We need to note at the outset *how important the fact of continuous recruitment is* to the Special Constabulary and to the police force of which it is a part. Not only does this aid the retention of existing Special Constables (particularly important at this time of increased financial stringency in the public sector), but also 'gearing' recruitment can link individual expertise to specialist deployment roles.

1.7.1.1 Avenues for recruitment

There are many ways in which Special Constables are recruited and the following text box, whilst not definitive, provides many examples of ways that police forces are reaching out to potential Special Constables:

- Newspaper advertisements
- Radio advertisements
- TV
- Police force's own website

- Special Constabulary website (for example, through Google)
- Generic police websites
- Volunteer websites
- Community events, fetes and fairs
- Posters
- Newspaper articles
- Local advertising
- Attendance at career fairs
- Talks at schools, colleges and universities
- Police station open days
- Community safety events
- Open evenings for potential recruits
- Blogs, Twitter, Facebook, Bebo, MySpace, MSN, etc.

These are all legitimate avenues for recruitment and many can be initiated and populated by current Special Constables themselves; after all, who is better to extol the pleasures or frustrations of the role than those already doing it? Furthermore, some of the examples listed require very little or no expenditure and that has real resonance in a time of financial constraints. When a police force provides local media with a 'good news' story, there is also a real opportunity to include a sentence about how local people can apply to become Special Constables.

1.7.1.2 Example of a Special Constabulary recruitment campaign

The Metropolitan Police has been running a recruitment campaign with the strap line, 'Extraordinary People: Special Constables' since 2007. This provides a series of case studies from a 'first-person' perspective, using serving Special Constables. The campaign focuses on six motivational strands:

- To escape the 'rat race'
- To acquire new skills
- To gain job satisfaction
- To wear the uniform
- To be part of the team
- To make a difference.

The campaign features high-profile posters across the London Transport network, including buses and the Underground, as well as advertisements in free newspapers, and is cleverly targeted at the commuter population at its most receptive, travelling into and out of the capital.

1.7.1.3 **Basic eligibility criteria**

For *all* police forces, no matter which avenue of recruitment, there are basic eligibility criteria for joining the Special Constabulary:

> Basic eligibility requirements are the same for the specials [*sic*] as for joining the regular police force; you must be over the age of 18, and there is no upper age limit, although you will need to be reasonably fit and in good health. In addition:
>
> - there are no minimum or maximum height requirements
> - there is no formal educational requirement, but applicants will have to pass written tests
> - only applications from member states of the European [Union], or other nationals who have leave to enter or remain in the UK for an indefinite period, will be accepted
> - convictions or cautions will probably make applicants ineligible, but this will depend on the nature and circumstances of the offence
> - applicants must be judged physically and mentally able to undertake police duties.
>
> (<http://policerecruitment.homeoffice.gov.uk/special-constables/index.html> and <http://www.npia.police.uk/en/10040.htm>; both accessed 20 January 2012)

Of particular note is that membership of some organisations is incompatible with being a police officer; specifically being a member of *any* organisation that promotes or accepts racial discrimination, or 'whose constitution, aims, objectives or pronouncements are incompatible with the duty to promote racial equality'. Police officers, including Special Constables, must satisfy the provisions of the Equality Act 2010, including s 149 which places a duty on public service employees to 'tackle prejudice and promote understanding'.

It is important that you satisfy all these criteria before making an application; otherwise you will be wasting your own time. If you are uncertain whether you will meet all the criteria, discuss this with the recruitment department (usually in Human Resources or 'Personnel') of the force you wish to join. In particular, you must be aware that certain occupations can preclude you from becoming a Special Constable because of the potential for problematic cross-over in responsibility. One example is if your full-time job is a PCSO. It would be confusing for any community to have the same person in two different uniforms, with two differing responsibilities and two differing sets of powers, patrolling the same neighbourhood at different times. Other 'police' jobs may not preclude you.

1.7.2 **Selection, interview, vetting**

The Police Recruitment website is an excellent source of information for those wishing to become Special Constables.

1.7.2.1 **Selection**

The document 'Special Constables: Eligibility for Recruitment' (<http:// policerecruitment.homeoffice.gov.uk/documents/npia-01-2011.html>; accessed 20 January 2012), gives access to information on how to apply to be a Special Constable, whilst the document 'Specials Recruit Assessment Centre—Information for Candidates' (<http://policerecruitment.homeoffice.gov. uk/documents/specials-ac-info.html>; accessed 20 January 2012) includes the application form to be a Special. Both are easily accessible online and are a generic means to apply, but the forms are often customised by individual forces for local use. The normal set of forms may come as an application pack with 16 or more pages to complete, along with medical and financial questionnaires and separate vetting forms.

1.7.2.2 **Interview**

If your application successfully negotiates the sifting phase then you will be invited to an interview/assessment centre. Again this will vary in time and place in the overall recruitment process, depending on which force you are seeking to join. There tend to be two approaches to a Special Constable interview:

- the Police Initial Recruitment (PIR) approach or
- an assessment centre approach.

More forces are beginning to use the latter as it encompasses a more holistic approach to recruitment and provides the force with a greater opportunity to assess candidates against a wide range of competencies. These can include:

verbal and written communication

problem solving

respect for race and diversity

team working

effective communication.

Generally, the following will make up the various components of a Special Constable interview/assessment process, although the actual structure of the day will vary:

- a competency-based interview, consisting of four questions; this seeks to establish if you have the competencies, or potential skills, to be a police officer)
- a written exercise (to examine your written and reasoning skills)
- a 'situational judgement' test (this test gives you a situation and asks you 'multiple choice' type questions about it: the aim is to establish if you can make appropriate judgements in the realistic circumstances of being a Special Constable. There are examples in the information online, with which you should be familiar before you attend the assessment).

It is crucial that you check with the force to which you wish to apply what procedures they will use, so that you can plan and revise accordingly. Forces will often have more candidates than available spaces, so use your opportunity wisely.

1.7.2.3 Vetting

The generic police role entails working with vulnerable persons and children, involves access to sensitive material, sometimes includes work with 'restricted' personal data from partnership agencies or police operations, and could involve working with intelligence material and accessing databases ranging from local force systems to the Police National Computer (PNC). It is therefore imperative that the police scrutinise applicants so as to exclude those who are unsuitable for the role. The risk otherwise is that criminals may seek to gain secret access by planting a 'mole' within the police. The vetting forms will ask questions about you and your family members and will also include a financial questionnaire. You should complete these honestly because any undeclared offences or irregularities which later come to light may damage your application, or require you to resign if you have concealed anything. If you are uncertain as to whether events in your past may exclude you from applying, then *ask*.

1.7.2.4 Fitness and medicals

Applicant Special Constables are subject to a fitness and medical assessment. Given the nature of police work, applicants need to be fit and healthy so that they can cope with the wide variety of tasks involved in being a police officer. Dealing with confrontation or chasing a fleeing suspect requires levels of fitness and stamina that an office worker does not need (at least in a work capacity). Check with your intended force what its fitness requirements are and, because the recruitment time can be lengthy, you have a chance to get yourself up to standard if you are not already there.

1.7.2.5 Fitness test

All forces require their Special Constable applicants to take a fitness test, but the timing of this within the recruitment process can vary. Most forces will use the same test as that used for regular applicants and it will involve two distinct aspects:

1. **Endurance** (the 'bleep test')—this involves running between two fixed points on a measured track with a set time limit indicated by bleeps, which become faster as the test progresses.
2. **Dynamic strength** (the 'push/pull test')—this requires you to do five seated chest-pushes and five seated back-pulls on a machine designed to measure your strength.

1.7.2.6 **Medical**

Similarly, all forces will require Special Constable applicants to undergo a medical examination. This will probably be the same test that regular officers take, involving a medical assessment by a practice nurse or medical advisor, and is likely to include sight/ vision/hearing tests. If you are uncertain what the requirements are for your chosen force, then check, as there can be subtle differences in application processes. If you have a medical condition that you think might preclude you from becoming a Special Constable, then check before applying. All queries will be treated confidentially and certain conditions, if managed correctly, do not prevent someone from having a long and fulfilling career within the police. Forces are used to applicants asking such questions. For example, some eyesight problems will exclude applicants, others will not. Some physical conditions may not disbar you if they are not severe, such as allergies. Others will. One point worth making is that *forces are looking for fit and healthy people who take their physical conditioning seriously and maintain sensible fitness levels.*

1.8 **Considering Employment and Employers**

In 2008, Martin Stuart, Deputy Chief Constable of Bedfordshire Police wrote this:

> As a business proposition the Special Constabulary is difficult to beat. Not only is it extraordinarily cost-effective, but it is more representative of the community (socio-economic groups and businesses) than any other body delivering policing services. It therefore brings greater involvement and improved communication with members of the public and the business community.

> (Executive Summary, *National Strategy*, 2008)

It is worth turning our attention to the employer for a moment and looking more specifically at the relationship between the employer and the Special Constable (whether about to join or already a Special: the same considerations apply). There will be times when the needs of the employer and the needs of the police are in collision, and often the expectation is that the higher sense of duty engendered by membership of the Special Constabulary will take precedence over any purely commercial concerns. Further, it is assumed that employers actually *like* the idea that members of their workforce have a calling to serve the community. And, of course, most of the time for most employers that is perfectly true.

What is also true is that the employer gets back, into the workplace, someone whose skills are being developed extensively at someone else's expense, which is a hefty bonus for Special Constable and employer alike. Yet it is entirely reasonable for an employer, faced with the effects of having a Special Constable in his/her workforce to ask: **what is in this for me?** The question may very well be asked of you, quite literally, if you approach your employer with a request for time off for additional police duties, or with a request that s/he support you to join the Special Constabulary. Even if the question is not asked by your employer, it may be asked by colleagues at work, and so it is sensible for you to have responses well considered and prepared. The remainder of this section suggests *precisely* what is 'in it' for the employer, when you become a Special Constable, so make sure that you understand the value of the arguments.

1.8.1 The return-on-investment of a Special Constable

The society in which we live depends upon peaceable circumstances to be able to function. The 'work' undertaken by any organisation, whether in public service or in private enterprise, flourishes under conditions of good order and withers under conditions of lawlessness (such as the riots in summer 2011) or lack of social control. This is true whether the product or service being delivered is education or furniture, animal welfare or scientific research, trading standards or computer software.

The Special Constabulary plays a significant part in sustaining or creating those conditions in which private and public businesses can thrive and develop. It follows that all of us, as citizens, have a **vested interest** in seeing the Special Constabulary (and the rest of the policing family) succeed in reassuring the public, carrying out visible patrol, dealing with nuisance, disorder and anti-social behaviour and being instrumental in crime prevention, crime detection and the arrest and prosecution of criminal offenders. It follows equally that employers should have the same investment in those of their employees who become Special Constables.

The important thing is that no organisation and no employer exists outside society: we are all citizens, we all belong to communities (sometimes to many of them), and we all have an obligation to support each other.

1.8.2 What's in it for the employer?

Having a Special Constable on the staff is actually beneficial to staff morale. Most employers will agree that a motivated employee, with a high sense of social responsibility, treated like an adult and equal partner and given flexibility and trust, is more likely to work productively than one who has none of these things. At least with Special Constables on their staff, employers may be assured that positive treatment will result in positive outcomes.

1.8.2.1 Don't forget the force

The force for which you work can also influence your employer for good. Mention of the sponsoring organisation when publicity is generated about the work of a Special Constable is one way in which the force can 'pay back' the employer's support, as can mentions on the Special Constabulary section of the force website. There are many ways to 'spin' the force's involvement with the Special Constabulary/employer and most will reinforce the strength of the 'triangular relationship' between force, employer and Special Constable with which we began (Figure 1.1). Further sponsorship of police activity may also be a force benefit, once positive links with employers are made, and there's nothing to stop your employer making it clear to shareholders, stakeholders, customers, communities, neighbourhoods, boards, trusts and oversight committees that s/he strongly supports Special Constables. Altruism is sometimes very good business.

1.8.2.2 **What's in it for both you and your employer?**

It is worth summarising here the very positive outcomes of the relationship between an employer and the Special Constable (please use this freely to persuade and influence):

- Staff enjoy flexibility: it works both ways, so a flexible employee is an added benefit to an employer
- Having additional positive things to note at an appraisal is helpful to the employer's assessment of the staff member
- Favourable publicity for the Special Constabulary is also favourable publicity for the employer: sponsorship of the Special Constable with a company logo, for example, is very cost-effective advertising
- Staff want *work–life balance*: encouraging membership of the Special Constabulary is a direct contribution to that balance
- The employer gets a person with continuously enhanced skills, for which s/he did not have to pay.

1.8.2.3 **Positive outcomes: Special Constables and their employers**

- It is mutually beneficial: both sides gain
- The employee's skills levels are enhanced in many ways and new skills learned, all of which can positively affect an employer's bottom-line profitability or efficiency
- It generates positive images (and good publicity if well handled) for the employer, which directly assists in the 'marketing' of his/her organisation
- Flexibility and understanding are needed on both sides, the outcomes of which are very positive in terms of productivity and employment relations
- Employers appreciate being informed of likely impacts of police work, whilst Special Constables appreciate reciprocity in planning their duties
- A Special Constable demonstrates qualities which employers value, not least of which are loyalty and commitment; whilst a Special Constable relishes working for a flexible and compassionate organisation aware of its community obligations
- Each needs to sustain an open dialogue

- The police force can support both sides and can play an important part in 'oiling the wheels' by showing sensitivity and understanding. After all, the force is an employer too.

DISCUSSION POINTS

Do you agree with these positives? If not, what do you think the benefits to an employer are in having Special Constables on his/her staff? If you do agree, to what extent should all police forces promote these 'mutual benefit' solutions to local employers?

1.9 Summary

This chapter has been about the role and place of the Special Constable, not just in the police force which s/he joins, or the 'Extended Policing Family' of which s/he is a part, but as one drawn from the community to serve the community, reinforcing the historical link between the police and the policed.

TEST BOX 1

Now, before you go to look at the joining process and training, it is time for you to self-test, or as the police call it, 'knowledge check' what you have learned in this chapter:

1. What was called 'a manifest sign'?
2. What are the three components of the 'volunteering equation'?
3. Name four members of the extended policing family.
4. Identify three things which PSVs can do to help police forces.
5. With PCSOs, what is the difference between standard and discretionary powers?
6. What does CSAS stand for?
7. What disadvantages might apply to the CSAS scheme?
8. What in some forces is the regular police 'equivalent' of an SC 'Area Officer'?
9. How many 'home' police forces are there?
10. What recruitment criteria apply to applicants to become Special Constables from member states of the European Union?

Further Reading

Caless, B. (ed.), 2010, *Blackstone's PCSO Handbook*, 2nd edn. (2010, Oxford: Oxford University Press)

Crawford, A., *Plural Policing: The Mixed Economy of Visible Patrols in England and Wales* (2005, Bristol: Policy Press)

Neuberger, J. (Chair), *Report of the Commission on the Future of Volunteering and Manifesto for Change* (2008: London, HMSO)

Police recruitment website at <http://policerecruitment.homeoffice.gov.uk/documents/npia-01-2011.html>

Report of the Working Group on the Special Constabulary in England and Wales 1995–96 (1996, London: Home Office Communication Directorate)

2

Joining and Training

2.1 **Special Constable—The Main Role**

The following is an extract from a Home Office recruitment site for Special Constables—you will probably already be familiar with it—which seeks to provide a broad 'job description'. What is immediately noticeable is its breadth and depth: this is not a role that can be handily condensed to one side of A4, even if the SC National Strategy can be (see Introduction). Furthermore, the activities described will vary from day to day, from force to force, from operation to operation. Despite being generic, the description shows how important the role of the Special Constable is and how central that role is to the business of visible and 'reassurance' policing. After all, if somebody wishes to volunteer his/her time, to make a gift of it, and can cover all of these areas, how much of a boon is that to the police force?

KEY POINT

Generally speaking, a [Special Constable's] main role is to conduct local, intelligence-based patrols and to take part in crime prevention initiatives, often targeted at specific problem areas.

In many forces, Special Constables are also involved in policing major incidents, and in providing operational support to regular officers.

Depending upon their individual force, Special Constables can:

- conduct foot patrols
- assist at the scene of accidents, fights or fires
- enforce road safety initiatives
- conduct house-to-house enquiries
- provide security at major events
- present evidence in court
- tackle anti-social behaviour
- tackle alcohol related incidents
- spend time at local schools educating youths about crime-reduction and community safety.

(Extract from Home Office website <http://policerecruitment.homeoffice. gov.uk/special-constables/whats-it-like-to-do-the-job/index.html>; accessed 20 August 2012)

Let's look at a couple of these elements.

2.1.1 **Tackle anti-social behaviour**

Anti-social behaviour is a problem that blights the lives of many people and the fear that such behaviour generates can have a huge impact on the quality of life for many neighbourhoods. It is therefore important that, once identified, this problem is tackled firmly, tactics for which are explored in greater detail later when we look more closely at Neighbourhood Policing. It is not surprising, then, that the Special Constabulary is involved in such high-profile activity, as the following example demonstrates:

Case study: Sending a strong message in Gloucestershire

Operation Ballymore was undertaken by the Stroud Police 'Safer Community' Team. This operation was mounted in response to residents' complaints about speeding, anti-social behaviour and criminal damage, principally by young people within their area. Having identified these local priorities, an integral component of neighbourhood policing, the Safer Community team provided high-visibility policing with strong enforcement capability. Twelve Special Constables were drafted in to assist their regular colleagues with reassurance patrolling and speed checks, and thus helped to play a key part in the successes, where arrests were made, cautions given and fines imposed, bringing a sharp decrease in the behaviours complained of. The successes were noted not just by the police but by the residents themselves.

(Adapted from: <http://www.gloucestershire.police.uk/Latest News/ PressReleases/2009/July/item12440.html>; accessed 24 August 2009)

2.1.1.1 Spend time [...] educating youths

Another key strand of both the previous and the Coalition governments has been the **inclusion** of young people in a series of projects designed to help them to avoid becoming victims of crime, to engage them in crime prevention or to deter them from embarking on a career in crime. Such projects include going into schools or youth projects to deliver talks on road safety and 'stranger danger', or helping with National Curriculum citizenship projects on community safety. All forces employ specialist officers to deal with youth offending, but local PCSOs, Neighbourhood Policing Officers and Special Constables can make a significant impact, as the following example demonstrates:

Case study: After-school café

In South Yorkshire, a team of Special Constables and community volunteers is running an after-school programme, the Dinnington ROC (Redeeming Our Communities) Café which provides facilities and activities for pupils from the local school. These pupils gain extra achievement points at school for their attendance at the 'Café' and gain additional awards for working in the local community. The team has recently set up a new project to get the young participants looking at the issue of 'distraction burglaries' in the area.

(Adapted from *Specials, the Voice of the Special Constabulary*, NPIA, April 2009)

2.1.1.2 Fitting this into the minimum of four hours' duty

The issue of hours is not set in stone, because volunteering requires flexibility both in the hosting organisation and in the individual. The police increasingly recognise that Special Constables have other commitments—work, family, studies, social lives (maybe all four)—so most forces will adapt to your needs. It is not unknown for police supervisors to order Special Constables to go home, because the latter have volunteered for too many shifts and need a break. You, working alongside your family, your employer and the police, must determine how many hours you can commit to and when. What you offer, of course, is an 'added value' to each force; so it may make more sense for you to think not simply about the number of hours you put in, so much as the qualitative difference you can make when volunteering.

2.2 Uniform

The British police uniform, particularly the traditional pointed police helmet, is one of the most recognisable uniforms in the world (so much so that it is used for souvenir purposes, as any visitor to the tacky souvenir shops in central London can testify). This distinctive image is perhaps diminishing, as patrol uniforms across the country are adapted to deal with the requirements of 21st-century policing: all officers on patrol or working outside police stations now routinely wear stab vests/body armour, for example, as the threat of 'sharps' has become more pronounced.

Some forces have adopted a black polo shirt instead of the traditional white shirt and black tie, and some forces have moved wholesale from the time-honoured tunic with silver buttons to the 'blouson' jacket (known irreverently in Special Constabulary circles as the 'bumfreezer'). Many officers wear high-visibility vests when on duty. The development of police uniform and equipment is one that has been going on since police officers were first introduced in 1829 and changes reflect the environment within which policing occurs. The whistle has given way to the Airwave radio, the truncheon to the ASP baton, and so on. North Wales Police has issued its officers with polo shirts (with special anti-sweat protection) instead of shirts and ties, together with cargo trousers and even baseball caps (*The Sharp End*, 28 July 2007). These changes may not prove universally popular, especially with those people more used to the appearance of the traditional 'bobby'; but for the advocates of the newer, less formal, uniform, polo shirts and baseball caps are reflective of the need to adapt.

Whilst American influence might be regrettable, it is worth noting that firearms officers have been wearing baseball-type caps for some years now, without provoking much adverse comment. These changes have also been incorporated within the Special Constabulary uniform, which is virtually identical to that of regular officers (except for rank designation, see Chapter 1). It is clear that there is more to the Special Constabulary uniform than items of occupational or protective clothing. Actually, in our experience, nothing in policing is more likely to produce a long and sometimes heated discussion than the topic of uniform and equipment. We do not take sides in any debate, but we have devoted some of this chapter to uniform and basic equipment, largely because it looms so large in many officers' experience. No doubt you too will be drawn into discussion of preferences and whether 'hi-sole tab-backed boots' are preferable with or without 'splash tread'. It is a topic which can become very arcane.

2.2.1 **Uniform standards**

All forces will have a force policy on uniform standards, and these apply equally to members of the Special Constabulary, and will include details of what uniform should be worn for what occasion, as well as details about hair colouring, body jewellery, tattoos and even the number of tiepins or badges an officer may display.

2.3 **'Going Equipped'—Police Equipment**

Whilst the make, model and style of police equipment may differ from force to force, all provide the following equipment to Special Constables as a minimum. It is obligatory to carry with you the following:

2.3.1 **Airwave radio**

Every operational police officer is required to carry a personal radio (PR), when on duty: these may be personal issue or from an equipment pool. PRs are essential and invaluable pieces of equipment. Not only do they allow you to pass and receive timely information about the events you are attending, or intelligence or warning markers on persons or vehicles stopped, but they allow you to call for emergency assistance should a situation deteriorate and urgent back-up be required. Earpieces (on 'curly-wurly' wires) are now becoming standard issue with the handsets to safeguard the integrity and security of information passed over the radio network.

'Airwave' is the operational name for the police service's encrypted digital trunked radio system that replaced the old analogue radio. Distribution of Airwave was completed in May 2005 and currently every territorial police force in the United Kingdom, including British Transport Police, the National Crime Agency and other policing organisations, make use of the technology. Both the fire and rescue and the ambulance services received Airwave radios at the end of 2009, so that in the event of a national emergency, or major incident (such as the flooding in Cheshire in November 2009), all three emergency services are able to coordinate resources and responses, using a communication system common to all (NPIA, 2009).

2.3.2 Hi-visibility jackets/tabards

The Health and Safety at Work Act 1974 places a statutory responsibility on both the employer and each individual employee to ensure his/her health, safety and welfare (see the NOS in Chapter 3), so the police service provides its staff with the necessary protective equipment for them to be able to carry out their work safely and to minimise any risks they might face on duty. 'High-visibility' ('hi-viz') jackets and tabards are provided because they enhance officers' visibility to others. This has the dual advantage of increasing public awareness of a police presence (whilst patrolling a neighbourhood foot beat, for example), and also enhances officers' safety on roads and motorways (at the scene of a road traffic collision, say). Hi-visibility jackets are waterproof, and ordinarily come with a detachable, quilted inner lining for additional warmth. These versatile jackets are quickly replacing the black 'town beat' coats used in the past by officers when patrolling on foot.

2.3.3 Body armour—'stab vests'

In most forces the wearing of body armour when on duty away from the police station is mandated by force policy to meet the legislative provisions of the Health and Safety at Work Act 1974. Failing to wear issued body armour not only risks injury, but it also endangers your colleagues because, if you are wounded, you cannot help them. The standard body armour has been designed to provide a level of protection against knife, glass, blade, slash, spike and other sharp-instrument attacks. Body armour also substantially safeguards an officer from sustaining an injury from the effects of 'blunt force trauma' during a physical attack from punches, kicks, dog bites, pinching or weapons that might be used against them such as bats, sticks or stones. Standard body armour offers *some* protection against the ballistic impact from light firearms.

2.3.4 Load vest/duty belt

Load vests and duty belts are a means of carrying police equipment whilst on patrol. A **load vest** is simply an adjustable webbing mesh worn over body armour which has sewn-on 'docks' and 'holsters' for storing the Airwave radio, ASP baton, rigid handcuffs, incapacitant spray, mobile telephone, torch, disposable gloves and first-aid pouch, whereas the **duty belt** carries holsters for this same equipment on a webbing belt worn around the waist. In some forces new officers may have the choice of either a load vest or a duty belt and it is very much personal preference which is selected. Both have advantages and disadvantages. Increasingly, load vests are being favoured by police forces because of the perceived future long-term risks which duty belts might pose to an officer's lower spine. Load vests can feel very heavy and may obstruct officers because they restrict movement, or get in the way if you have to climb obstacles. A duty belt is less of a problem. Moreover, it allows the ASP baton to be drawn from the hip, which is often the preferred and natural way to pull out a defensive weapon (rather than from the chest which is how you draw it from a load vest). Duty-belt holsters also allow for extendable batons to be carried either in their 'open' or 'closed' modes.

2.3.5 **Baton**

The symbolic yet impractical wooden truncheon has been replaced with a variety of different police batons modelled mostly on American law-enforcement designs such as the PR–24 telescopic baton, the side-handled tactical baton or the ASP extendable baton. Each baton has a set of strikes and techniques for safe and effective use. These will be taught to you by specialist staff safety trainers during your officer safety training phase. Batons are provided to all operational Special Constables as defensive weapons and form part of an officer's 'personal protection equipment' (PPE) and must be carried when booked on duty and in the public domain. They are usually uniquely identifiable to an individual officer because of an etched serial- or collar-number marking on the base. Lawful authority to be in possession of such an article ceases when the officer books off duty. Whilst police officers are authorised by law to use force on other people in certain circumstances, the decision to deploy or utilise a baton is the officer's own, and s/he alone is accountable for justifying its use in court and to supervisory officers.

2.3.6 **Rigid cuffs**

Rigid 'speed' or 'quick' cuffs have replaced the 'bracelet'-style handcuffs. The major advantage with modern rigid cuffs is that they restrain a non-compliant subject effectively and can also be used to force a person to the ground if necessary to allow officers to gain better control. The application of handcuffs to another person amounts to use of force and must be justified and recorded in your pocket notebook. Handcuffs should always be checked for tightness on a person's wrist and then double-locked to prevent the cuff from closing and tightening further.

2.3.7 **Incapacitant spray**

Incapacitant sprays, whether of the CS 'teargas' or PAVA (synthetic pepper spray) varieties, form part of a Special Constable's PPE. Both sprays are classified under s 5 of the Firearms Act 1968 as **prohibited weapons** and accordingly very few people have lawful authority to possess such items. Special Constables are authorised to do so, *but only when booked on duty*. The aim of incapacitant sprays is to enable Special Constables to gain control over a violent or non-compliant subject so that an arrest or other procedure can be executed swiftly and as safely as possible for everyone involved. Incapacitant sprays are useful tools for enforcing compliance, or as a distraction, allowing an officer time to disengage from a violent subject and employ a different tactic, or call for back-up. Sprays are generally thought of as the safest and lowest levels of force an officer can utilise because there are no lasting physical effects on a person after use.

2.3.8 **Personal equipment or property**

Finally, you should *never* supplement force-approved equipment with your own. Should any incidents occur whilst you are on duty at which you are found to have used equipment not approved or issued by your force, you might be liable in any possible future litigation, and might have made void any claims by you for compensation. Similarly, you should think twice about wearing expensive rings or watches in case of loss or damage. It is unlikely that police forces will offer you compensation for the loss of such items. Cheap substitutes worn for duty purposes are much easier to replace and have much less sentimental value.

A 'knowledge check' on this section:

TEST BOX 2

1. What does the Home Office say a Special Constable's main role is?
2. Name three other things a Special Constable can do operationally.
3. What preceded the ASP-type baton?
4. What American influence can be seen in British police firearms teams?
5. What is the operational name for the police's encrypted, digital, trunked radio system?
6. What does standard body armour protect against?
7. What is a load vest?
8. What alternative is there to a load vest?
9. What is meant by PPE?
10. Under what legislation are CS or PAVA sprays classed as 'prohibited weapons'?

2.4 **Training and Learning**

This part of the chapter moves on from how you are equipped to discussions about the kinds of training and learning you will receive as a Special Constable. We deal with generic training and learning issues here, based upon the Initial Learning for the Special Constabulary (IL4SC) outline which forms the national curriculum. Individual forces may have different emphases in particular areas, so always ensure that you check with your training staff about things that vary from the standard.

A common approach in police training of all kinds is KUSAB. This stands for:

K	Knowledge
U	Understanding
S	Skills
A	Attitudes and
B	Behaviours

Police learning is designed to capture one or more of these categories. Clearly, you need to **understand** the law, in order to perform your duties as a Special Constable, and you need **knowledge** of individual pieces of legislation appropriate to any situation in which you find yourself. You may need to render first aid to the victim(s) of an accident, and your **skills** in doing so might sometimes mean the difference between life and death, whilst an equal skill exists in subduing and arresting someone who is 'fighting drunk', without causing either of you any damage.

Your approach to the people you deal with, and to your colleagues, is an important part of who you are, and how you are perceived by others. For example, calm reasonableness, backed by a steely resolve, is almost an 'ideal' prescription for a Special Constable, and your **attitudes** to the work and the people you meet will have reverberations beyond the job. Finally, your **behaviours** in dealing with what you encounter on patrol, or in the other duties you are called upon to exercise as a Special Constable, may determine the success or failure of your performance as a police officer.

For example, until comparatively recently (say, up to ten years ago), some police forces had difficulty in investigating homophobic crime. Gay communities, conscious of thinly veiled or open antagonism towards them from the police, would not cooperate. Now, there is a more enlightened attitude, added to which is the recognition of homophobia as a crime in itself. Relations with gay and other minority communities have improved (they are still not perfect) but enough of a change has been effected for investigation of homophobic crime and other crimes against the gay community to stand a far better chance of successful prosecution because the two sides have learned to cooperate. This is where a Special Constable's behaviours and attitudes are crucial. All the knowledge, skills and understanding in the world will not help you to investigate and solve a crime, if your attitudes and behaviour alienate the very people you should be helping.

KUSAB do not come in watertight compartments. They overlap and curl around each other so that there is often a blurring between what you think and what you do (**attitudes** and **behaviours**) or between your learned **skills** and your internal **understanding**. To illustrate the point, here are some basic Special Constable's topics for learning.

Using the topics in the box below, discuss how you might assign an individual KUSAB attribute to each one.

DISCUSSION POINT—WHICH KUSAB APPLY?

Your powers in law
Discretion
Structure and organisation of your police force
The criminal justice system
Anti-social behaviour
House-to-house enquiries
Missing persons enquiries
Human rights
Standards of Professional Behaviour
Relations with your community
Dealing with the vulnerable
Communications
Negotiating and persuading
Developing partnerships
Working as part of a team

If you think that some of these learning topics entail overlaps between various parts of KUSAB, you would be right. This is our suggested answer:

Key point	KUSAB elements
Your powers in law	K, U
Discretion	K, U, A
Structure and organisation of your police force	K, U, A
The criminal justice system	K, U, A
Anti-social behaviour	K, U, A, B
House-to-house enquiries	K, U, S, A, B
Missing persons enquiries	K, U, S, A, B
Human rights	K, A, B
Standards of Professional Behaviour	K, U, S, A, B
Relations with your community	U, A, B
Dealing with the vulnerable	U, A, B (maybe K too)
Communications	K, U, S
Negotiating and persuading	K, U, A, B (some S too)
Developing partnerships	K, U, S, A, B
Working as part of a team	K, U, A, B

We can think of many instances across the entire range of learning topics for Special Constables in which all the elements of KUSAB apply at some point, for the simple reason that *knowing and understanding something modifies your behaviour and attitude towards it.* Often, a skill of some mechanical or intellectual kind is needed to ensure that the **K** and **U** are able to modify the **A** and **B**. None of what we learn takes place in isolation, and in policing that is especially so, since knowledge is **applied** to situations and circumstances unlike, say, some kinds of academic knowledge where the knowledge sought is the thing itself (some abstruse 'large-number' theoretical mathematics, say, or the function of colour symbolism in late medieval English literature): better known as 'knowledge for its own sake'.

We can summarise the nature of **applied learning** through this case example:

Case Example—Applied Learning

Offence: Domestic violence

K Knowledge—the law, the circumstances, police powers

U Understanding—common causes for domestic violence, common inhibitors, awareness that injured party often subsequently declines to prosecute (knowing that 27 is average number of assaults before first reporting)

S Skills—calming a situation, rendering first aid, encouraging assailant and victim (separately) to talk to you, taking notes, collecting evidence (including prompt photographing of alleged injuries)

A Attitudes—no assumptions, not demonising any of those involved, but alert to evidence, ready to caution

B Behaviours—calm, authoritative, non-judgemental, protecting children or the elderly

---

There are many other examples of how KUSAB applies 'across' your actions as a Special Constable, and it is rare that one single aspect of KUSAB applies in isolation.

2.4.1 Special Constables' training

Significantly, when they see a police uniform the public do not distinguish between experienced and novice, any more than they distinguish between a regular police officer and a Special Constable. Whether it is your first tour of duty after your initial foundation training or whether you are a seasoned veteran; in any given crisis or emergency, the public will assume that the person wearing the uniform can and should cope, ensuring everybody's safety and well-being. The sole exception is probably a firearms incident, but even there the public would expect uniformed police officers, Special or not, experienced or not, to contain the situation, get the public into safety and call for support. One might argue that the same applies to a terrorist incident, but there the police are generally dealing with the aftermath, not the threat. The scene of a terrorist attack is the same as any crime scene, needing to be contained and those within taken to safety or given first aid and comfort. The difference is scale, and the threat of further devices. Special Constables might be involved in containment, evacuation or treatment activities, or all of these, but we are discussing basic training, not specialised deployment.

2.4.1.1 Initial foundation-level training—a synopsis

Before you are let loose to perform operational police duties, you will receive initial foundation-level training (nationally designated as **Initial Learning for the Special Constabulary** or 'IL4SC') from your chosen force. This usually takes place at police headquarters, or in another designated police training establishment operated by trainers. The average initial foundation training course lasts between 12 and 16 weeks, with at least one and probably two evenings and a weekend day each week. There is an expectation that you will be able to commit to, and attend all of, these training sessions. There is usually a limited 'run' of training courses at various points throughout the year, often following a recruitment drive. It is important that you choose a course at dates that you are able to commit to fully, without diversion, previous arrangements or leave. You also need to ensure that your employer is aware of your commitment, so that you are not subject to in-work pressures at the same time.

Because you are to perform identical duties, hold exactly the same powers and share the same responsibilities as a regular police officer, your foundation training is very intensive, bearing in mind your volunteer status, and the fact that a probationary police constable's initial taught training is approximately 36 weeks in duration (Bryant *et al* (eds.), 2012). The typical training timescale outlining key milestones in your development as a Special Constable might look like Table 2.1 overleaf (based on IL4SC).

Timescales to achieve independence will, of course, vary depending on the number of hours you are able to work as a Special Constable, your availability to perform duties, the activities and training modules that you complete satisfactorily and reflection on the experiences you gain when on duty, allied to your levels of confidence, skill and knowledge. It is not a race to force you into independence, though it is anticipated that most Special Constables, under average conditions, will be able to achieve Independent Patrol status in 12 months.

The police generally believe in the 'accretion of experience' as an adjunct to, and reinforcement of, training, and you might not be allowed to progress to any other kind of policing unless you first prove yourself capable and resourceful as a patrol officer. If you diversify into a new specialism, for example into roads

Table 2.1 Typical initial training contents (basis for IL4SC)

Induction	Laws, Policies and Guidance
Ethics and Values	Assault
National Occupational Standards	Public Order Offences
People's rights	Theft, robbery and burglary
Developing knowledge and practice	Taking a vehicle without the owner's permission ('twocking')
Health and safety	Criminal Damage
First aid	Drug Awareness
Partnerships and Neighbourhood Policing	Stop & Search (PACE)
	Related Offences
Citizen Focus	Drunk in a public place
Community Safety Partnerships	Firearms awareness
PACT	Arrest and detention
Neighbourhood Policing Teams	Pocket Note Book
Crime prevention	Police communications
Environmental Visual Audits (EVAs)	Powers of entry
Signal Crimes	Summons and warrants
	Taking statements
	Counter-terrorism
	Breach of the peace
	Lost & found property
	Discretion
	Cautions and 'Significant Statements'
	Interviews
	Professionalising the Investigative Process (PIP)
	Road traffic collisions
	Fixed Penalty procedures
	HORT/1 (stopping a vehicle and obtaining documents)
	Driving licences
	Vehicle Defect Rectification Scheme (VDRS)
	Tyres and Lights
	Racially and religiously aggravated offences

KEY POINT

This is an outline version of the IL4SC which we expand upon significantly in Chapters 3, 4 and 5. We might observe at this outline point that the IL4SC 'syllabus' is nationally agreed, usually delivered in-house and is calibrated to represent the commonest events and activities and knowledge that you are likely to encounter early in the job of being a Special Constable. We explain more at the beginning of Chapter 3, where we look at **Induction** (IND) learning and Chapters 4 and 5, where we examine in detail the **legislation, policies and guidelines** (LPG) that you will need to work effectively from the outset of your first patrol. The aim of all your training, both Initial and Follow-Up, is to bring you to the point of **Independent Patrol**—in other words, functioning efficiently and completely as a police officer.

policing, or if you are promoted within the Special Constabulary, then you will be expected to undergo further intensive training and learning. Furthermore, much of the background study and understanding of the context in which you work must be done in your own time (or whatever is left from your normal job and your duty time as a Special Constable). Can't take a joke, shouldn't have joined.

Training courses are most likely to be held and delivered on weekday evenings after 1830 hours and on weekends. This derives from the traditional nature of volunteering, in which the majority of volunteers work conventional weekday 'nine-to-five' jobs and perform their volunteer duties in their spare time—evenings and weekends. These times may be problematic for those of you who work on weekday evenings, or whose duties normally include weekend working, or are tied to a rotating shift pattern. It may also be an issue for those of you who have young children or dependants to care for at home.

In recognition that some Special Constables today don't adhere to the traditional 'nine-to-five' working environment, some forces have attempted to mitigate these problems by providing intensive Special Constabulary foundation training courses in blocks lasting between one and three weeks, with an increasing number of forces likely to implement them in the near future. The aim is to make the training more flexibly available for potential recruits alongside their other work, their family and personal commitments. You should consult your local force to find out if this is an option for you. *Make no mistake though: whether your training is spread out across the year with regular short training slots, or delivered in one or more intensive study sections, there is a lot to learn and a lot of reinforcement learning that you will have to do on your own.*

Your training as a Special Constable often begins from the moment you are successfully accepted as having passed all of the recruitment phases. Your chosen force is likely to send you a list of informative 'pre-reads' (material you should study in advance) and other information forms for you to complete and return. This is so that the force can learn more about you and how you like to learn, and also ascertain which training course you are able to commit to and attend. Moreover, the 'pre-reads' equip you with the knowledge that you will need before attending the first session of your initial foundation-level training course, including what to wear and what to bring.

KEY POINT

We do not suggest that this book is a substitute for your formal training in force as a Special Constable. Rather, *it is an aid and support to your training*, and a companion thereafter, where you can refresh your memory, anticipate situations, read up on things you have not yet done and make sure that you understand key policing concepts, conflicts, controversies and content.

2.5 **Police Training**

Training in the police is designed to be interactive, and uses a variety of teaching and delivery techniques to cater for the widest possible audience and the diversity in each individual's learning style, educational background and life experience. Some of you may not have experienced a formal learning environment since you were at school, but perhaps are highly practical in terms of skills, such as driving or IT; others may be fresh from college or university and used to study, familiar with individual learning and experienced at expressing themselves verbally or in writing, but lacking in practical skills.

Neither position is enough on its own: neither the lately academic, nor the lately practical, has a monopoly on understanding police training. It is a mixture of both, with more added. In order to develop your personal communication skills, confidence and KUSAB, police training *delivery* usually comprises a mixture of:

- **Pre-reads**—are designed to maximise the contact time you have with your trainers and equip you with the knowledge you need before attending a training session, to aid your understanding, ask any questions you may have, to clarify any non- or mis-understandings and to develop better interaction
- **'Board blast'**—discussions led by training staff where responses are invited from students and are written down on a board or flipchart. These responses are assessed and discussed throughout the lesson. The disadvantages are that they allow less confident members of the group to hide behind those more vocal in their contributions. Moreover, given the lack of previous policing experience, it is likely that the list of responses may need to be augmented by the trainers to cover each of the lessons' learning points
- **Case studies**—using a practical example of a police-related problem, you may be invited to read or watch the material and form conclusions about its content to show your understanding and awareness of the subject matter or any issues presented
- **Demonstration**—your tutor will demonstrate to the group how to perform an action so that you can repeat it at a later stage, for example demonstrating the correct procedure when arresting a suspect
- **Small-group work**—in small groups you will be asked to research a set topic, analyse and discuss it amongst the group and present your findings to the rest of the class. The trainers will usually act as facilitators to ensure that the key learning points are drawn out to aid the students' understanding of the topic
- **Individual work**—you may be set individual tasks to ensure that you can work unsupervised. These might include reading your 'pre-read' notes, revising for a knowledge check, giving a presentation to the rest of your group about your findings on a set topic or (less formally) asking questions to clarify any learning points and consolidate your understanding during lessons
- **Lectures**—usually kept to a minimum, though sometimes they are an important way of getting across key learning points quickly, effectively and without confusion

- **Electronic learning**—using computer-based learning (CBL) packages designed by your force or by the National Centre for Applied Learning Technologies (NCALT) system. E-learning aims to present topics in an interactive audio-visual manner that asks questions of the user to check his/her understanding of the material. The advantage is that the user can progress with the training at his/her own pace

- **Presentations**—used for certain topics such as aspects of the criminal law. A speaker will present and discuss the key points, whilst the presentation itself acts as a reference point for those who prefer to learn by reading rather than by listening. Presentations also aid those who wish to take concise training notes. Copies of the presentations may be given out as paper notes or as disks after the session

- **Role-play**—often used to simulate a set scenario, for example performing a stop and search or making an arrest. Student Special Constables play one of the roles in the scenario—for example, the lead police officer, the support police officer or the suspect—and will follow the scenario through to its conclusion. Role-plays are normally used when students have sufficient knowledge and understanding of police procedure and the law to make scenarios meaningful. They are useful in consolidating this knowledge and understanding by allowing you to practise your skills actively in a safe learning environment. A trainer or assessor will oversee the role-play and will conduct a debrief at the end explaining how well you performed and any learning points that need to be highlighted for your awareness, to learn from or bear in mind, when you perform the procedure, possibly in a real situation, next time

- **Practical sessions**—usually first aid, radio and Officer Safety Training are the key practical or physical elements of training based on the 'learning by doing' philosophy. Student Special Constables will be shown a technique and then practise it in pairs and alone until judged proficient. There will be many 'reinforcement' sessions to consolidate what you have practised so that the **S**kills and **K**nowledge (remember **KUSAB**?) involved are firmly embedded, and ranges from the use of rigid handcuffs to cardio-pulmonary resuscitation (CPR)

- **Facilitated/led discussions**—very useful when exploring attitudes, values and behaviours. Often a facilitated/led discussion will be stimulated initially by a film or DVD clip, or by reflecting on a written passage, or by a guest speaker's presentation. The trainer will encourage student Special Constables to discuss, share views, feelings and thoughts in the safe learning environment of the classroom. It is important that confidentiality is maintained since participants might disclose personal, private or sensitive matters that they may not wish others outside the training environment to know about. That said, remember that students will constantly be assessed, monitored and observed by trainers and directing (or 'Di') staff. The safe learning environment of the classroom does not protect or insulate anyone from any disciplinary proceedings for inappropriate language, attitudes or behaviour.

In most cases, foundation training courses are delivered to a maximum of 20 student Special Constables with a class ratio of approximately one trainer to ten student officers or fewer, though other assessors and trainers are brought in to monitor smaller groups, for example when performing role-plays, as appropriate.

You will have plenty of quality contact time with your trainers and they will normally show interest in your progress.

2.5.1 Assessment

Assessment is an ongoing process throughout your training period. You will be visually assessed, monitored and observed by your trainers from the outset of your training. It is therefore essential that you take a professional and mature approach to your training. Whilst you are not attested as a Special Constable immediately on commencing to train, the force will almost certainly view you as a voluntary employee of the police authority and also as a trainee police officer. You are therefore subject to the same professional and organisational standards as the regular police, police staff and police authority employees, and other volunteers. Most importantly, this includes the Standards of Professional Behaviour for police officers. Any inappropriate language, attitudes or behaviours are likely to incur disciplinary proceedings.

Furthermore, the first aid, radio and Officer Safety Training (OST) elements of your training are thoroughly assessed by your trainers and are pass/fail aspects of training because of their importance to your personal safety and that of the public. Should you not reach the required standard in any of these training elements, your trainers will conduct a debrief with you to identify why you have difficulties and discuss what you can do to develop for next time. You would probably be 're-coursed' (that is, put through the training for that particular element again) so that you can attempt this practical aspect of your training with a greater understanding of what is expected of you. Your trainers may also provide additional training notes and perform one-to-one training with you to iron out any shortfalls and improve your performance next time. Having to start again at the beginning (a complete 'back course') is unusual but not unknown—but failure to reach the required standard a second time might mean that you are asked to leave. Every effort will be made to help you to succeed—no one wants to see you fail after all the effort that has been put into your learning, not least by you.

More common and regular forms of assessment are **knowledge checks**. These written or verbal tests are designed to assess whether you have attained the required levels of knowledge and understanding about your role, responsibilities, powers, procedures and other material covered by your foundation training. These knowledge checks take place periodically throughout your foundation training period, culminating in a final written knowledge check covering all aspects of the course before you will be deemed suitable for attestation. Incidentally, and as you've already seen, it is a technique we use in this book to help you to check what you have read and learned. This will be a good 'litmus test' for you to see if the knowledge is going in! Answers to each of the knowledge checks are at the back of the book.

Whilst these assessments should not be viewed as exams to get stressed about, they *are* important for your trainers to gauge whether you have the levels of knowledge to be able to carry out your role as a Special Constable and support your police colleagues safely and effectively when you are attested and deployed on your police area. Written knowledge checks are also used throughout your training to gauge your understanding of the criminal law.

2.6 **Attestation**

Your attestation is the formal ceremony in which you take the oath of office in front of a magistrate, your family, a command officer in the force you have chosen to serve, your Special Constabulary chief officer and other invited guest representatives from the community, the police service or other community safety partnership agencies. Making the oath of attestation in front of the magistrate marks your formal swearing-in as a 'warranted' police officer. You will receive your warrant card and from this moment you hold full police powers. You will be viewed as a police officer by the public, your friends and family, and the police service. The ceremony is a prestigious event and is the culmination of your foundation-level training, and recognises all your commitment, work and learning to date. Ordinarily, it will take place after you have completed your initial foundation training on about week 12 or 13, when you *demonstrate sufficient fundamental policing knowledge, understanding and vocational skills to merit being granted your executive police powers.*

2.7 **Supervised Patrol, Tutoring, Mentoring and Performance Reviews**

Once you are attested, you are able to perform operational police duties, but you will not yet be capable of **Independent Patrol**. As a Special Constable, you may be allocated to a section of Special Constables, usually between five and ten strong, and each with different lengths of service and experience levels. The section may be supervised and led by a Special Sergeant or by a regular police sergeant, or very occasionally by a senior regular constable. It is the supervisor's job to look after your welfare, to monitor your performance and to help your professional development.

The Special Sergeant will usually assign you to an experienced Special Constable, or one who has undergone additional mentor training, or request the help of a regular police officer to take you on a tour of the police station, get you fully equipped with the forms that you will need and take you on a tour of the district you will now police, highlighting problem areas or crime hot spots. The 'mentor Special' or 'tutor constable' (terms vary) may arrange to perform duties with you for a set period, so that you get used to wearing your uniform and performing your core skills such as radio use, stop accounts and searches. All this will be under the experienced officer's eye and with his/her gentle help, which will include basic things such as filling in your pocket notebook (PNB), and completing statements for witnesses of events, to evidential activities or actions that you perform at a crime scene.

It is probable that you would remain with a mentor Special Constable for approximately three months; however, this is flexible and will be determined by your experience, skills, knowledge and confidence levels, the number of hours that you are able to work as a Special Constable and the speed at which you learn and pick things up. There are no hard-and-fast rules, and practice in forces will vary considerably.

KEY POINT—SUPERVISED PATROL

After you have completed your tutored patrol period and have become more proficient in exercising your powers, performing police duties and interacting with suspects and the public with confidence, you will be able to perform Supervised Patrol duties with your regular officer colleagues on patrol or in neighbourhood teams to support them in their work.

Supervised Patrol allows you to gain experience of routine police work, using your police powers and undertaking standard policing procedures.

However, you will almost certainly do this under the observation or supervision of an independent Special Constable or a regular police officer who might take over from you if necessary. This acts as a buffer for you should you encounter a situation that you are unfamiliar with or not yet confident enough to deal with without additional guidance or support. Informally, of course, you will continue to learn from your colleagues as you work with them.

At three-monthly intervals, your section Special Sergeant should conduct tutorials and performance reviews with you. These tutorials and performance reviews should be an open, honest, two-way process in order to ensure that your performance and development are given maximum encouragement. Your personal welfare will also be a consideration. For your Special Sergeant, it is a formal opportunity to provide you with a synopsis of the feedback s/he has received from your mentor, or other officers you have worked with, and there is also the chance to highlight any learning points for you to develop.

Your Special Sergeant will also review your Professional Development Profile (PDP) to monitor how far you are progressing towards Independent Patrol status. S/he may also discuss other relevant or appropriate matters with you concerning your welfare, performance, work, discipline or professional development. For you, these regular tutorials provide the opportunity to discuss any matters that preoccupy or concern you, and give you the chance to describe how you feel you are getting on in the role, any issues you have, any further training that you feel that you would like to receive to support you in your duties and any areas that you feel you would like to develop. It is a dialogue between you. Your Special Sergeant may decide to draft an action plan to help you to develop particular aspects of your work or else provide an opportunity for extra training, or an attachment to a specialist unit, such as to tactical CID or its equivalent, the Roads Policing Unit or the Specialist Search Team (descriptors will vary), to enhance your understanding in these areas of policing by working with those who actually do the job on a daily basis. This can be a fundamental and highly enjoyable learning experience, but it also gives you the chance to see what other kinds of policing there are outside patrol and community policing.

2.8 **Policing Skills and Core Competencies**

There is an expectation that you will have achieved *all of your core training* within six months of attestation as a Special Constable and that you will have achieved *Independent Patrol status* within 12 months of the same. After the IL4SC comes the skills-evidencing stage. This is where your PDP plays an important role. It is one thing to have received training in an aspect of policing, for example in how to carry out an effective stop and search, but it is quite another to do one yourself whilst complying with your legal obligations, ensuring your personal safety and that of your colleagues, communicating with the detained person and trying to locate the object of your search.

Your PDP contains a list of key operational policing skills and core competencies that you must attain before you will be considered for Independent Patrol status. These skills and competencies are termed the **Police Action Checklist** (PAC) and comprise a series of headings, each with a list of sub-skill headings. You will be required to evidence each PAC heading and each of its sub-skills a number of times (usually three to four), or as many times as you feel necessary for you to become proficient and confident.

The evidence of attaining each skill will come in various forms. It could be evidence from your PNB, from any forms or 'tickets' you have competed or issued during your tour of duty, written witness testimony from colleagues who have observed you performing one of your PAC skills or from any forms or reports generated from your actions, such as arrest summary reports. Collecting the evidence is far from difficult, because it is simply the collation and grouping of the actions and activities you perform on every duty. Part of the skill is organising the mass of evidence you will quickly accumulate into the appropriate PAC heading or subheading. Most officers find the taxing part is recording the evidence in their PDP; however, this is usually because they do not keep on top of their PDP and do not record the evidence as they achieve it. This makes it a fairly hefty job later on, so:

KEY POINT—BEST PRACTICE

Best practice is to record your PDP/PAC evidence as you go, and write it up at the end of each tour of duty you perform.

2.8.1 Continuous professional development

In addition to your operational policing hours, most forces run weekly or bi-weekly, uniformed Special Constabulary training or 'parade' nights at your police station, or the main district station in larger BCUs. Your attendance is expected, and should take precedence over performing operational police duties. Not only are these meeting nights an invaluable chance to catch up on any administration or process that you might have outstanding, but they are also an opportunity for your supervisory special officers or Area Special Constabulary Coordinator (ASCC) to share important information with you, such as impending operations, or events that extra officers are required at and that you might wish to take part in, or to advise you about important area news, changes to force policy or indeed the law. They might also conduct an intelligence briefing so that you are aware of the BCU priorities, crime hot spots and prolific offenders relevant to your patrol during the forthcoming duty.

Sometimes training inputs are arranged to enhance officer skills on a specific offence or aspect of policing, such as the completion of crime reports or common problems in dealing with a road traffic collision. On other occasions, other specialist departments (such as Fraud, or Professional Standards) might come along to inform you about their work and how your work as a Special Constable can support them. Essentially, this ongoing training is about keeping you as up to date as possible, bearing in mind that crime and policing can change very quickly. It is also valuable, as you have more limited exposure to these experiences since you are not a regular officer and can only commit a limited number of hours each week or month to performing policing duties.

Ongoing training and learning might include:

- **Safety**—including dynamic risk assessments and use of radio
- **Information management**—including intelligence reporting in accordance with the National Intelligence Model (NIM)
- **Patrol**—including crime reporting, knowledge of offences and abilities to deal with them
- **Search**—safe and competent skills at searching persons, vehicles and property
- **Investigation**—including evidence gathering, writing and taking statements, accurate note taking in your PNB, use of caution and arrest procedure

- **Disposal**—including reporting for summons, Penalty Notice for Disorder (PND) and street cautions
- **Custody procedures**—including booking in a prisoner
- **Finalise investigations**—including charging suspects, giving evidence at court and submitting case files
- **Roads policing**—including issuing Fixed Penalty Notices (FPNs), HORT/1s and VDRS and dealing with drink-drive offences
- **Property**—including dealing with found and special property, handling, preserving and managing physical evidence.

2.8.2 Independent Patrol status and advanced training

At about 12 months' service, you should be ready for Independent Patrol status, if you have not already achieved this.

KEY POINT—INDEPENDENT PATROL

Independence allows you to patrol unsupervised—that is, without the direct supervision of another independent Special Constable or regular officer—and allows you to patrol solo, or take out up to two other non-independent Special Constables to help them to achieve their independence, and act as lead officer when dealing with incidents or emergency situations.

Whilst achievement of Independent Patrol status would seem to make the Special Constabulary more flexible for you, it does carry increased responsibilities. By patrolling as an independent officer, you will take ownership of everything you deal with. You should not rush to achieve independence: rather, you should wait until you feel able enough to deal with any given incident by yourself, confident that, as a result of your training and learning, and the consolidation of your experience, you will get it right.

2.9 The National Occupational Standards (NOS)

The NOS are intended to show what a Special Constable can do competently, what s/he cannot do quite so well and where the consequent learning gaps are (see also 3.3 on technical/specialist NOS). The problem with the NOS is that evidencing each of the skills to the competency required involves lots of cross-checked paperwork, analysis of and reflection on examples, 'expert' and specialist assessment ('testimony') and the investment of considerable amounts of time to ensure the completion of the paperwork. Since the Special Constable's time is limited, this seems to many commentators and practitioners to get in the way of operational policing rather than complementing it. It is in this context that we wish briefly to explore the subject of NOS—which, to be fair, do exactly what it says on the tin:

KEY POINT—NATIONAL OCCUPATIONAL STANDARDS

National occupational standards describe the **standards of performance** that people are expected to achieve in their work and the **knowledge and the skills** they need to **perform effectively**. National occupational standards have been developed to cover most occupational areas [of work] in the UK.

(Skills for Justice, 2006: 3; emphases added)

There can be no doubt that the key terminology here is that which we have highlighted in the box—*standards of performance, knowledge and skills, perform effectively*. Therefore it is not surprising that police forces, the Home Office and Skills for Justice (the organisation that administers and develops NOS) have placed great emphasis on individual Special Constables achieving such competence (see also 3.3).

2.9.1 Developments within NOS

At the time of writing, there are quite profound developments taking place in the world of NOS and no one knows precisely where it will end. It is quite possible that, by the time you read this, the details which we outline in the following sections may have changed. The onus is on you to check out any changes, additions, amalgamations or omissions with either your in-force training or local personal development units. At the moment, there are five Personal Qualities Standards which a Special Constable is expected to demonstrate. They are:

Decision-making

Assimilates complex information quickly, weighing up alternatives and making sound, timely decisions. Gathers and considers all relevant and available information, seeking out and listening to advice from specialists. Asks incisive questions to test facts and assumptions, and gain a full understanding of the situation. Identifies the key issues clearly, and the interrelationship between different options at a local and national level, assessing the costs, risks and benefits of each. Prepared to make the ultimate decision, even in conditions of ambiguity and uncertainty. Makes clear, proportionate and justifiable decisions, reviewing these as necessary.

Professionalism

Acts with integrity, in line with the values and ethical standards of the Police Service. Delivers on promises, demonstrating personal commitment, energy and drive to get things done. Defines and reinforces standards, demonstrating these personally and fostering a culture of personal responsibility throughout the force. Asks for and acts on feedback on own approach, continuing to learn and adapt to new circumstances. Takes responsibility for making tough or unpopular decisions, demonstrating courage and resilience in difficult situations. Remains calm and professional under pressure and in conditions of uncertainty. Openly acknowledges shortcomings in service and commits to putting them right.

Leadership

(a) Openness to change

Positive about change, adapting rapidly to different ways of working and putting effort into making them work. Flexible and open to alternative approaches to solving problems. Finds better, more cost-effective ways to do things, making suggestions for change. Takes an innovative and creative approach to solving problems.

(b) Service delivery

Understands the organisation's objectives and priorities, and how own work fits into these. Plans and organises tasks effectively, taking a structured and methodical approach to achieving outcomes. Manages multiple tasks effectively by thinking things through in advance, prioritising and managing time well. Focuses on the outcomes to be achieved, working quickly and accurately and seeking guidance when appropriate.

Public service

Promotes a real belief in public service, focusing on what matters to the public and will best serve their interests. Ensures that all staff understand the expectations, changing needs and concerns of different communities, and strives to address them. Builds public confidence by actively engaging with different communities, agencies and strategic stakeholders, developing effective partnerships at a local and national level. Understands partners' perspectives and priorities, working cooperatively with them to develop future public services within budget constraints, and deliver the best possible overall service to the public.

Working with others

Builds effective working relationships through clear communication and a collaborative approach. Maintains visibility and ensures communication processes work effectively throughout the force and with external bodies. Consults widely and involves people in decision-making, speaking in a way they understand and can engage with. Treats people with respect and dignity regardless of their background or circumstances, promoting equality and the elimination of discrimination. Treats people as individuals, showing tact, empathy and compassion. Negotiates effectively with local and national bodies, representing the interests of the Police Service. Sells ideas convincingly, setting out benefits of a particular approach and striving to reach mutually beneficial solutions. Expresses own views positively and constructively. Fully commits to team decisions.

(Adapted from the *Policing Professional Framework*, Skills for Justice, available at <https://www.skillsforjustice-ppf.com/?rg_id=13&r_id=135#re>; accessed 20 August 2012)

2.9.1.1 The ten professional NOS for a Constable (see 3.3)

In 2011, a new consolidated and truncated set of ten NOS was developed for the police service; this reduced the original number of 22 NOS for a constable and formulated according to the rank and responsibility of the individual. There is no distinction between the competences required of a regular police constable and those for a Special Constable:

1. Provide initial support to victims, survivors and witnesses and assess their need for further support
2. Gather and submit information that has the potential to support law enforcement objectives
3. Provide an initial response to incidents
4. Arrest, detain or report individuals
5. Conduct priority and volume investigations
6. Interview victims and witnesses in relation to priority and volume investigations
7. Interview suspects in relation to priority and volume investigations
8. Search individuals and their personal property
9. Carry out systematic searches of vehicles, premises and open areas
10. Manage conflict.

(See Skills for Justice, available at <https://www.skillsforjustice-ppf.com/?rg_id=8&r_id=1#re>; accessed 20 August 2012)

DISCUSSION POINTS

How do you ensure that volunteer police officers are assessed as being competent for their role, as they should be, whilst not making their limited volunteering hours all about assessment? How do you ensure a balance between attaining NOS and doing the job?

It could be quite dispiriting for a Special Constable to spend his/her designated 16 hours per month of volunteering in a continual round of NOS completion and form filling. It is fair to acknowledge that a balance is being sought through a dialogue between ACPO, the Special Constabulary Strategic Command and Skills for Justice. What balance will be struck, however, is not yet clear. Some might argue that attaining the NOS *is* doing the job.

2.9.1.2 How could NOS be used in the Special Constabulary?

By themselves, NOS do not improve individual performance; they need to be put into a *performance management* context. This requires the NOS to become part of the annual appraisal process and, in particular, they are crucial in the first year to 18 months, during which a new Special Constable works towards independence (see 3.3). Furthermore, the NOS need to be utilised in all forms of training for the Special Constabulary, so that competence can be assessed and gaps in knowledge or skills promptly identified, and then addressed. Only then can the NOS begin to be used correctly for the benefit of both the individual and the organisation, in what is a cyclical process as outlined Figure 2.1.

Figure 2.1 NOS as cyclic skill determinants

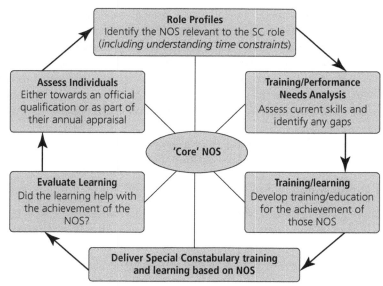

Source: adapted from Skills for Justice, 2006: 5

2.9.1.3 Some difficulties in utilising the NOS within the Special Constabulary

- **Time constraints**—Special Constables volunteer to help with policing, and might be frustrated by continuous and bureaucratic assessment. They might see the NOS as getting between them and the job, rather than being an effective way of evaluating how well they do the job

- **Use of regular officer NOS**—these are not bespoke for the Special Constabulary and therefore do not take into account the unique volunteering perspective
- **Achievement of NOS**—a Special Constable may find it difficult to achieve all the NOS in a specified period, particularly if s/he does not encounter some given or routine situations upon which the NOS are predicated
- **Assessing the NOS**—as Special Constables predominantly work in the evenings/weekends, some assessors might not be available to observe the Special Constable in action and to assess completion of a NOS indicator
- **Training the NOS**—as with the previous point, it can be difficult for training to be given to Special Constables in a standard 'Monday–Friday, 9–5' training context; weekend training tends to be crammed anyway
- **Utilising the NOS**—many Special Constables do not receive annual appraisals that take the NOS into account. This lack reduces the effectiveness, relevance and utility of the NOS.

2.9.1.4 Delivering on the NOS

It is evident that, as a species of work-based assessment, the NOS can be used to the benefit of individual performance and therefore can contribute to the achievement of overall organisational aims. Furthermore, used within a training context, the NOS can help with retention and 'job satisfaction' by providing Special Constables with access to training and assessment that truly matters—individual Special Constables will feel valued by their forces as a consequence of a substantial investment in their skills and development. However, this can tend to the utopian.

Bureaucracy still dominates the NOS and there are many difficulties in properly utilising them within the Special Constabulary.

2.9.1.5 Conclusion

Competence is, of course, the *minimum* level of attainment of NOS by the Special Constabulary that the public should expect. However, it remains to be seen how Special Constables can be 'assessed for competence' under the NOS (full or 'core') without making individuals dissipate their available time in pursuit of a paper exercise. The NOS must be made brisker, more practical and more meaningful to the Special Constabulary without compromising operational effectiveness and without devaluing the Special Constables' gift of time. See 3.3 for more detail on the technical and specialist competences in the NOS.

TEST BOX 3

Now we want to help you to check that you have understood about training and development.

1. What does KUSAB stand for?
2. Approximately how long will your initial learning take?
3. What are 'pre-reads'?
4. Name three other techniques which your training staff might use.
5. What is the commonest form of assessment?
6. What happens at Attestation?
7. How often are you likely to have a tutorial and performance review with your section Special Sergeant?
8. What does your PDP indicate to your supervisor?
9. Why might 'parade nights' be important for you?
10. What are NOS?

Further Reading

ACPO, *Guidance on the Use of Incapacitant Spray* (2006, London: ACPO)

——, *Guidance on the Use of Handcuffs* (2009, London: ACPO)

Bryant, R. and Bryant, S. (eds.), *Blackstone's Handbook for Policing Students 2013* (2012, Oxford: Oxford University Press)

Caless, B. (ed.), with Bryant, R., Spruce, B. and Underwood, R. *Blackstone's Police Community Support Officer's Handbook*, 2nd edn. (2010, Oxford: Oxford University Press)

Carroll, G. and Boutall, T., 'Guide to Developing National Occupational Standards' (2009, Skills for Justice, available at <http://nos.ukces.org.uk/Guidance%20Documents/0611%20Guide%20for%20Developing%20NOS%20Final%20Version%202%20June%202011.pdf>; accessed 20 August 2012)

NPIA, 'Airwave Radio' (2009, NPIA, available at <http://www.npia.police.uk/en/10506.htm>; accessed 13 November 2012)

Skills for Justice, *A Guide to the Development of Education and Training Using the National Occupational Standards* (2006, Sheffield: Skills for Justice)

Induction

3.1 **Introduction**

This chapter is designed to complement the outline of the *Initial Learning for the Special Constabulary* (IL4SC) programme; itself a basic frame for a Special Constable's 'police syllabus' in England and Wales, which we introduced in the previous chapter (2.5). The IL4SC is in three parts, of which we cover two in this book: (1) **Induction** and (2) **legislation, policies and guidelines (LPG)**. The third element is **operational policing**, which self-evidently, we cannot cover (though we do give it a context throughout the book). In this chapter, we cover the main Induction Modules and in the next two chapters, we look in some detail at the legislation, policies and guidelines.

3.1.1 **Police Initial Learning Programmes**

With a view to standardising the initial learning and development of *all* uniformed members within the police family, the National Police Improvement Agency (NPIA) designed an 'Initial Curriculum' in 2011 for England and Wales, comprising three programmes:

- Initial Police Learning and Development Programme (IPLDP) for **regular officers**
- Police Community Support Officers National Learning Programme (for **PCSOs**)
- **Initial Learning for the Special Constabulary** (IL4SC).

The national curricula for each of the three programmes are derived from generic modules. Consequently each programme may share modules with another, but each of the three will vary in the number of its modules, according to the needs of the learners. This can seem confusing in isolation, because numbering will not seem sequential (but numbering *is* sequential when all three programmes are considered together).

As noted, there are three groups of generic modules. The first two are designed to be learned in a 'safe environment' such as a classroom, whereas the third is more likely to be learned during accompanied patrol, which obviously we cannot replicate in this book. Instead, we aim to provide you with the underpinning knowledge and understanding for the Induction and the legislation, policies and guidelines modules of the IL4SC. In other words, we have taken the generic bits of initial policing learning and development which relate to the Special Constabulary, and analysed and commented on them for you; presenting them in the chapters which follow.

KEY POINT

Abbreviations and acronyms are everywhere in policing. Check the Abbreviations section at the front of the book if you are unsure or forget what the apparently random groups of initials mean.

3.2 (IND1) Underpinning Ethics and Values of the Police Service

There are ten general 'professional standards' which govern police behaviour, breach of any part of which will render you liable to disciplinary proceedings. As noted, the Standards are enshrined in law, and you must observe them in your everyday conduct, as you would observe any other law.

3.2.1 The Standards of Professional Behaviour

Police Regulations which gave guidance for ethical behaviour were revised in 2008 and a Schedule (No 3) was added in a Statutory Instrument (SI No 2864) which reflected a new emphasis. The following are the revised **Standards of Professional Behaviour**, full details of which may be found at <http://www.legislation.gov.uk/uksi/2008/2864/contents/made>.

In each case we have used the SI 2864 'headline' wording in italics, and followed it with our own brief commentary and explanation.

3.2.1.1 Honesty and integrity

Police officers are honest, act with integrity and do not compromise or abuse their position.

This is about probity (ethical or 'right' action), and is part of the 'Nolan Principles' which govern proper behaviour in public office, and include: selflessness, integrity, objectivity, accountability, openness, honesty and leadership (by which Lord Nolan meant 'example', see further reading at the end of the chapter). Without honesty, a Special Constable cannot be trusted; without integrity, the job s/he does will be partial or biased in some way; and the position of the sworn officer is one where considerable powers are granted in the expectation that those powers will be applied 'without fear or favour'; in other words, the Special Constable should never do something because of feeling obligated or under pressure to do someone a favour.

3.2.1.2 Authority, respect and courtesy

Police officers act with self-control and tolerance, treating members of the public with respect and courtesy. Police officers do not abuse their powers or authority and respect the rights of all individuals.

'Abuse of powers' is among the major public complaints about police officers' actions, manifested often as high-handedness, incivility and arrogance. Nick Hardwick, then Chair of the Independent Police Complaints Commission (IPCC), said this in 2008: 'It is unacceptable that nearly half of all complaints [against the police] involve neglect or rudeness. There is absolutely no excuse for being rude to the public.' (See <http://www.telegraph.co.uk./news/uknews/3074592/Police-rudeness-attacked-by-watchdog.html>; accessed 14 November 2012.)

Mr Hardwick includes the Special Constabulary, PCSOs and other members of the extended policing family in his reference to 'complaints against the police'. It is sometimes difficult, in the face of deliberate provocation or abuse from the public, for a Special Constable to remain cool and calm, but the abiding characteristic of the 'good copper' is imperturbable fairness and impartiality, not loss of temper or abuse of power. 'Respecting the rights of all individuals' is much easier to write about than to do; and it does not simply refer to people who are different in terms of skin colour, or gender, or sexual orientation. Discriminatory behaviour of any kind has no place in the Special Constabulary, or anywhere else in policing. However, treating a paedophile or child murderer with tolerance and respect *can be very difficult*, and some crimes which Special Constables have to investigate are abhorrent by any civilised standard. For all one's individual feelings of repugnance and disgust at what people might have done, the external treatment of and attitude towards such offenders must still be exemplary.

3.2.1.3 **Equality and diversity**

Police officers act with fairness and impartiality. They do not discriminate unlawfully or unfairly.

We noted earlier that discrimination is not tolerated in the Special Constabulary, and this extends to age, disability and belief, as well as to skin colour or race, gender or sexual orientation. Indeed, most of these forms of discrimination are unlawful.

But **diversity is about difference**, and the positive way to approach difference is to accept it and learn from it, not to oppose it or seek to act prejudicially against it.

3.2.1.4 **Use of force**

Police officers only use force to the extent that it is necessary, proportionate and reasonable in all the circumstances.

Most forces have a mnemonic or handy reminder of the principle of proportionality guiding the use of force or compulsion. The most common is **PLAN**:

P Proportionate
L Legal
A Authorised
N Necessary

---

but there are other examples which say more or less the same things. This professional behaviour standard is about what is right and appropriate to do in the circumstances, and the majority of Special Constables have plenty of common sense to guide them. Occasionally, the use of force is authorised, for example to compel protesters to move away from obstructing a highway, in order to allow access to emergency vehicles; but in almost every instance except aggressive resistance, it is better to persuade someone to do something than to make that person do something. Much criticism was directed at the Metropolitan Police, for example, because officers used anti-terrorist powers to deal with protesters at the G20 economic summit in London in April 2009. There is a spectrum of responses which usefully illustrates the point, as shown in Figure 3.1 (adapted from Caless (ed.), 2010: 417):

Figure 3.1 Aggression response spectrum

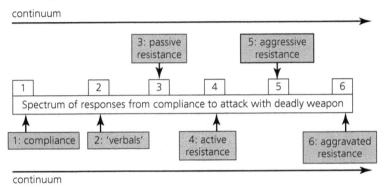

or we might remember the point behind this deceptively simple model, where sometimes (but importantly, not always) your aggression *can* provoke aggression; your incivility *can* produce an equally dismissive response. There are other times when you will have to cut across this pattern, impose your will and make an arrest. See Figure 3.2:

Figure 3.2 Betari's Box

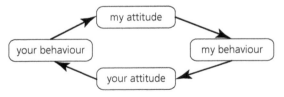

With care, common sense and some luck, such occasions ought to be uncommon.

3.2.1.5 Orders and instructions

Police officers only give and carry out lawful orders and instructions. Police officers abide by police regulations, force policies and lawful orders.

Special Constables should only ever give **lawful orders** and instructions, and only ever receive them. You cannot hazard the safety of members of the public, for example by telling them to cross a busy road or to drive faster than the speed limit, except under highly unusual conditions such as the urgent and overriding need to save lives. Common sense plays a large part in the orders and instructions which a Special Constable gives and receives; but always, at the back of any action or order, is the spectre that, if things go badly wrong, it might be in the dispassionate and clinical atmosphere of a court that such actions and orders are scrutinised. Remember the police shooting of Jean-Charles de Menezes in London in July 2005, and how the media coverage, consequent inquiry, accusations and strong emotions surrounding that unfortunate event completely overshadowed the excellent work which the Metropolitan Police and the other emergency services had performed in dealing with the aftermath of the terrorist attacks on public transport on 7 July 2005.

3.2.1.6 Duties and responsibilities

Police officers are diligent in the exercise of their duties and responsibilities.

The technical legal term for not doing what you should do in public office is **non-feasance**: this applies to diligence, or 'careful and persistent industriousness'. A Special Constable should never ignore situations where someone is breaking the law, creating a nuisance or upsetting other people. That said, whilst there is always an absolute duty to save life, a Special Constable can exercise discretion whether or not to apply the law in some circumstances. That is *not* the same as turning a blind eye. In addition, diligence entails enthusiasm for the job of policing, a readiness to take responsibility and a willingness to go into places and to do things which ordinary members of the public might reasonably refuse to do (such as stopping a fight, defusing an angry quarrel, going into a rowdy pub, entering a house where death is suspected and so on).

3.2.1.7 Confidentiality

Police officers treat information with respect and access or disclose it only in the proper course of police duties.

Relationships between Special Constables and the media (particularly a friendly local journalist who often casts the police in a favourable light), have to be carefully managed, to avoid crossing the line between protecting information and improperly disclosing it. In general terms, **confidentiality** means that Special Constables should not discuss any police activity with anyone from the media, always referring enquiries to the force media spokesperson or media centre. The principle of **need to know** should be paramount: as a police officer, you only tell someone something confidential about policing if s/he *needs* to know it in order to do his/her job. We only need to recall the sorry saga of the phone-hacking scandal which dominated media/police relations in 2012, to be aware of how easy it is for officers, in too close a relationship with the media, to fail to 'treat information with respect' (see <http://www.levesoninquiry.org.uk/>; accessed 14 November 2012).

3.2.1.8 **Fitness for duty**

Police officers when on duty or presenting themselves for duty are fit to carry out their responsibilities.

This is a straightforward principle about being able, physically or mentally, to do the job, and not doing something (or refraining from doing something) which would compromise that ability. The classic example is being unfit through drink to drive a car, and in some forces police officers face dismissal if convicted of drink-driving. Other forces are more tolerant, but there can be no reasonable excuse for turning up for rostered duty impaired by drink. The same principles apply to drugs, with the additional observation that the taking of illegal drugs is a criminal offence.

3.2.1.9 **Discreditable conduct**

Police officers behave in a manner which does not discredit the police service or undermine public confidence in it, whether on or off duty. Police officers report any action taken against them for a criminal offence, any conditions imposed on them by a court or the receipt of any penalty notice.

A Special Constable who has a court order for bankruptcy proceedings must declare it, as must one who has been ordered by a court not to approach an ex-partner, for example. A Special Constable convicted of a crime may be dismissed if the offence is grave enough: normally crimes of deception, theft, sexual predation or violence fall into the dismissal category, depending upon severity and any court ruling or comment. In its less severe form, this standard is about being sensible on social networks (not uploading nude photographs of yourself or others, for example); and in your private life, making sure that your actions do not discredit the force or bring policing into disrepute. You should realise by now that a higher standard of behaviour and social responsibility is expected of you as a police officer than of society as whole.

3.2.1.10 **Challenging and reporting improper conduct**

Police officers report, challenge or take action against the conduct of colleagues which has fallen below the Standards of Professional Behaviour.

This is an internal measure, designed to ensure that Special Constables treat their colleagues in the rest of the Constabulary, and in the extended policing family, with respect. It is important that the kinds of attitude which characterised Mark Daly's exposé of racist police trainees in the BBC's *The Secret Policeman* in 2003, are challenged internally by colleagues and fellow officers, so that discrimination and intolerance are eliminated from the police service. This applies as much to any other form of discriminatory behaviour as it does to racism, and will cover bullying, intolerance and offensive language as well as behaviour. This is not intended to create a breed of police 'informants' but to ensure that the police become and remain non-prejudiced non-discriminators. **There is no place in policing for sexism, racism or prejudice.**

3.2.1.11 Police Regulations apply in their entirety to Special Constables

The Explanatory Note in the Police (Conduct) Regulations 2008 makes it clear that '[t]he Regulations establish procedures for the taking of disciplinary proceedings in respect of the conduct of members of police forces and special constables' (SI No 2864). In other words, whatever applies to the regular police officer in terms of required behaviour and professional standards applies equally *in law* to the Special Constable, which is, of course, how it should be.

3.3 **The National Occupational Standards (NOS)**

Now we move from police conduct governed by law to ways in which you are assessed in performing your duties. These are the **National Occupational Standards**, which have lately undergone some revisions and necessary pruning and shortening, and which we considered earlier in 2.9 in the learning and training context. What used to be something of a bureaucratic exercise for Special Constabulary joiners in their first years have been trimmed and polished so that the 'NOS' now relate better to the work that a Special Constable will do. The NOS are about competence to do the job, so you either attain that competence or you do not. There is no 'nearly'.

DISCUSSION POINTS

You should be aware that the NOS do not distinguish in competences between a regular officer and a Special Constable: in other words, there is no allowance for the fact that you work part-time. Do you think that there should be such a distinction? How might you angle or modify the NOS so that the Special Constables' hours of work are taken into consideration? Does it matter?

In the sections which follow, we present the NOS individually, examine the sorts of competence expected of you and then comment on ways in which you might do it. This is a guide, not a crib, and there is no substitute for you completing your own work in order to demonstrate your abilities and behaviours. Remember that attaining Independent Patrol status will depend very much on how well you demonstrate your NOS competency. The following NOS are part of the Induction modules in IL4SC.

3.3.1 **(IND2) Foster people's equality, diversity and rights**

The first three 'performance criteria' (what you need to show you can do) could be completed using separate incidents/events, but in terms of completing the NOS portfolio it makes sense to use one event or situation to evidence several criteria:

1. Recognise a person's right to make [his/her] own decisions and acknowledge [his/her] responsibilities
2. Interpret the meaning of rights and responsibilities consistently with existing legislative framework and organisational policy
3. Provide **information**, which is up to date and takes account of the complexity of the decision which people might need to make.

The third criterion comes with two 'range statements', **written** and **unwritten**.

3.3.1.1 Appropriate help

The performance criterion within this unit is: 'Give **appropriate help** to people who are unable to exercise their rights personally'. This has two range statements attached—(a) speaking on behalf of the person when s/he is not able to do so, and (b) seeking support from someone else to help in the exercise of rights.

DISCUSSION POINTS

Why might some people be unable to exercise their rights personally?
What benefits and/or problems could arise from helping people to exercise their rights?

Example

Take the situation of a refugee family living in your area who do not speak fluent English and who have no contact with other people from their country of origin to assist them. They might have a problem with their housing and nervously approach you as you patrol, or in the margins of a community meeting. If you then speak to the housing association/local authority/landlord on their behalf, you are meeting this criterion along with range statement (a). If you put the family in touch with a refugee help group or community group that has access to an interpreter for their particular language or dialect, you are meeting range statement (b).

3.3.1.2 Support, record, inform

The next three criteria can also be bracketed together as a further illustration of the evidential value, within the context of the NOS portfolio, of events that you deal with:

4. Acknowledge and provide **appropriate support** towards the resolution of **tensions** between rights and responsibilities
5. Ensure that the necessary records relating to the promotion of rights and responsibilities are accurate, legible and complete
6. Provide the necessary information to people who wish to make a complaint about an infringement of their rights.

Criterion 5 comes with four range statements, the first two relating to the **appropriate support** portion. These are (a) **direct challenges to the people concerned** and (b) **help sought from others towards a resolution**. The two relating to the **tensions** aspect are (c) **within people** and (d) **between people**.

Task

Using the following example, place the performance criteria and the range statements so that they can be used as evidence within your NOS portfolio.

Example

At a community surgery, a couple approach you. They are having problems with their neighbour over the issue of a replacement fence. They claim that the fence is the responsibility of their neighbour and is shown on their property deeds as such. This fence is in poor repair and the neighbour's dog is forever getting through and fouling their garden. They state that when they speak to their neighbours they receive abuse. The couple have resorted to chucking the dog mess back over the fence because they are fed up with this situation.

You advise the couple that throwing the mess back over the fence only makes the situation worse and explain that this is a civil issue and that they need to speak to a solicitor. You also advise them to contact the Environmental Health Agency, or that part of their local council that deals with environmental health issues, and offer to find out if there are mediation services available to help to resolve these tensions. You make full notes in your PNB throughout.

3.3.2 **Respecting people's rights**

The NOS criteria will require you to

1. Show consistency with people's expressed beliefs and views and acknowledge the benefits of **diversity**
2. Promote anti-discriminatory practice in ways which are consistent with legislative frameworks and organisational policy
3. Take **appropriate action** to minimise the impact of discrimination and oppression on people
4. Promote equality and diversity and seek advice and guidance when difficulties arise

5. Record information which is consistent with the promotion of equality and diversity.

Criterion 1 has two range statements attached—(a) individual and social characteristics, (b) values and beliefs. There are also two range statements for criterion 3—(a) challenge the source of discrimination, (b) seek the support of others to challenge discrimination.

Task

Rather than provide you with an example to illustrate the practicality of these issues, this time we want you to do some research on your own:

1. What are the six strands of diversity?
2. What legislation applies to each of these strands?
3. Within your own force, identify the policies relating to each of these strands and where they can be found.
4. Consider what agencies/support groups exist within your community for each of the six strands of diversity.
5. Look at what anti-discriminatory activities are taking place in your area and consider what role you could play in promoting and upholding these.

Undertaking this within your community and within your police force, on your own or with other colleagues, will then provide you with all the tools and information for the successful completion of this unit, and help to ensure your professional commitment to the principles of embracing diversity and promoting it wherever you are and whatever you do.

3.3.3 (IND3) Develop one's own knowledge and practice

The following section is necessarily brief because there is no one set way to develop your own knowledge and practice. In order to become a 'reflective practitioner' there is some signposting we can do but if this were to be too prescriptive, ironically, it would be pointless given that no other person can be your reflective guide; this has to come from within you.

However, there is one starting point that we can state: reflective learning = interest in practice = increased professionalism. You will encounter many experiences as a Special Constable and you need to develop the means to digest, process and learn from those experiences.

This can be expressed through the Experiential Learning Cycle which you may well have come across in your education, training or day job (Figure 3.3).

Figure 3.3 Experiential Learning Cycle
Source: adapted from Kolb, 1984, see Further Reading at the end of the chapter

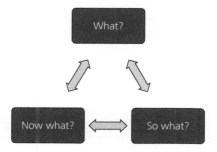

This emphasises how learning is cyclical and never-ending and how you take experiences and relate them to future ones. It may be a cliché, but it is often true of the best police officers that they never stop learning.

Task

Consider the ways that you as an individual can develop your reflective practitioner skills.

There are numerous ways you can develop your reflective skills, so the following is not exhaustive:

- Talk to colleagues or discuss experiences
- Talk to trusted friends and family (mindful of confidentiality issues)
- Write a reflective diary
- Attend training—an important part of being a Special Constable is to maintain current knowledge
- Use your (annual) evaluation process to highlight strengths and to consider ways of addressing areas for development
- Be honest about your performance
- Consider the use of online training—**please remember to be aware of your own force's rules on online behaviour**
- Use the facilities of your force to develop further—peer mentoring, probationer development trainers, experienced colleagues, additional training etc.

We did say this section was brief because the main impetus for self-development must come from the individual. We cannot make you a reflective practitioner but can point you to the benefits of being so. In short, a reflective practitioner is a better practitioner and if you get used to thinking critically and objectively about your actions, the benefits will stay with you throughout your time in the Special Constabulary and beyond.

3.3.4 **(IND5) Ensure your own actions reduce the risk to health and safety**

This unit has two distinct elements, which seek to identify and reduce the health and safety risks that exist in your workplace or within your role. Read about **dynamic risk assessment** so that you are familiar with both the process and the reasons for doing it. Several of the elements in this NOS will be particular to your own individual workplace and the role you will be expected to perform in your area, and so this section needs to be general rather than specific. As with the other NOS sections, it is about highlighting potential avenues for exploration rather than providing actual events.

Definition of dynamic risk assessment

A dynamic risk assessment is one that develops as a situation changes. It entails identifying hazards, taking actions which reduce or eliminate risks, making continuous assessments and monitoring what is happening all the time. By actively engaging in this way, it may be possible to stop a bad situation getting worse.

DISCUSSION POINTS

What health and safety training were you given on your Special Constable training course, or since?

Do you have access to handouts, booklets, advice sheets or course notes that may help you to complete this unit?

Were you informed of the main legislation in relation to health and safety?

If the answer to any of these questions is no, try to find out which legislation is applicable in your workplace (a good place to start this research would be the website of the Health and Safety Executive—<http://www.hse.gov.uk>).

3.3.5 **Hazards and risks in the workplace**

The first element of this unit is **4G2.1**, *Identify the hazards and evaluate the risks in your workplace*. This is divided, for ease of understanding, into seven distinct performance criteria; but they do not have to be evidenced individually. It may be that one event could be used to evidence several simultaneously:

1. Correctly name and locate the person(s) responsible for health and safety in the workplace
2. Identify which workplace policies are relevant to your working practices
3. Identify those working practices in any part of your job role, which could harm you or other people
4. Identify those aspects of the workplace which could harm you or other people

5. Evaluate which of the potentially harmful working practices and the potentially harmful aspects of the workplace are those with the highest **risk** to you or to others
6. Report those hazards which present a high **risk** to the persons responsible for health and safety in the workplace
7. Deal with hazards with low **risks** in accordance with workplace policies and legal requirements.

The last three criteria have five range statements attached to them—(a) use and maintenance of machinery and equipment, (b) working practices which do not conform to established policies, (c) unsafe behaviour, (d) accidental breakages and spillages, and (e) environmental factors.

3.3.5.1 Evidencing your responses to risk

The first four criteria could be evidenced within your initial period on station or Basic Command Unit (BCU). It may be that you receive a welcome pack or a structured introduction which could identify most of these points, such as who the nominated health and safety representative is (**1**), or how to access your force policy on health and safety (**2**). Given that your 'workplace' includes your patrol area and community, these too can be taken into account when completing this section. If a formal risk assessment has been completed, then this could serve as substantive evidence because it would identify potential risks for your policing role (**3**) as well as physical or environmental risks in the area itself (**4**). If your arrival in your BCU does not include a structured induction, then you could still meet the performance criteria by finding out for yourself the answers to the questions, remembering of course to commit the answers to some form of evidential trail.

3.3.5.2 The remaining criteria to evidence your responses to risk and hazard

The final three criteria, along with the five range statements, require a substantive approach by you so that they can be evidenced fully. Perhaps the best way to achieve this is to look at the range statements and identify ways to evidence them. They can then be 'bolted on' to one of the remaining three criteria.

Task

Identify within your policing role, or within the wider policing or community context, potential evidence for these range statements:
(a) Use and maintenance of machinery and equipment
(b) Working practices, which do not conform to established policies
(c) Unsafe behaviour
(d) Accidental breakages and spillages
(e) Environmental factors.

A model response

Our suggested answers to this rather complex task would include the following:

(a) **Use and maintenance of machinery and equipment**—using a police vehicle; operating mobile CCTV equipment; operating computers

(b) **Working practices, which do not conform to established policies**—working at night in a poorly lit area

(c) **Unsafe behaviour**—incidents where the behaviour of others has led you to call for police assistance

(d) **Accidental breakages and spillages**—photocopier toner; chemicals; fuel on the road after an accident; blood and broken glass

(e) **Environmental factors**—specific hazards in your area, such as rivers, ponds; heights; unsafe buildings; building sites, derelict areas and poorly lit areas.

Conclusions about responses to risk and hazard

Therefore, if you were asked to operate any equipment and you then read the health and safety instructions pertaining to the equipment, you would satisfy criterion 5 and range statement (**a**). Calling for assistance when confronted with a potentially dangerous situation, such as a rowdy group of drinkers leaving a nightclub and fights breaking out, would satisfy criterion 6 and range statement (**c**). If you were on the scene of a road traffic collision, noticed that there was fuel on the road, and arranged for it be cleaned off or hosed down, you would have evidence of criterion 7 and range statements (**d**) and (**e**).

In all of these situations, you would need evidence to show that the criteria had been met before ticking them off your portfolio checklist.

3.3.5.3 Reducing the risks to health and safety

The second element of this unit is *Reduce the risks to health and safety in your workplace*, in which the onus on you switches from merely identifying risks to actually reducing them. This element has eight criteria:

1. Carry out your working practices in accordance with legal requirements
2. Follow the most recent **workplace policies** for your job role
3. Rectify those health and safety risks within your capability and the scope of your job responsibilities
4. Pass on any suggestions for reducing risks to health and safety within your job role to the responsible persons
5. Ensure that your personal conduct in the workplace does not endanger the health and safety of you or other people
6. Follow the **workplace policies** and suppliers' or manufacturers' instructions for the safe use of equipment, materials and products

7. Report any differences between **workplace policies** and suppliers' or manufacturers' instructions as appropriate
8. Ensure that your personal presentation at work
   - ensures the health and safety of you and others
   - meets any legal duties
   - is in accordance with **workplace policies**.

3.3.5.4 The criteria in detail

The four criteria in which workplace policies are identified have five range statements attached—(a) the use of safe working methods and equipment, (b) the safe use of hazardous substances, (c) smoking, eating, drinking and drugs, (d) what to do in the event of an emergency, and (e) personal presentation.

Your evidence must show how you reduced risk to health and safety

In order to evidence these criteria and range statements, the emphasis is on showing how you reduce the risks to health and safety. For example, in making sure that your day-to-day activity is in conjunction with your risk assessment, you can evidence criterion **1** and if you encounter a situation in which the risk assessment needs to be updated, you are satisfying criterion **4**.

Examples of how you amass evidence

In the previous unit, we used the example of calling for police assistance in a situation that had gone beyond your personal ability to control. If you could also show that your behaviour in this situation was calculated to *avoid* confrontation, for example you showed politeness and respect, you were non-judgemental and so forth, then criterion **5** could also be included.

3.3.5.5 The remaining four criteria

This leaves four remaining criteria and the range statements to complete before the unit can be evidenced.

Task

Use the following statements to identify which remaining criteria and range statements they could evidence (our suggestions are in bold after the statement).

1. As a Special Constable, you always go on patrol wearing your personally issued and fitted body armour in conjunction with your force's policy. (**Criterion 8, range statements (a) and (e)**)
2. A member of the public reports that there is a fire in a building nearby. You immediately use your radio to seek fire brigade assistance. Upon reaching the building, you use the correct fire extinguisher having read the instructions. (**Criteria 2 and 6, range statements (b) and (d)**)
3. You find a hypodermic syringe in a children's play area. You cannot leave it there and so pick it up safely and arrange for its disposal at a nearby doctor's surgery. (**Criteria 2 and 6, range statements (b) and (c)**)

> 4. When on patrol in a very hilly area, you request a load vest rather than a belt because it is proving difficult to move easily wearing a belt. (**Criterion 7, range statement (a) and possibly (e)**).

These are by no means the only evidential interpretations of the scenarios and you may feasibly have a different set of answers. These too can be used for NOS completion, provided always, of course, that they can be evidenced.

3.3.5.6 Linking health and safety with other NOS

This section has looked at the health and safety aspects in isolation but you will be able to evidence them in conjunction with an incident or event that has already been used for another NOS.

Task

Go back through the NOS sections covered thus far and use the scenarios to identify where health and safety criteria could also be evidenced.

3.3.6 **(IND9) Administer first aid**

This is the only NOS which can be achieved through simulation. It would be remiss of the police force to allow you to wander the streets waiting for accidents to happen, or to go 'ambulance chasing', so that you could use the casualties to evidence your NOS portfolios. A group of new Special Constables queuing to assess a casualty with their folders at the ready, might be something that would send out the wrong signals to the public.

Professional training in first aid is a must. In order to achieve completion of this unit, you will need to attend a professionally managed first-aid course, which covers the following four units. If it is not part of your induction training, you should book yourself on a course as soon as possible. St John Ambulance run frequent courses in basic first aid, as do the Red Cross and some Health Trusts (using paramedics) and Primary Health Care centres. **Don't rely only on a book:** first aid is something you have to practise with a 'casualty' in a proper, structured, learning environment (hence we do not try to teach first aid in this book).

This unit is divided into four elements:

Element **4G4.1**: respond to the needs of casualties with minor injuries

1. Check the area for danger and respond accordingly
2. Ask the casualty for the history and symptoms of the injury
3. Assess the casualty and establish the nature and extent of the injury
4. Apply first-aid treatment appropriate to the type and severity of the injury
5. Call for additional help as appropriate
6. Inform the casualty of action taken and sources of further help.

Element **4G4.2**: respond to the needs of casualties with major injuries

1. Assess the extent and severity of the casualty's injuries
2. Place the casualty in an appropriate position of rest to maximise blood flow to vital organs
3. Protect the casualty from heat or cold
4. Comply with hygiene procedures and avoid infection
5. Control bleeding by applying direct or indirect pressure and appropriate dressings or bandages
6. Check for, and where possible maintain, circulation beyond bandaging
7. Immobilise and support injuries in line with current practice
8. Call for additional help promptly.

Element **4G4.3**: respond to the needs of unconscious casualties

1. Check the area for danger and take the appropriate action
2. Check casualty's level of consciousness and breathing
3. Assess the casualty and establish the nature and extent of any injury
4. Check for presence of any life-threatening conditions
5. Move the casualty to the recovery position in accordance with current practice
6. Call for help promptly
7. Monitor the casualty's condition and note any changes.

Element **4G4.4**: perform cardio-pulmonary resuscitation (CPR)

1. Check for danger and take the appropriate action
2. Open the casualty's airway by head tilt and chin lift, and position the casualty correctly for ventilation
3. Check for breathing and remove any obstructions from the mouth
4. Apply CPR at the correct rate, depth and ratio
5. Apply chest compressions in the correct position and at the correct rate
6. Demonstrate that you recheck for circulation
7. Call for additional help promptly.

3.3.6.1 Making sure that the training fits the requirement for competence

When you attend a first-aid course or refresher, it is crucial that this unit is not merely seen as an NOS exercise, because one day the knowledge gained could be crucial in dealing with a casualty or even saving someone's life. Whether it's bandaging a grazed knee or applying CPR, your actions need to be decisive, prompt and necessary. *Remember that because you are wearing a uniform, the public will expect you to know what you are doing* and that your intervention 'to save life or limb' is not an option: you must do this as part of your essential duty.

3.3.6.2 What *must* be in the training?

It is not for us to prescribe what you learn, and your force will have its own policy on first aid and the competence of its staff, but you cannot go far wrong if *you really thoroughly learn*:

- How to deal with hygiene and prevention/barriers to infection methods
- How to apply CPR and give mouth-to-mouth resuscitation
- How to deal with injuries such as fractures
- How to deal with wounds and bleeding
- How to make a casualty comfortable and safe
- Calling for appropriate help.

3.3.6.3 Practice

Practice may make you competent, but it will not make you perfect. Any paramedic or nurse will tell you that unused first-aid skills degenerate over time, and, for example, where once you knew how to deal effectively with a casualty with a fractured leg, the procedure for immobilising the affected limb may get a bit rusty if you don't practise. Your force will probably provide refresher first-aid programmes every year or so, but if this is not provided for you, you will have to ensure that you keep your skills polished.

Always double check with a health professional after you have administered first aid.

Incompetent first aid is worse than no first aid at all; and you could be liable to proceedings in law by the affected person (injured party) if you make a major blunder. This is why we urge you that, even when you have administered first aid, you still call for a paramedic to check the casualty, or you take the casualty to a doctor's surgery or to a hospital's Accident and Emergency Department. You may not be able to assess internal bleeding or diagnose trauma. Make sure that the casualty sees practitioners who can do these things. And write up your PNB at the first opportunity; litigation or a criminal investigation may follow the initial accident.

TEST BOX 4

We want you now to do a 'knowledge-check':

1. What does 'IL4SC' stand for?
2. What are the three generic modules?
3. What Statutory Instrument (SI) established the Police Standards of Professional Behaviour in law?
4. What is meant by the 'Nolan Principles'?
5. Who said 'There is absolutely no excuse for being rude to the public'?
6. What does PLAN mean?
7. What is '**non-feasance**'?
8. What is reflective learning?
9. What is the Experiential Learning Cycle?
10. What is a dynamic risk assessment?
11. What is CPR?

3.4 **(IND11.5) Partnerships and Neighbourhood Policing**

The major part of your initial work as a Special Constable will entail Neighbour-hood Policing and working with others in partnership. This section is therefore of central relevance to your role and has real resonance for your effectiveness as a police officer.

3.4.1 **Neighbourhoods and communities**

Criminologists often refer to policing occurring in cycles where the collective focus is on one current way of thinking or operating. The late 20th century saw the dawn of neighbourhood policing and this still persists well into the 21st century; partly because of its persuasive qualities and partly because of its politi-cal expediencies. The recent HMIC report into the effects of austerity on policing *Policing in Austerity: One Year On* (2012) makes clear that the flexibility of the Special Constabulary provides an excellent opportunity to increase visibility at key times; one of the key variables within Neighbourhood Policing. Every police force in England and Wales has as part of its central rationale a commitment to Neighbourhood Policing (NP) and it is therefore of importance to all Special Constables.

3.4.2 **What is the difference between 'neighbourhood' and 'community'?**

In a report on progress in establishing Neighbourhood Policing, the Home Office wrote this:

> A 'neighbourhood' to an inner-city resident is very different from someone living in a rural area. For the former, their neighbourhood could be a few streets or the estate where they live; for the person in the country, it could be their village, or group of villages, or parish. Local communities, police forces, police authorities and partners are deciding what neighbourhoods mean—rather than being told by the Government—but typically, we would expect it to cover one or two local authority wards.
>
> (Baggott and Wallace, 2006)

Neighbourhood, then, is about **place**, the physical location where people live, and consists of buildings: houses, flats, streets, shops and other kinds of physical dwelling. It is tactile and dimensional. You can touch it, see it and it remains more or less constant, though the human inhabitants of the neighbourhood may move in and move out regularly. People who live in a neighbourhood might actually have very little or nothing in common, even supposing that they know each other.

Community, by contrast, is more about **combinations of things which people have in common**. It is a much vaguer, looser term altogether because we can be members of several communities simultaneously.

Task

Write down how many different communities you belong to.

Your list may have included some or all (and more) of the following:

Communities

Work (community of occupation)

Profession, skills or knowledge (medicine, the law, retail, teaching, the military, building trades, maintenance, IT, civil engineer, commerce and so on)

Professional or work associations (other members of the extended policing family, law enforcement agencies, professional institutions, trades unions, trade/skills 'guilds' or organisations, membership of professional bodies such as Chartered Management Institute, Institute of Electrical Engineers, British Forensic Association)

Interests (Special Constabulary, charity work, voluntary organisations, 'drop-in' centres, youth work, fund-raising)

Demography (age group)

Education/learning (nursery, school, college, apprenticeship, university, qualifications, adult education)

Faith or belief (church or religious groups, humanist societies)

Identity and ethnicity (race, nationality, ethnic origins, languages, history, genealogy (family tree))

Shared past experiences (Royal British Legion for ex-Service personnel, school reunions, alma mater associations from university, youth groups, cadet forces, 'Old Boys' clubs for cricket, rugby or football)

Shared internet 'clubs' (Twitter, Facebook, Friends Reunited, chatrooms, Bebo and MySpace)

Shared hobbies (allotments, arts and crafts, collecting things, choirs, quilting, carpentry, driving, motor clubs)

Sports (team and individual sports from archery to yachting, golf to snooker)

Common problems (fear of crime, social isolation, mobility, lack of transport)

Impairment (forms of disability or physical/mental impairment, illness, terminal and other forms of disease, charities and associations such as Mind and Cancer UK)

Politics (local or national, party or social)

Clubs and pubs (disparate communities of drinkers, darts players, quiz aficionados etc)

> **Gender** (groups like the Women's Institute (WI), working men's clubs and Mother and Toddler groups tend to be gender-dominant, but there are signs that this is changing).

We won't have included everything, but this gives you a fair notion of how membership of communities can overlap and interrelate even at the individual level. If you raise this to a family level, or to groups in a community, the network of cross-relationships and interdependence becomes very complex and forms part of the 'social web' of relationships.

In order to put this into the realm of Special Constabulary policing, we look in more detail later in the chapter at Community Safety Partnerships (CSPs) and Neighbourhood Policing Teams (NPTs), both of which are integral to the Special Constabulary policing of neighbourhoods and management of the public's expectations about crime and disorder. It would be helpful at this point to describe a context for local policing, and indicate why understanding community and neighbourhood is important to those who police them.

3.4.3 Local policing: context and importance

In 2004, the Labour Government produced a consultation paper called *Building Communities, Beating Crime*, which canvassed views from people on how the police (with local authorities and other partners) could work with communities to address anxieties about crime and disorder. The argument which emerged from the public consultation went something like this:

> the police respond to crime, not to low-level disorder or anti-social behaviour. Even when the police attend incidents, like 'joyriding', it is likely to be all over by the time they get there. The public is uneasy about levels of anti-social activity and bad behaviour and the police are not listening. No one knows the 'local copper' any more; it's all too remote.

For their part, the police generally responded rather defensively: they knew how to deal with crime, but they were not social workers, and it was the responsibility of others to deal with broken windows and poor street lighting. The police did their best, but there were not enough of them and not a lot that they could do in the context of general crime and disorder.

The following year, the Government published a national *Community Safety Plan* which incorporated much of what had been outlined in *Building Communities, Beating Crime*, but added in the results of the various consultations. The new plan gave *key priorities and actions to the police* to deliver in partnership with other agencies and with communities themselves, to make neighbourhoods safer:

Community Safety Plan—desired outcomes

- Reducing crime and anti-social behaviour
- Making neighbourhoods safer and stronger
- Protecting the public and building confidence in the police
- Improving people's lives so that they are less likely to commit offences or to reoffend.

This represented a major shift in policing priorities and attitudes. No longer is policing something which is 'done to' people in a neighbourhood, but policing is a partnership—a consensus—with those being policed. This has resulted in a greater simplicity about the police function. There are now essentially two kinds of policing in Britain: **protective services** (including all the specialist and major investigations into serious, organised and major crime, as well as public order and traffic policing) and **neighbourhood** or **'community' policing**. The latter is formed in direct response to public unease and has been in active existence now for about nine years (see O'Connor, *Closing the Gap*, details in Further Reading at the end of the chapter). Some areas and police forces are continuing to create Neighbourhood Policing Teams, even though there is reduction in police budgets and there is no doubt that some still have a long way to go to attain the confidence and trust of those being policed, but a substantial start has been made.

To keep this rather optimistic picture in context, there are instances of police and partner failure to deal with anti-social problems, as this case study from September 2009 illustrates:

Case study: the victimized family

Fiona Pilkington, bullied and harassed over a long period by groups of 'feral' teenagers who also assaulted and attacked her children, in despair killed herself and her disabled daughter in 2007. At the inquest in Loughborough in 2009, the coroner severely criticised Leicester Police for not responding adequately to Mrs Pilkington's 33 separate requests for help over three years, 13 of which were in the ten months before her suicide, for not linking the complaints, and for occasions when police did not attend.

For their part, the police admitted that they had wrongly downgraded her complaints to anti-social behaviour and had not regarded the family's victimisation as crime (though now, in 2013, the persecution of the family would be regarded as 'hate crime').

The controversy which followed the deaths and the coroner's inquest, together with much media commentary, suggested that there was a long way to go yet in some communities before the concerns of the highly vulnerable were met by resolute police action.

3.5 **Citizen-Focused Policing**

As the performance management regime of the 1990s and early years of this century diverted police attention into a narrow band of quantitative measurable objectives, policing was seen to have become detached from its local foundations. 'Citizen Focus' was seen as the method by which this gap is bridged, in concert with a new way of measuring police performance in the community. The return of 'law-abiding citizens' to the centre pivot of locally delivered policing is not without its political appeal to all sides, particularly in Parliament.

Definition of citizen-focused policing

Citizen-focused policing means reflecting the needs and expectations of individuals and local communities in decision-making, service delivery and practice. The objectives of citizen-focused policing are to improve public confidence, to increase satisfaction of service users and to increase public involvement in policing.

The Citizen Focus approach goes to the heart of the policing culture and requires of the police a change to a more *customer-orientated* approach. This is illustrated in the 'We asked, You said, We did' campaigns that many forces have adopted to show the public what they are doing in response to locally identified problems, as this example from Newcastle shows:

> Police in Newcastle launched their campaign to quell disorder during the summer months in particular and off-licences in Benwell agreed to withdraw drinks popular with underage youngsters from their shelves. Now the traders have agreed not to sell 75cl bottles of sparkling perry wine during the summer holidays... Posters have been displayed in the participating shops' windows telling customers they are taking part in the scheme... It's part of Northumbria Police's ongoing We Asked, You Said, We Did campaign.
>
> (*Newcastle Evening Chronicle*, 23 June 2008)

3.5.1 **Principles of Citizen Focus**

In a 2008 report ACPO identified four main focus areas for citizen-focused policing:

- Understanding people
- Understanding services
- Designing services and
- Delivering services.

A series of 'hallmarks' (guarantees of quality and trust) were then designed to assist forces with implementation:

Table 3.1 ACPO hallmarks for Citizen Focus

Understanding people	Understanding services
This hallmark incorporates: (a) Understanding the people a force serves (b) Understanding staff, and the internal culture of the force (c) Understanding partners, stakeholders and regulators—their differing influences, motivations and levels of cooperation	This hallmark incorporates: (a) Staff understanding the force vision and values and their contribution to achieving them (b) Understanding the quality of the service expected and delivered from the public perspective (c) Staff understanding what services are provided by the [force] and the standards expected of them in developing and delivering [those services] (d) Leaders and staff understanding how their areas of work impact upon the overall experience that [members of the public] have with the [force] (e) Clarifying responsibility and accountability with partners to align services and make them as effective as possible (f) The public understanding what services the police deliver, how to access [those services] and what standards of service they can expect

Designing services	Delivering services
This hallmark incorporates: (a) Considering the actual or potential impact of services on people as part of the design and review process (b) Providing opportunities for staff, the public, and partners to be involved in decision-making processes at appropriate levels (c) Giving staff, the public and partners access to relevant information and the support necessary to be effective in their involvement (d) Coordinating public engagement activity with partners (e) Providing clear and accessible feedback to staff and the public on actions taken as a result of their involvement	This hallmark incorporates: (a) Delivering adaptable services driven by public demand and priorities (b) Encouraging and training staff to improve service delivery (c) Agreeing service standards with the public, partners and stakeholders, and achieving them (d) Evaluating the effectiveness of service delivery from the public perspective (e) Including a wide range of partner agencies in delivery

(ACPO, 2008: 5–8; our additions and glosses are in square brackets. The original text tends to be incoherent at times)

The phrase 'Citizen Focus' may have lost some of its resonance with the transition to a Coalition government but the principles remain the same and are enshrined in concepts such as localism and 'Big Society'. Policing should be for the benefit of the people who are most in need of its services.

3.6 **Community Safety Partnerships (CSPs)**

The emphasis in both Neighbourhood Policing and Citizen Focus on establishing local partnerships and producing multi-agency responses to locally identified problems, takes place through the **Community Safety Partnership** (previously entitled the Crime and Disorder Reduction Partnership—CDRP). This body *coordinates the public sector response to crime and disorder in an area* as it is now well established that such problems are not solely within the care of the police. This approach led to legislation to obligate local authorities and others to cooperate in producing solutions as part of their everyday activity. Section 17 of the Crime and Disorder Act 1998 imposed a duty on every local authority:

> without prejudice to any other obligation imposed on it—[to] exercise its function with due regard to the need to do all it reasonably can to prevent crime and disorder in its area.
>
> (Crime and Disorder Act 1998, s 17)

3.6.1 **Membership of a CSP**

Five bodies have statutory responsibility for attending the CSP and working towards its objectives—the police, the police authority (now the Police and Crime Commissioner), the fire and rescue service, the local authority and the area primary health care trust. Not all problems relating to crime and disorder can be solved by these five organisations alone, so other organisations can be brought into the CSP orbit, either as permanent or ad hoc members.

Task

Are there any other organisations you would want to work on a CSP?

Consider what each could bring 'to the table' and what effect they could have on reducing crime and disorder in your area.

The lifeblood of the CSPs is the flow of information about crime and disorder from *all* the partnerships as we demonstrate in Figure 3.4. It is equally pertinent to suggest that in the same way that information flows into the CSP so actions flow back out (Figure 3.4):

Figure 3.4 CSP relationships

Task

Turning the priorities into actions

Consider how you would use a CSP to deal with a particular problem: under-age drinking.

Information suggests that the problem of under-age drinking is becoming a real ASB nuisance within your area. The local media have run some stories and have alleged that little is being done to combat the nuisance.

You must include roles for all the statutory CSP bodies and include any other partners you feel could help.

Our suggested answer:

Under-age drinking—CSP partnership approach

The CSP start the process by collecting the data and intelligence available to them, as well as highlighting those areas where information is sparse.

The following actions are then tasked to the five statutory CSP agencies:

Police—provide an enforcement response to the problem by taking home to their parents youths found drinking; enforce any designated no-drinking zones allocated by the local authority; use intelligence sources to identify retail premises that may be selling alcohol to under-age persons.

Police and Crime Commissioner—monitor the activity of the police and link in with other partners to assist in the process.

Local Authority—consider implementing designated no-drinking areas; use licensing and trading standards officers to enforce legislation prohibiting sale of alcohol to those who are under age; use cleaning services to remove debris left behind by those drinking; install CCTV if appropriate.

Fire & Rescue—start an education programme on the dangers of drink-driving; look at problem of under-age drinking and fire starting and enforce accordingly.

Primary Care Trust—provide education and literature to children and young people and their parents of the dangers of under-age drinking.

The following partners may be engaged under the aegis of the CSP to add the following:

Local drug and alcohol charities to provide appropriate support and guidance to those affected by these problems.

Youth offending teams to provide positive support to young people, including diversionary activities.

Public Prosecution Service to ensure that convictions are sought for those found to be selling to under-age drinkers.

Voluntary community groups to enforce this message and to engage with communities to help to provide solutions to the problems this can cause.

There is no one answer to the problem and our suggestions are merely illustrative of the approach a CSP may take.

3.6.2 Some observations about CSPs

Whilst it is well established that a multi-agency approach is one that works well with minor crime and disorder reduction, there are still many problems associated with CSPs. The practical nature of partnership work can be very difficult, especially if one agency seeks to dominate or another seeks to abrogate its responsibilities. The mechanics of getting all agencies on board and working towards specific problems can be very time-consuming. Rogers & Prosser (2006: 12), for example, tell us that 'Deep structural conflicts exist between the parties that sit down together in partnerships', which can make the whole process very frustrating. This is even without considering the potentially corrosive elements of local politics, and the even more damaging atmosphere created by a perceived imbalance in resource allocation.

3.6.3 **Police and Crime Commissioner**

The policing landscape has changed with the introduction in 2012 of an elected Police and Crime Commissioner (PCC) to replace the old Police Authority. We cannot comment yet on potential effects on partnership entailed by the PCC, however, what is known and what is worth keeping an eye on is the fact the PCC will rule the Community Safety roost and will have the power, should s/he choose to exercise it, to direct CSP activities and even merge them if that represents better value for money. The election of PCCs is the biggest public change in policing for several decades and it is within the community safety arena that its impact may be felt the most.

3.7 **Partners and Communities Together (PACT)**

Partners and Communities Together (PACT; sometimes confusingly but erroneously referred to as *Police* and Communities Together) is a part of Neighbourhood Policing in some police forces. It is impossible to provide a generic description of PACT because it functions differently in each force. This is not a sign of a lack of standardisation, rather that neighbourhood policing *should* vary across the country, for without this variation how can the police properly respond to local concerns? The concerns and preoccupations of every neighbourhood will be different; it follows that the partnership arrangements to meet local needs in that locality will be different too.

3.7.1 **What is PACT?**

PACT is a process, not a series of fixed and timed events. It is reflective of the attempts made by the police and partnership agencies in any given community to seek to understand the priorities that exist in that area.

KEY POINT

PACT provides a series of opportunities for forces to understand what problems the local residents want the authorities to solve.

3.7.2 **How does it work?**

One example of the PACT process is provided by Devon and Cornwall Police explaining to the public what elements can be used in a PACT:

PACT Environmental Visual Audit (EVA)—checking the locality for signs of deterioration
PACT Surgeries—these are drop-in surgeries at advertised locations and times where members of the public can [...] speak to a police or local authority

---

representative. Some [BCUs] use mobile police stations so that they can capture priorities from areas with a high 'footfall'

PACT Panel Meetings—often follow a public meeting at which local residents [identify] the three top priorities for their community. The panel is made up of representatives from the community and partnership agencies and allocates these tasks accordingly

PACT Surveys—can be door-to-door or [used] in areas where lots of people will be, and [can] capture local concerns but without the formality of a public meeting

PACT Postcards—allow residents who cannot, or do not, attend meetings and surgeries to identify their concerns; instead post them in boxes that are then collected by the neighbourhood policing team (NPT)

PACT Response Mailing—similar to the postcards but with prepaid envelopes that can be sent direct to the appropriate NPT.

This spread of projects for PACT is not unique to Devon and Cornwall, of course, (though it is a good example) and we know that such methods are replicated across England and Wales to a greater or lesser degree, with many forces showing considerable ingenuity in seeking to capture information on community priorities. Furthermore, in some forces there may already be mechanisms that can be utilised for identifying PACT priorities. As we noted earlier—each PACT arrangement will be different, in the same ways that priorities and communities are different.

3.7.3 **Problems with PACT**

There are problems that can bedevil such a process. Not all are insurmountable, but they do represent a challenge to the Neighbourhood Policing Teams, which are often charged with other busy tasks and which cannot devote all their time to PACT matters:

Possible problems with PACT

- Public meetings can be very time-consuming to manage, requiring a chairperson, an agenda, a venue, publicity, quorate membership, resolutions and actions
- Public meetings do not appeal to all sections of the community. Such events tend to favour those who are comfortable with public speaking and with formal discussions
- Public meetings can be hijacked by groups which have a single issue or political agenda that may not fully represent the views of the community, but about which they are vociferous (for example, by-pass roads and environmental concerns)

- Public apathy—meetings and surgeries can be sparsely attended (which lets the 'single-issue zealots' exercise disproportionate influence sometimes)
- Partnership non-attendance—the police is often the organisation with the dedicated resources for the locality and it often falls on them to persuade other partners to attend; even the local authority can drag its feet
- How representative can PACT be? Does a public meeting of 25 people identifying local priorities reflect the will of the whole community?
- Costs—there may be costs associated with postcards, surveys, prepaid envelopes etc
- It must be a problem-solving process, not a 'talking shop'
- How is feedback provided to the residents of the locality? (Feedback is crucial as it can demonstrate success and may drum up further support)
- Will PACT always focus on the low-level problems?

These are by no means the only problems with PACT but they do demonstrate some of the potential pitfalls that need to be considered throughout the process. More positively, many police forces are establishing 'social identity PACTs' in order to capture the priorities of diverse and minority groups, as this example from Lancashire shows:

> What we're finding is that, as we develop PACT, the specific communities with specific issues are also coming under the PACT umbrella...we have a very active lesbian and gay PACT in Blackpool which talks about the issues that community are facing. We've recently initiated deaf PACT meetings for the deaf community.

(ACC Cunningham, Lancashire Police quoted in *Police Professional*, 2006: 24)

3.8 Neighbourhood Policing Teams (NPTs)

Neighbourhood Policing is predicated upon responses to local issues and identifying local solutions for the priorities of residents in a given neighbourhood. Neighbourhood Policing should not only be different in Manchester and Harwich, *it should be different in differing neighbourhoods in the same town or police BCU*. It follows that the teams which deliver Neighbourhood Policing in all these localities should match the needs of the locality, not conform to any generic model.

3.8.1 The role of NPTs

That said, there will be a common theme running through the work of most NPTs and this has been articulated by the Home Office as follows:

What does a local NPT do?

Neighbourhood policing teams are involved in proactive or preventative work to tackle low-level crime and anti-social behaviour that may be a persistent issue or concern in the local community:

* communities can now expect to see increased numbers of PCSOs patrolling their streets, addressing anti-social behaviour issues and building relationships with local people
* communities should also have information about how their local force will be policing the local community, and have a point of contact for their neighbourhood team
* local people will have the opportunity to tell the police about the issues which are causing them concern and help shape the response to those issues.

(Home Office, <http://police.homeoffice.gov.uk/community-policing/ neighbourhood-policing>; accessed 25 October 2009, now no longer available, but a useful research report (No. 28) on the Home Office website gives detail of continuing support for NPTs; see <http://www.homeoffice.gov.uk/publications/ science-research-statistics/research-statistics/police-research/horr28/ horr28-summary?view=Binary>; accessed 23 November 2012)

There are some key themes that inform the activities of an NPT and will determine their composition:

* **Work is both proactive and preventative**—an NPT requires an enforcement capacity but also focuses on crime reduction/prevention
* **Tackling anti-social behaviour**—partnership needed with local authorities as they have the lead responsibilities on many of the issues that ASB encompasses, such as noise, litter, dog fouling
* **PCSOs**—any NPT must embrace the 'extended policing family' as part of its remit; PCSOs have effective powers to deal with low-level nuisance
* **Local people/local community**—the priorities of local people are paramount and therefore partnership must involve the community, not only in identifying problems but also in implementing long-term solutions.

(See Hughes and Rowe, 2007, in Further Reading for more analysis of NPT.)

3.8.2 **The importance of visibility**

A key aspect for any NPT is ensuring that the public is aware of what it does and who the individual team members are. Police forces have published details of who patrols which neighbourhood, with photographs of NP officers and PCSOs as well as their official contact details (force email addresses and force mobile phone numbers). Many police forces have functions on their websites that allow access to details of the local NPT, and this is also available via Directgov—a website that puts access to all public services in one place: see <http://www.direct.

gov.uk>. This function has been supported by Crimemapper—see <http://www.police.uk>—which at a click can reveal details of crime in one's area, based on post codes, as well as outcomes and ongoing issues. This is policing accountability at a street level. This accessibility is also linked to the tasking of NPTs to undertake patrols in their areas/neighbourhoods (Figure 3.5):

Figure 3.5 The NPT 'square'

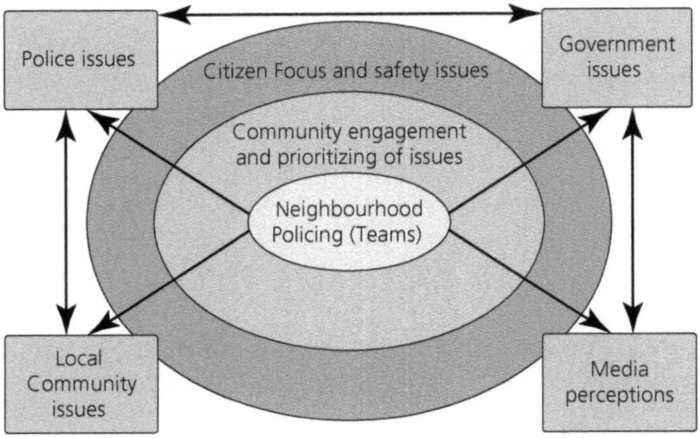

3.8.3 **Composition of an NPT**

Figure 3.6 describes those generic factors that may appear in an NPT.

The composition of some NPTs may not fit into this neat, nicely delineated model, proud though we are of it. The local truth for your NPT will be more complex and will often be based on changing priorities. However, the essence in our model is crucial: the composition of an NPT must involve more than the police, and whilst partnership agencies and the voluntary sector are not formal members, they are important partners, without whom community engagement could not be achieved.

3.8.4 **Success factors for an NPT**

The composition of an NPT is only one factor. Getting the right blend of partners and an environment in which community engagement can flourish are factors that turn a good idea into an achievable event. Communities do not necessarily care about the foundation or rationale for Neighbourhood Policing,

Figure 3.6 Components of NPTs

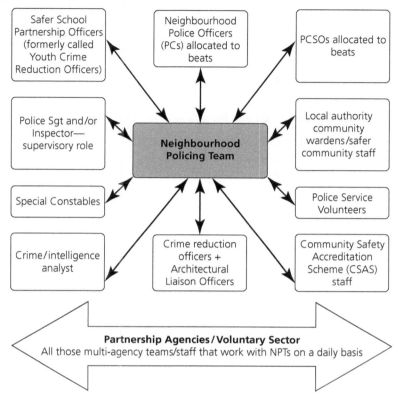

they simply want to see results. An academic study highlighted what success factors may be:

- An organisation-wide community policing ethos
- Decentralised decision-making
- Locale-based accountability
- The involvement of auxiliaries
- Proactive tactics oriented to crime prevention
- A problem-solving approach and
- Sincere engagement in inter-agency partnerships and public involvement.

(Fielding, 2009: 9)

Task

Consider each of the success factors outlined in the previous paragraph.

How will you as a Special Constable ensure that you can contribute to each of these?

> What can you bring to the role that will benefit community engagement for your force?
>
> We believe that if you examine your motivations for being a Special Constable (whether it involves making a difference, or performing some form of public service, or even in eventually becoming a regular officer), then you will fit into this community engagement rationale.

3.8.5 **The Special Constable and Neighbourhood Policing**

As both our model and our task have illustrated, there is a pivotal role for the Special Constable within Neighbourhood Policing, and in particular in community engagement. After all, what are these other than listening to communities and responding to their needs? If the Special Constabulary is to deliver all it can to policing, then it must enthusiastically embrace Neighbourhood Policing. Indeed, Sir Peter Fahy, ACPO Lead for the Special Constabulary, suggests that Special Constables are uniquely placed to do so:

> The neighbourhood teams are all about building confidence and developing active communities. What better way to achieve this than by recruiting Specials who are citizens first and foremost and have those community links? And because Specials are flexible, committed, high-quality individuals, they are in great demand by the neighbourhood teams.
>
> (*Specials*, April 2009: 11)

3.9 **Crime Prevention/Reduction**

One of the key activities within Neighbourhood Policing is that of crime prevention. It is not acceptable for crime prevention to be considered a specialist function; surely all warranted officers, PCSOs and police staff have an innate responsibility to prevent and reduce crime, including Special Constables? It is increasingly important in a citizen-focused environment to consider the needs of victims and potential victims and this must include crime reduction/prevention initiatives.

One way of looking at crime prevention is in terms of its **situational** or **social** contexts. Some work in this area has been undertaken by Tonry and Farrington (1995) and Clarke and Homel (1997), which suggests that to make crime prevention effective, the Special Constabulary needs to focus on:

Situational crime prevention

Increasing risk: making it harder for the thief, vandal or graffitist to succeed in what they are trying to do (enhanced CCTV images for evidential purposes is a case in point)

Increasing effort: thieves and petty criminals have to try to overcome obstacles, locks, shutters and other kinds of impediment to committing their crimes (anti-intruder paint is an example)

Reducing reward: making it more difficult to sell on stolen items, working with manufacturers to render technology ineffective if damaged (such as SIM cards in mobile phones, or the cancellation of credit cards)

Reducing provocation: finding ways in which the provocation to steal or vandalise is diminished (putting displays of digital cameras or jewellery out of casual reach, not presenting easy 'blank canvases' for graffitists and so on)

Removing excuses: rule setting and publicising generally, taking away the defence of 'I didn't know' or 'it wasn't clear'—of particular use when potentially hazardous obstacles, such as razor wire, are used protectively.

(Adapted from Byrne and Pease, 2003, summarising Clarke and Homel, 1997)

All this is predicated on offenders making rational choices, but you might think of alcohol, long-term unemployment, conspicuous consumption and so on, any of which may provoke *irrational* offending. Some critics see situational crime prevention as merely 'target hardening'. *Displacement of crime* (the 'squishy balloon' effect), where offenders simply move elsewhere, giving some other part of the area the headache of dealing with them is another criticism, as is the 'fortress mentality' adopted by gated communities which exacerbates the inhabitants' already high fear of crime, both of which can dominate the crime prevention tactics used by local authorities and the Special Constabulary.

Social crime prevention, usually working in parallel with situational crime prevention, addresses the long-term motivation of the offender, often on the basis that early intervention may help to deflect potential offenders away from crimes, or that combined agency and partnership working, for example the Special Constabulary with social services, may offer alternatives to offending and role models other than criminals for younger people to emulate. Factors such as child abuse, neglect, poor or absent parenting, health, education and aspirational issues may be taken into account, and alternatives offered, to reduce the risk of later offending.

If crime prevention is a series of measures, situational and social, designed to reduce offending, then **crime reduction** is the term given to all such strategies and methods, based on 'what works' in reducing crime. Needless to say, this is a huge area of academic research and applied thinking, best accessed through the Home Office Crime Reduction website: <http://www.crimereduction.home-office.gov.uk>.

Crime prevention and crime reduction have become big business in the United Kingdom, not surprisingly since the cost of crime itself in 2009 was estimated to be **£78 billion** (Chambers *et al*, 2009, but see the Home Office report of September 2011, available at: <http://www.homeoffice.gov.uk/publications/crime/reducing-reoffending/IOM-phase2-costs-multipliers?view=Binary>;

accessed 22 October 2012, where the complexities of estimating the economic costs of crime are discussed).

However, it is not just private companies, local authorities and concerned citizens who have an interest in crime prevention; there is an obvious incentive for the government to reduce the cost of crime (particularly in the current economic climate) and has real resonance for the Special Constabulary.

3.9.1 Areas for crime reduction/prevention

Table 3.2 details those types of crime, crime audit and local amenity for which the Home Office has published practical crime reduction advice ('toolkits') that are accessible to the public.

Any one of these areas has ramifications, since they are all areas in which Special Constables operate. Crime reduction/prevention should be at the heart of policing and it is one area in which Special Constables need to be competent, not least because the public will expect them to have specialist levels of knowledge, or be able to direct them to access that knowledge.

Table 3.2 Crime reduction—areas of concern

Vehicle crime	Street crime and robbery
Domestic burglary	Repeat victimisation
Using intelligence and information-sharing	Alcohol-related crime
Anti-social behaviour	Rural crime
Motor salvage operators regulations	Public transport
Racial crime and harassment	Communities against drugs
Mentally disordered offenders	Trafficking in people
Fear of crime	Business and retail crime
Arson	Safer schools and hospitals

(From <http://www.crimereduction.homeoffice.gov.uk/toolkits/index.htm>, accessed 11 October 2009; updated and revised at <http://www.homeoffice.gov.uk/publications/science/cast/crime-prev-community-safety/>; accessed 22 October 2012)

3.9.2 Crime prevention products

Many local authorities will have sector or charitable schemes that can assist with crime prevention. Forces too will distribute free products such as shed alarms or purse chains at community safety events, so it is worth Special Constables becoming familiar with the initiatives and resources on offer:

Table 3.3 Crime prevention products

Alarms	CCTV	Property marking (UV/ SmartWater)
Security guards	Lighting	Signage
Door and window security	Layout design	Access control
Stop locks	Fake storage tins	Purse chains
Shredders	Safes	Gates
Barriers	Hedges	Intercoms
Identification badges	Vehicle tracking equipment such as 'Tracker' beacons	Nominated neighbour schemes

(See the 'Crime Matters' website for further details: <http://www.crimematters.com>)

However, technical knowledge alone is not enough in crime prevention and the risk factors that lead to criminality must also be explored, assessed and actions taken to address them.

3.9.2.1 **Risk factors for criminality**

Figure 3.7 overleaf highlights some of the risk factors involved in criminality, whilst the circles identify possible preventative measures.

3.10 **Environmental Visual Audits (EVAs) and Neighbourhood Concerns**

In order to link Neighbourhood Policing and crime reduction, one of the activities undertaken by neighbourhood Special Constables and PCSOs is that of the EVA and

> [it] is the insight that to an extent public anxiety and confidence reflects the nature of the physical environment they inhabit. The method of environmental audit is an attempt to capture the central features of the policed environment to which the law-abiding public responds.
>
> (Fielding *et al*, 2002: 6)

This makes EVA a powerful tool, particularly when many of the problems identified might not previously have found their way on to the police neighbourhood 'radar', either because the problems were not deemed to be important enough, or because they were seen as 'belonging' to the council or to someone else. Thus, an EVA provides a window on to a community and in doing so provides a more holistic problem-solving approach because the problems identified are those that cause people the greatest concern:

What to the police may seem low-level, trivial and routine behaviours or disrepair can to the public represent serious threats to their sense of comfort and well-being. The method of environmental audit is an attempt to gauge the public's sensitivities and to provide an information base with which to accommodate these in partnership interventions whose outcome the public will regard as effective.

(Fielding *et al*, 2002: 7)

Figure 3.7 Risk factors and solutions for criminality

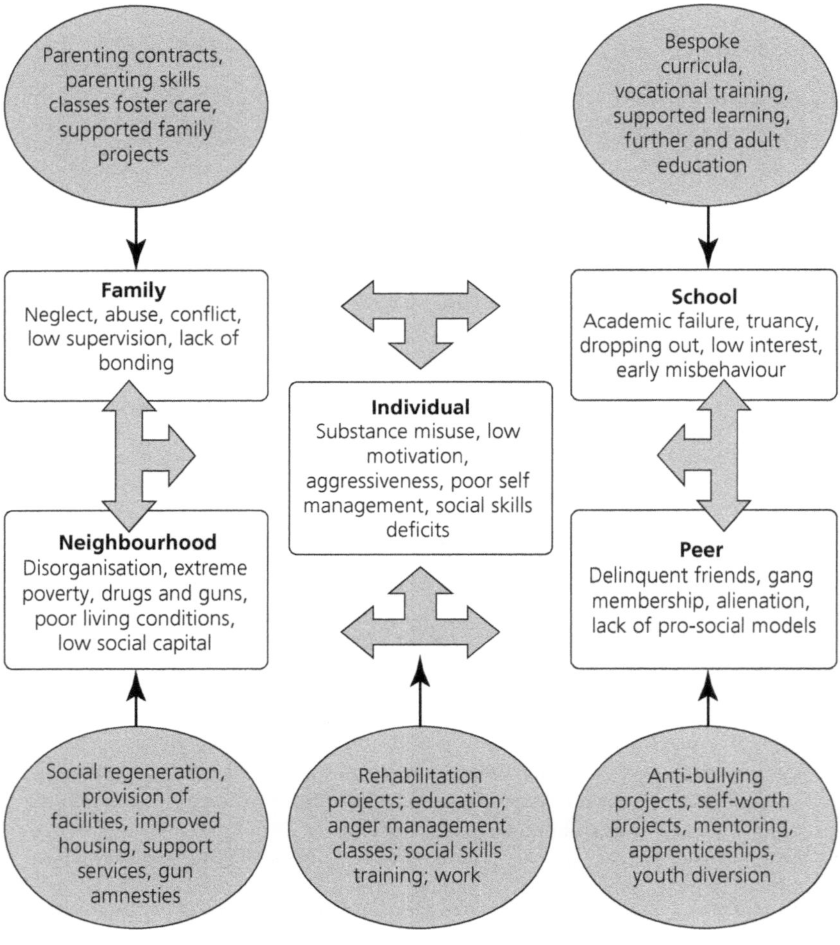

3.10.1 **Signal crimes perspective**

In 2002, Dr Martin Innes (from the University of Surrey, working alongside Surrey Police) developed the concept of a 'signal crimes perspective' which sought to demonstrate that *some crimes and acts of anti-social behaviour make people feel disproportionately unsafe within their community*. These 'signal' crimes act as a social barometer for feelings of safety. The kinds of activity we are talking about are often low level, even trivial in police terms, but Innes's work demonstrated that dealing with these lower level issues was crucial to improving public perceptions of safety. Examples of signal crimes include:

- Litter
- Dog fouling
- Nuisance noise
- Signs of criminal damage/vandalism
- Young people congregating (as perceived by others)
- Graffiti and
- Abandoned cars.

The 'signal' is not a simple equation where **act + unease = police intervention**. The psychological processes involved are actually rather complex, and this is reflected in the complexity of the signal itself. Innes identified four elements to the signal crimes perspective—the *expression*, the *content*, the *effect* and the *control signal*:

The signal crimes perspective—the constituent parts

Expression—the act of disorder or crime that gives concern for the person seeing it, or hearing about it.
Content—how it made that person feel about safety in his/her community.
Effect—what happened as a result of this incident.
Control signal—what the authorities did to deal with this issue (or, in not doing something, what have they signalled to the community?).

An example

When I leave my house in the morning to walk to work I often have to walk past the empty alcohol cans and bottles left by the groups who gather to drink at night nearby (the **expression**). In the winter, when I return I worry that they may be gathered in the street and I worry about how they will react when I go by (the **content**). When I saw these groups, I often walked home a longer way round so as to avoid them (the **effect**). When this was highlighted by me and others at a public meeting, the police increased their patrols and the local authority made the vicinity a designated 'no-drinking area' (the **control signals**).

3.10.2 **Signal crimes and Neighbourhood Policing**

The relevance of the signal crimes perspective to Neighbourhood Policing is obvious, given that it deals with people's perceptions of safety, and this has been recognised by many police forces, which are alerted to act when examples are brought to their attention. This approach has been recognised as being complementary to the aims and objectives of Neighbourhood Policing:

> The Signal Crimes Perspective is equally valid in neighbourhood policing. The primary focus of the SCP is that some incidents of crime and disorder can act as warning signs to the public about the distribution of risks to their security in everyday life. Some crimes and disorderly behaviours will, therefore, have a disproportionate impact on public perception of risk.
>
> (ACPO, 2006: 6)

Signal crimes—an example

In Lambeth, south-west London, Clapham Park was chosen as a New Deal for Communities (NDC) regeneration project. Part of the problem was that the benches in housing blocks, which [originally] had been provided for elderly people, were used by drug dealers, drug takers, prostitutes, and those drinking alcohol. The debris [left by] these activities, and [concerns about the people] using the area, had made the benches a no-go area for the elderly residents. The way the benches were being used became the signal crime. When removed, the criminal and anti-social activity stopped and the complaints stopped. This was the control signal the community needed.

(*Police Professional*, 2009: 16; our explanatory additions in square brackets)

3.10.3 **What will be on an EVA?**

Each EVA will reflect a different set of individual, local or parochial concerns but there may be similarities and overlaps in some areas: for example, many urban centres will highlight problems with graffiti or criminal damage. In terms of EVAs, geography matters:

> Members of a community frame their sense of neighbourhood using geographic markers such as streets, buildings or natural land formations as boundaries...this proximity connects community members to the same experiences—good or bad...
>
> (Wilson and Brown, 2009: 30)

The actual capture of the issues is only one part of the overall strategy of engagement. Table 3.4 highlights many of the issues that could feature on a 'typical' EVA; many of these issues are signal crimes:

Table 3.4 Environmental issues that could feature on an EVA

Graffiti	Boarded-up premises	Abandoned premises
Heavy security shutters	Lots of CCTV	Overgrown gardens
Rubbish outside houses	Broken windows	Poor street lighting
Used condoms	Evidence of public urination	Loud music/noise
Homeless people	Begging	Congregations of large groups of people
Litter	Drugs paraphernalia	Broken bottles
Speeding cars	Illegal parking	Dog fouling
Stray dogs	Unlit alleyways	Signs of vandalism/criminal damage

3.10.3.1 Engaging with young people

The following example shows an innovative way to engage with young people. Including them (and their families) in consultation on what problems may exist in a community is an excellent way to reach consensus solutions, as well as community ownership of those solutions:

KEY POINT—COMMUNITY INVOLVEMENT IN AN EVA

An example of community involvement in an EVA is provided by Thames Valley Police:

Katesgrove neighbourhood policing team will be conducting an Environmental Visual Audit (EVA) around Katesgrove Primary School with children from the school.

The EVA, which aims to identify issues that impact on the quality of life of local residents such as graffiti and fly-tipping, will be carried out in partnership with Reading Borough Council and the local community.

This is a follow-up to an earlier EVA conducted in September 2008 with children from the school, which was considered very successful in identifying a number of issues. West Mercia Police encourage community members to undertake their own EVAs and report findings to their local NPT (see <http://ripassetseu.s3.amazonaws. com/www.westmercia.police.uk/_files/documents/dec_09/wmp__1260372226_ PACT_Environmental_Visual_Audi.pdf>; accessed 23 November 2012).

3.10.4 **Conclusion**

In its more formal adoption, the EVA is clearly a useful tool within Neighbourhood Policing itself, but its central tenets have applicability to the wider Special Constable role. If you understand the signal crimes perspective and realise that certain issues/disorders have a disproportionate effect on individual and communal perspectives of safety, then you understand why community engagement is central. Furthermore, in understanding this approach, you can begin to become part of the solution. After all, what better control signal is there than the Special Constabulary volunteers who wish to make a difference in their community? In time, we envisage that the corollary to Martin Innes's signal crime will be the Special Constabulary's **signal solution**.

TEST BOX 5

To conclude this chapter, here is your 'knowledge check' on the second part:

1. What is the difference between 'neighbourhood' and 'community'?
2. Give five examples of a community of interests.
3. Name two of the desired outcomes from Community Safety plans.
4. What is a CSP?
5. Which five bodies have statutory responsibility for being at a CSP?
6. What does PACT mean?
7. Name three of the possible problems with PACT.
8. Name two components of 'situational crime prevention'.
9. What does an EVA try to do?
10. Give an example of a 'signal crime'.
11. What are the four central components of signal crimes perspective?
12. Who developed the theory of signal crime?

Further Reading

ACPO, *Citizen Focus Hallmarks Summary* (2008, NPIA), available at <http://cfnp.npia.police.uk/files/cf_hallmarks_summary.pdf>; accessed 14 November 2012

——/NPIA, *Practice Advice on Professionalising the Business of Neighbourhood Policing* (2006, Wyboston: National Centre for Policing Excellence, part of NPIA), available at <http://cfnp.npia.police.uk/files/np_neighbourhoodpolicin.pdf>; accessed 14 November 2012

Baggott, M and Wallace, M, *Neighbourhood Policing Progress Report* (May 2006, London: Home Office)

Brantingham, P and Faust, F, 'A Conceptual Model of Crime Prevention' in (1976) 22 *Crime and Delinquency* 284–98

Brogden, M and Nijhar, P, *Community Policing: National and International Models and Approaches* (2005, Cullompton: Willan Publishing)

Byrne, S and Pease, K, 'Crime Reduction and Community Safety' in Newburn, T (ed.), *Handbook of Policing* (2003, Cullompton: Willan Publishing), Part III, pp 286–310

Caless, B (ed.), with Bryant, R, Spruce, B and Underwood, R, *Blackstone's Police Community Support Officer's Handbook*, 2nd edn. (2010, Oxford: Oxford University Press)

Casey, L, 'Engaging Communities in Fighting Crime' (2008, Cabinet Office Crime and Communities Review), available at <http://www.cabinetoffice.gov.uk/newsroom/news_releases/2008/080618_fighting_crime.aspx>; accessed 1 March 2010

Farrell, S, *Experience and Expression in the Fear of Crime* (2007, Swindon: Economic and Social Research Council (ESRC))

Felson, M and Clarke, R, 'Opportunity Makes the Thief: Practical Theory for Crime Prevention', Police Research Series, Paper 98 (1998, London: Home Office)

Fielding, N, 'Getting the Best out of Community Policing', The Police Foundation, Paper 3 (May 2009)

——, Innes, M and Fielding, J, *Reassurance Policing & the Visual Environmental Audit in Surrey Police: a Report* (2002, Guildford: University of Surrey)

HMIC, *Policing in Austerity: One Year On* (2012), available at <http://www.hmic.gov.uk/publication/policing-in-austerity-one-year-on/>; accessed 3 September 2012

Home Office White Paper, *Building Communities, Beating Crime* (2004), available at <http://police.homeoffice.gov.uk/publications/police-reform/wp04_complete.html>; accessed April 2008

Hughes, G and Rowe, M, 'Neighbourhood Policing and Community Safety: Researching the Instabilities of the Local Governance of Crime, Disorder and Security in Contemporary UK' (2007) 7(4) *Criminology and Criminal Justice* 317–346

Innes, M, Fielding, N and Langan, S, *Signal Crimes & Control Signals: Towards an Evidence-Based Conceptual Framework for Reassurance Policing. A Report for Surrey Police* (2002, Guildford: University of Surrey)

——, 'What's Your Problem? Signal Crimes and Citizen-Focused Problem-Solving' (2005) 4(2) *Criminology and Public Policy* 187–200

Kolb, D, *Experiential Learning, Experience as a Source of Learning and Development* (1984, Englewood Cliffs, NJ: Prentice Hall)

Nolan, Lord, *First Report of the Committee on Standards in Public Life*, Cm 2850-I (1995, London: TSO)

O'Connor, D/HMIC, *Closing the Gap: A Review of the Fitness for Purpose of the Current Structure of Policing in England and Wales*, HM Inspectorate of Constabulary (September 2005, London: Home Office)

Rogers, C and Prosser, K, *Crime Reduction Partnerships* (2006, Oxford: Oxford University Press)

Specials (2008), 'Cafe Culture Combats Crime', NPIA (August 2008)

—— (2009a), NPIA (April 2009)

—— (2009b), NPIA (Summer 2009)

Thames Valley Police, 'Katesgrove Environmental Visual Audit' (2009), available at <http://www.thamesvalley.police.uk/yournh-tvp-pol-area-read-newsitem?id=90173>; accessed 9 November 2009

Tilley, N (ed.), *Handbook of Crime Prevention and Community Safety* (2005, Cullompton: Willan Publishing)

Tonry, M and Farrington, D, *Building a Safer Society: Crime and Justice, A Review of Research*, Vol 19 (1995, Chicago, IL: University of Chicago Press)

Wilson J and Kelling G, 'Broken Windows' (1982) 249 *Atlantic Monthly* 29–36

Legislation, Policies and Guidelines

4.1 Introduction—IL4SC Part 2: Legislation, Policies and Guidelines (LPG) Modules

The laws in this chapter that we summarise for you are the commonest that you are likely to encounter, but even here we can't include everything in the criminal law and every contingency you are likely to meet. We strongly advise that you look at the laws themselves in greater detail in *Blackstone's Police Operational Handbook: Law*, edited by Ian Bridges and Fraser Sampson (2013, Oxford: Oxford University Press) or in Michael Jefferson's huge *Criminal Law*, 10th edn. (2011, London: Pearson Longman). We also look throughout at factors like your powers and duties as they impact on your role as a Special Constable.

We need to emphasise that what follows here is a basic summary of the law followed by our notes and comments on what that means to you, the Special Constable, out in the street and needing to apply the right law to the right offence. This is what it says: a reference **guide**. It is *not* a substitute for you reading the law thoroughly and understanding the case law that attends it, as well as the significant milestones in interpretation, which we have space only to allude to.

It is worth repeating that this book uniquely introduces you to both your role as a police officer *and* to the context in which you do your policing. You cannot separate what you do from why you do it.

4.2 (LPG1_1_01) Assaults

Here we cover several different types of offence:

- **Common assault and battery** under s 39 of the Criminal Justice Act 1988
- **Assault occasioning actual bodily harm** under s 47 of the Offences Against the Person Act 1861
- **Assault on a constable** under s 89(1) of the Police Act 1996
- **Wilfully obstructing a constable** under s 89(2) of the Police Act 1996
- **Obstructing or hindering certain emergency workers responding to emergency circumstances** under s 1 of the Emergency Workers (Obstruction) Act 2006
- **Obstructing or hindering persons assisting emergency workers** under s 1 of the Emergency Workers (Obstruction) Act 2006
- **Assaulting a constable with intent to resist arrest** under s 38 of the Offences Against the Person Act 1861.

4.2.1 Common assault/battery offences

Under s 39 of the Criminal Justice Act 1988 there are two possible offences:

- Common assault—this is not a physical attack, but is instead any act (for example, a threat) which makes a victim understand s/he is going to be immediately subjected to some personal violence. An example of this would be: 'I'm going to smash your head in!'
- Common assault by beating or battery—this involves the actual use of force by an assailant on a victim but only results in very minor or no perceivable injury.

These are alternative offences and therefore should never be charged together (see *DPP v Little* [1992] 1 All ER 299). In *Fagan v Metropolitan Commissioner* (1968) 52 Cr App R 700; [1969] 1 QB 439; [1968] 3 All ER 442, it was suggested that 'an assault is any act which intentionally or recklessly causes another person to apprehend immediate and unlawful personal violence.' In *Haystead v Chief Constable of Derbyshire* [2000] EWHC QB 181, a battery is 'an act by way a person intentionally or recklessly applies force to the complainant.' An intentional act is one which is done in such a way that is calculated to leave the victim in no doubt that s/he will be subjected to personal violence. A suspect is reckless if s/he foresees the possible consequence of his/her conduct, but still continues.

These common assault offences are triable summarily only, and the penalty is six months' imprisonment. Note that these offences can be racially or religiously aggravated (see 5.18).

4.2.2 **Defences**

There are several defences to assault. Self-defence (often referred to as 'common law self-defence') may be used as a legal defence. It is not defined by statute and therefore it is a question of fact for the courts to decide. In *Dewar v DPP* [2010] EWHC 1050 (Admin) it was reaffirmed that there is a two-part test to self-defence.

KEY POINT

Two-part test to self-defence:
(a) that the individual believes that s/he was acting in self-defence and
(b) that the force used was reasonable in the circumstances.

The general meaning of 'reasonable force' is covered in s 76 of the Criminal Justice and Immigration Act 2008. The more specific meaning of 'reasonable force' with respect to self-defence, arrest and crime prevention is covered in s 3(1) of the Criminal Law Act 1967. Another defence to assault is consent, for example being tattooed, having a piercing or being operated on for a medical condition.

4.2.3 **Actual occasioning bodily harm (AOBH)**

Section 47 of the Offences Against the Person Act 1861 states that 'whosoever shall be convicted upon an indictment of any assault occasioning actual bodily harm shall be guilty of an offence.' *R v Donovan* [1934] 2 KB 498 at 509; [1934] All ER Rep 207 suggested that 'bodily harm' has its ordinary meaning and includes any hurt or injury calculated to interfere with the health or comfort of the victim. Such hurt or injury need not be permanent, but must, no doubt, be more than merely transient and trifling. Hurt can also include psychiatric injury.

This offence is triable either way. The penalty if tried summarily is six months' imprisonment and/or a fine, and five years' imprisonment on indictment. This offence can be racially or religiously aggravated (see 5.18).

4.2.4 **Assault on a constable**

Section 89 of the Police Act 1996 states it is an offence for any person to assault (s 89(1)), resist or wilfully obstruct a police officer or any person assisting a constable in the execution of his/her duty (s 89(2)). It is not enough for the constable to simply be on duty, the officer must be in the lawful execution of his/her duties and exercising his/her powers with authorisation (see *Cumberbatch v CPS* [2009] EWHC 3353 (Admin)).

These offences are triable summarily and the penalties are a fine or imprisonment (six months for a s 89(1) offence and one month for a s 89(2) offence).

4.2.5 **Obstructing or hindering certain emergency workers responding to emergency circumstances**

Section 1 of the Emergency Workers (Obstruction) Act 2006, states that it is an offence for person (A), to obstruct or hinder person (B), without reasonable excuse, while (B) is responding to emergency circumstances.

4.2.6 **Obstructing or hindering persons assisting emergency workers**

Section 2 of the Emergency Workers (Obstruction) Act 2006 states that it is an offence for person (A) to obstruct or hinder person (B) who is assisting person (C) who is responding to emergency circumstances. Emergency workers include those involved in fire, ambulance, coastguard, RNLI and other similar duties. These offences are triable summarily and the penalty is a fine.

4.2.7 **Assaulting a constable with intent to resist arrest**

Section 38 of the Offences Against the Person Act 1861 states that 'whosoever shall assault any person with intent to resist or prevent the lawful apprehension or detainer of himself or of any other person for any offence shall be guilty of an offence.'

This offence is triable summarily and the penalty is two years' imprisonment.

4.2.8 **Charging standards for unlawful personal violence offences**

The Public Prosecution Service and the police will base their choice of the most appropriate charge for most assault cases on two factors: first, the level of injury and, second, the sentence that the court is likely to pass. Consequently in the first instance, where the injuries are not serious or non-existent, the offence will be Common Assault/Battery. In cases of serious injury and where there is a likelihood of a prison sentence exceeding six months, the charge will generally be ABH. Further details can be obtained at: <http://www.cps.gov.uk/legal/l_to_o/offences_against_the_person/>; accessed 30 June 2012).

TEST BOX 6

Now we need to test briefly what you have learned here.

Assault

1. Why should 'common assault' and 'common assault by beating or battery' never be charged together? Name two defences to charges of assault.
2. Is hurt or injury always physical?
3. Define the offence of assault on a constable.
4. What must a constable be doing in these circumstances?
5. How would the offence of **Obstructing or Hindering...Emergency Workers** be tried and what would be the penalty on conviction?
6. Cite the law which you would use against someone who tried to assault you in order to resist arrest.
7. What determines any decisions to charge someone with assault offences?

4.3 **(LPG1_1_03) Public Order Offences**

Here we cover several different types of offence under the Public Order Act 1986:

- Affray (s 3)
- Fear or provocation of violence (s 4)
- Intentional harassment, alarm or distress (s 4A)
- Non-intentional harassment, alarm or distress (s 5).

Before looking at the sections in detail, you might find it useful to consider the meanings of key terms used in the legislation as shown in Table 4.1:

Table 4.1: Terms used in public order offences

Key terms	Connotations or expansions
Abusive	Using or containing insulting or degrading language
Alarm	A state of surprise, fright, fear, terror and panic
Behaviour	Display of conduct involving the treatment of others
Disorderly behaviour	Rowdy, unruly, boisterous, loud, raucous or unrestrained conduct
Display	Show or exhibit for all to see, such as placing a sign or poster in a window
Distress	A feeling of suffering, anguish and misery
Distribute	To hand out, share out, give out or issue to a particular person or people, not just simply leave 'lying about'
Dwelling	Place of residence
Harassment	A feeling of annoyance, persecution, irritation, and aggravation
Insulting	Disrespectful, especially if done in a way that is offensive or suggesting that a person is beneath consideration (but in a way that is more than causing annoyance or bitterness)
Threatening	Describes a physical or verbal act which indicates that harm will be inflicted. It can also include violent conduct
Words	Spoken or shouted
Writing, sign or other visual representation	A notice containing lettering or other visible form of copied picture, text or image, leaflet, pamphlet or fly poster

4.3.1 **Affray**

Section 3(1) of the Public Order Act 1986 states that a person is guilty of an offence if s/he uses or threatens unlawful violence towards another and his/her conduct is such as would cause a person of reasonable firmness present at the scene to fear for his/her personal safety. It can be committed in private as well as in public places (s 3(5)).

A threat cannot be made by the use of words alone (s 3(2)) and the suspect must intend to use or threaten violence or be aware that his/her conduct may be violent or threaten violence (s 6(2)). Unlawful violence is not restricted to conduct towards a person causing or intended to cause injury or damage but includes any other violent conduct, for example throwing a full can of beer towards a person, even if it falls short (s 8)).

This offence is triable either way and the penalty is: summarily: six months' imprisonment, and/or a fine; on indictment: three years' imprisonment.

4.3.2 **Fear or provocation of violence**

Section 4 of the Public Order Act 1986 states that a person is guilty of an offence if s/he uses towards another person threatening, abusive or insulting words or behaviour or if s/he distributes or displays to another person any writing, sign or other visible representation which is threatening, abusive or insulting. The intent must be to:

- cause that person to believe that immediate unlawful violence will be used (against him/her or another) by any person or
- provoke the immediate use of unlawful violence (by that person or another)
- cause that person to believe it is likely either that such violence will be used or be provoked.

A police officer may enter any premises to arrest any person reasonably suspected of committing an offence under s 4 of the Public Order Act 1986 (s 17, PACE Act 1984: see 4.5). The offence is triable summarily and the penalty is six months' imprisonment and/or a fine. This offence can be racially aggravated (see 5.18).

4.3.3 **Intentional harassment, alarm or distress**

Section 4A of the Public Order Act 1986 states that a person is guilty of an offence if s/he uses threatening, abusive or insulting words or behaviour, or disorderly behaviour, or displays any writing, sign or other visible representation which is threatening, abusive or insulting, with intent to cause a person harassment, alarm or distress thereby causing that or another person harassment, alarm or distress.

Defences available to a suspect are as follows:

- s/he had no reason to believe his/her words, behaviour or conduct inside a dwelling could be seen or heard by a person anywhere outside, for example a poster hanging on an inside wall within a house was difficult to see from the road outside (s 4A(3)(a)) or
- his/her conduct was reasonable, for example if a person shouted at a group of people who were carrying out an unlawful act outside his/her home (s 4A(3)(b)).

This offence is triable summarily and the penalty is six months' imprisonment and/or a fine. This offence can be racially or religiously aggravated (see 5.18).

4.3.4 **Non-intentional harassment, alarm or distress**

Section 5 of the Public Order Act 1986 states that a person is guilty of an offence if s/he uses threatening, abusive or insulting words or behaviour, or disorderly behaviour, or if s/he displays any writing, sign or other visible representation which is threatening, abusive or insulting, and this is done within the hearing or sight of a person likely to be caused harassment, alarm or distress thereby.

There are three defences to this offence (listed in s 5(3)):

- that s/he had no reason to believe, whilst in public, that anybody could hear or see his/her conduct and had become harassed, alarmed or distressed as a result
- that s/he had no reason to believe, whilst inside a dwelling (place of residence), that his/her words, behaviour or conduct could be seen or heard by a person outside that same or another dwelling or
- that his/her conduct was reasonable and did not cause anybody to be harassed, alarmed or distressed.

This offence is triable summarily and the penalty is a fine. This offence can be racially or religiously aggravated (see 5.18).

4.4 **Important Differences Between the Offences of ss 4, 4A and 5**

Table 4.2 highlights important differences between the offences of ss 4, 4A and 5:

Table 4.2: Differentiating between offences

Evidential requirements	s 4	s 4A	s 5
Awareness and intentions of the suspect	Intends to cause fear of violence or to provoke violence	Intends to be threatening, abusive or insulting	No intention, but is aware that the conduct is threatening, abusive or insulting, but
Recipient of the conduct	Conduct aimed towards a specific person	Conduct does not have to be aimed towards a specific person	Conduct does not have to be aimed towards a specific person but has to be carried out in the hearing or sight of a person likely to be caused harassment, alarm or distress
Includes disorderly behaviour?	Does not include disorderly behaviour	Includes disorderly behaviour	
Distribution of material?	Includes distribution of material	Does not include distribution of material	
Outcome of the behaviour	No specific outcome is required to prove this offence	An identifiable person must be harassed, alarmed or distressed	No specific outcome is required to prove this offence

---

TEST BOX 7

Now let's see how much you can recall.

1. What makes behaviour 'disorderly'?
2. Distinguish between *abuse* and *harassment*.
3. What section of the Public Order Act 1986 deals with threats of unlawful violence such to make a person fearful of his/her safety?
4. How would you prove intent under s 4 of the Public Order Act 1986?
5. What are the possible defences to offences against the Public Order Act?

4.5 (LPG1_1_04) Theft Act 1968

Here we cover several different types of offence contained within the Theft Act 1968:

- Theft (s 1)
- Robbery (s 8)
- Burglary (s 9)
- Aggravated burglary (s 10)
- Taking a conveyance without consent (s 12)
- Aggravated vehicle taking (s 12A)
- Taking a pedal cycle (s 12(5)).

4.5.1 Theft

Section 1 of the Theft Act 1968 states that a person is guilty of theft if s/he dishonestly appropriates property belonging to another with the intention of permanently depriving the other of it. Each of five key concepts for theft are involved.

4.5.1.1 Dishonesty

Dishonesty is not defined by the Act, but s 2(1) of the Theft Act 1968 outlines when a person will *not* be treated as dishonest. The person is not acting dishonestly if s/he believes that:

- s/he had the lawful right to take the item (for example, a person mistakenly taking the wrong coat from a changing room, believing it was his/her own)
- s/he would have had the owner's consent if the owner had known of the circumstances and
- the owner could not have been discovered by taking reasonable steps.

But s 2(2) of the Theft Act 1968 states that a person may be treated as dishonest even though s/he was willing to pay for the property (for instance, where a person wants to buy a particular garden ornament but the shopkeeper cannot be found, so the person takes the ornament and leaves behind what s/he thinks it is worth in money). In the end, a court must decide whether a person acted dishonestly or not.

4.5.1.2 **Appropriation**

With reference to theft, the term 'to appropriate' is given the following meaning in the Theft Act 1968, s 3(1):

- assuming the rights of an owner of property by stealing it (for example, by shoplifting) or
- obtaining property innocently and later keeping it and using it as one's own (for example, hiring a piece of machinery and not returning it).

However, when an innocent purchaser pays the right price to a person who is selling some kind of property which later turns out to be stolen, the innocent purchaser will not have committed theft. For example, if a person buys a second-hand bicycle in good faith and then discovers it is stolen, the innocent purchaser will not have committed theft (s 3(2), Theft Act 1968).

4.5.1.3 **Property**

The definition of property (s 4, Theft Act 1968) is not straightforward. Property includes:

- *money*
- *personal property*, for example personal effects or pets
- *real property*, for example land and things forming part of the land, such as plants and buildings. However, land can only be stolen:
  - ○ by a trustee (someone who has the legal control over the land), for example during its transfer in some kind of a legal process
  - ○ by persons who do not own the land, for example by removing turf or topsoil, or digging up cultivated trees and shrubs
  - ○ by tenants, for example by removing fixtures and fittings
- *things in [an] action,* for example patents, copyrights and trademarks
- *plants or fungi growing wild*, but only if they are picked for sale, reward or a commercial purpose (and always consider other legislation that might prohibit such activities, such as the Wildlife and Countryside Act 1981)
- *wild creatures*, but only if they are tamed and have not been lost or abandoned since they were kept in captivity and
- *tangible property*, for example gas.

(Note that electricity is not included and cannot be stolen but is dealt with separately under s 13.)

4.5.1.4 **Belonging to another** (s 5) means that the person has:

- a proprietary right or interest, for example the owner of a computer that needs repair
- possession, for example the owner of the computer repair shop that the owner takes it to, or
- control, for example the person repairing the computer.

4.5.1.5 The intention permanently to deprive (s 6(1)) is shown by a person treating another person's property as if it were his/her own. This could include:

- lending and borrowing over an extended time scale (for example, borrowing a DVD from someone and then lending it to someone else) or
- pawning an item (for example, going to a pawnbroker's shop with another person's computer and receiving a loan of money in exchange).

The offence of theft is triable either way and the penalty is: summarily: six months' imprisonment and/or a fine; on indictment: seven years' imprisonment.

4.5.2 Robbery

Section 8 of the Theft Act 1968 states that a person is guilty of robbery if s/he steals, and immediately before or at the time of doing so, and in order to do so, s/he uses force on any person or puts or seeks to put any person in fear of being then and there subjected to force. First, note that a robbery must involve at least one of the following elements:

- force or a threat of force is used on any person, immediately before, or at the time of the theft, or in order to carry out the theft or
- any person is '*put in fear*' that force will be used to carry out a theft.

There are key concepts involved in robbery:

Steals: the entire key elements of s 1 of the Theft Act 1968 (see earlier) must be satisfied. If force is used but no theft takes place, then an alternative charge of assault with intent to rob could be considered.

Immediately before or at the time of doing so: if the force is used at any other time then alternative offences of theft and assault will be considered as alternatives.

In order to do so: the use of force must take place in order for the theft to be carried out.

Uses force on any person: the threat or use of force can be on any person and it can be a third person in order to create a situation in which the theft can take place.

Puts or seeks to put any person in fear of being then and there subjected to force: a threat to use force must be made at the time that the theft is committed with the intention that something should happen immediately.

The offence of robbery is triable on indictment only and the maximum penalty is life imprisonment.

4.5.3 Burglary

The offence of burglary is set out in s 9 of the Theft Act 1968 which states that a person is guilty of burglary if:

(a) [s/he] enters any building or part of a building as a trespasser and with intent to steal anything in the building or part of a building in question, inflict on any person therein any grievous bodily harm, or do unlawful damage to the building or anything therein; or

(b) having entered into any building or part of a building as a trespasser [s/he] steals or attempts to steal anything in the building or that part of it or inflicts or attempts to inflict on any person therein any grievous bodily harm.

Note that part (a) offences involve a person entering a building with the **intent** to steal or cause injury or damage (but these actions do not actually need to be carried out). For part (b) offences, the theft or injury must be **carried out** or at least attempted.

4.5.4 **Section 9(1)(a) burglary**

Certain terms, such as 'entry', 'building' and 'intent' need to be carefully defined in order fully to appreciate the range of activities that might count as burglary under s 9(1)(a) of the Theft Act 1968.

4.5.5 **Entry as a trespasser**

Trespass means entering without the consent of the owner (but see the following points). **Entry** can be gained in a number of clearly defined ways:

- *In person*, by walking or climbing into a building, either completely or by inserting a body part (such as an arm or a leg) through a window or letter box. However, there must be more than minimal insertion: sliding a hand between a window and frame from the outside of a building in order to release the catch would be insufficient
- *Using a tool or article* as an extension of the human body to carry out one of the relevant offences. In these circumstances, no part of the body needs to be inserted, only the article that is being used. Using a crowbar just to prise open a door would not qualify as the full offence, but a length of garden cane pushed through the letter box of a shop to hook a scarf from a display would qualify
- *Using a blameless accomplice* in a similar way to using an article as an extension of the suspect's body. Here, for example, a child below the age of criminal responsibility (ten years of age) could be lifted through a small window to obtain property from inside. On the other hand, if the child is used for the purposes of preparing an entry point for the burglar only, and nothing is stolen, then the full offence is not committed: it has only been attempted
- *Trespass* involves a person entering a building or part of a building (for the purpose of committing one of the relevant offences) in one of the following ways:

> ○ *entering a building* for a purpose other than that building's intended purpose, for example going into a shop with the intention to steal (rather than to browse or buy)
>
> ○ *entering by some kind of deception*, for example pretending to represent a utility company coming to read a meter and being invited into the building ('distraction burglary') or
>
> ○ *crossing over a demarcation* line of some kind, unlawfully and without invitation or permission, whether or not the owner knows that the person crossing the line is trespassing.

4.5.6 Intent ('*mens rea*'—the guilty mind)

The suspect must intend to commit certain specified offences (see 7.5). 'Intent' can be proved in a number of ways or in combination:

- during the interview of the suspect when s/he admits to having *guilty knowledge* or criminal intent to commit the offence
- when other suspects involved in committing the offence name their accomplices and the part these people played in its commission
- circumstantial evidence (including witness statements, observations of the arresting officer(s), retrieval of stolen property from the crime scene and forensic identification).

In summary, for a part (a) burglary, the suspect does not actually need to have committed any of the acts described in the following sections.

4.5.7 Section 9(1)(b) burglary

For part (b), the suspect has already entered the building or part of the building as a trespasser and commits the full offences as opposed to just having an intention to carry them out as in s 9(1)(a).

Steals: see 'theft' (4.5.2).

Attempts to steal: the act must be more than merely preparatory, for example the very last and final act before the full offence is committed.

Anything in the building or that part of it: this will include anything in the building into which the suspect entered originally as a trespasser or anything in another part of the building which the suspect entered as a trespasser having gained entry to the main part of the building lawfully.

Inflicts: not as restricted as assault but narrower than cause (see *R v Wilson* [1983] 3 All ER 448).

Grievous bodily harm: s 20 of the Offences Against the Person Act 1861 states that 'whosoever shall unlawfully and maliciously wound or inflict any grievous bodily harm upon any other person, either with or without any weapon or instrument shall be guilty of an offence.'

An offence under either subsection is triable either way and the penalty is: summarily: six months' imprisonment and/or a fine; on indictment: ten years' imprisonment (14 years' imprisonment if the building or part of the building was a dwelling) and three years' minimum imprisonment on conviction for a third domestic burglary.

4.5.8 Aggravated burglary

Section 10 of the Theft Act 1968 states that a person commits an offence of aggravated burglary if s/he commits any burglary and at the time, has with him/her, any firearm or imitation firearm, any weapon of offence or any explosive.

Firearm: includes an airgun or air pistol, and 'imitation firearm' means anything which has the appearance of being a firearm, whether capable of being discharged or not.

Weapon of offence: any article made or adapted for use for causing injury to or incapacitating a person, or intended by the person having it with him for such use.

Explosive: any article manufactured for the purpose of producing a practical effect by explosion, or intended by the person having it with him for that purpose.

This offence is triable on indictment only and the penalty is life imprisonment.

4.6 Taking a Conveyance Without Consent

Section 12(1) of the Theft Act 1968 states that it is an offence for any person who without having the consent of the owner or other lawful authority, takes any conveyance for his/her own or another's use or, knowing that any conveyance has been taken without such authority, drives it or allows him/herself to be carried in or on it.

Consent: must be genuine and not obtained under duress. A hirer will be the owner for the period during which an agreement is in place.

Lawful authority: includes individuals employed to remove vehicles contravening parking regulations and reclaiming vehicles under a hire-purchase agreement when the hirer has defaulted.

Takes a conveyance: any conveyance constructed or adapted for the carriage of a person or persons whether by land, water or air.

Drives it or allows him/herself to be carried in or on it: to 'allow him/herself', the suspect must know that the conveyance has been taken without the owner's consent.

A possible defence is available if the person believes that s/he has the consent of the owner or had other lawful authority (s 12(6)).

This offence is triable summarily and the penalty is six months' imprisonment and/or a fine.

4.6.1 **Aggravated vehicle taking**

Section 12A of the Theft Act 1968 states that it is an offence for a person who takes a mechanically propelled vehicle without consent and it is proved that at any time after the vehicle was unlawfully taken (whether by him/her or another) and before it was recovered, the vehicle was driven, or injury or damage was caused under the following circumstances (s 12A(2)):

1. that the vehicle was driven dangerously on a road or other public place
2. that, owing to the driving of the vehicle, an accident occurred by which injury was caused to any person
3. that, owing to the driving of the vehicle, an accident occurred by which damage was caused to any property, other than the vehicle
4. that damage was caused to the vehicle.

This offence is triable either way: summary: six months' imprisonment and/or a fine, on indictment: two years' imprisonment and/or a fine. If the accident (under s 12A(2)(b)) caused death, the penalty is 14 years' imprisonment.

4.6.1.1 **Taking a pedal cycle**

Section 12(5) of the Theft Act 1968 states that it is an offence for a person who, without having the consent of the owner or other lawful authority, takes a pedal cycle for his/her own or another's use, or rides a pedal cycle knowing it to have been taken without such authority. A possible defence is available if the person believes that s/he has the consent of the owner or had other lawful authority (s 12(6)). This offence is triable summarily and the penalty is a fine.

TEST BOX 8

Now we test you on theft and associated offences.

1. When is a person guilty of theft?
2. Section 2(1) outlines when a person will not be treated as dishonest. Give two examples.
3. Give four examples of property.
4. What does section 8 of the Theft Act 1968 describe?
5. What three things might 'aggravate' a burglary?
6. What constitutes a 'conveyance'?
7. What is the penalty for taking a pedal cycle?

4.7 **(LPG1_1_09) Criminal Damage Act 1971**

Here we cover several different types of offence contained within the Criminal Damage Act 1971:

- Destroying or damaging property (s 1)
- Threats to cause criminal damage (s 2)
- Having articles with intent to destroy or damage property (s 9).

4.7.1 **Destroying or damaging property**

Section 1(1) of the Criminal Damage Act 1971 states that it is an offence for a person who 'without lawful excuse destroys or damages property belonging to another, intending to destroy or damage any such property or being reckless as to whether any such property would be destroyed or damaged.'

A person would have lawful excuse if s/he had an honestly held belief that:

- s/he had permission from the owner of the property (or an appropriate person) to cause the damage, for example a recovery operator is authorised by a car owner to load the car onto a recovery vehicle, and damages it in the process. This would also apply if the operator believed that the owner would have given permission but is unable to do so (such as having been taken to hospital unconscious)
- that his/her own or another's property was in immediate need of protection by reasonable means if, for example, a car had slipped down a steep embankment and was likely to slip still further, and a recovery operator damages it when pulling it back up onto the road.

If the property is destroyed then it is no longer of any use and cannot be repaired. Therefore the cost of the damage will be equal to the cost of replacing the item. Damage, on the other hand, does not have to be everlasting nor does the item need to be beyond repair. The cost of the damage will be equal to the cost of the repair.

The damage must be to something 'real'; that is, something that you could touch, for example land ('real estate') or personal items including money (a bundle of notes for example). The property must belong to another person who has custody, control, a right, an interest or is in charge of the property. The person carrying out the offence must either intend to cause the damage, or be reckless as to whether the property would be damaged.

In *R v G and another* [2003] UKHL 50 it was decided that a person acts recklessly with respect to a circumstance or a result. For example, knowing that heavy objects can break glass on impact, a person throws a barrage of large stones towards a glass panel bus shelter, intentionally disregarding the possibility that the panes might smash if they come into contact. Subsequently,

111

one or more of the stones do hit the glass and cause it to break. Alternatively, having read the instructions on a packet of weed killer and knowing that it should not be used near fish, a person deliberately ignores the risk to his/her neighbour's fish pond and allows the spray to drift over to next door, killing all the fish.

A power to search for articles made or adapted for use in the course of or in connection with an offence under s 1 of the Criminal Damage Act 1971 is provided under s 1(2)(a) of the PACE Act 1984.

This offence is triable either way. If the value of the property damaged or destroyed is less than £5,000, the offence is tried summarily (s 22, Magistrates' Courts Act 1980). The penalty is six months' imprisonment and/or a fine if tried summarily, and ten years' imprisonment on indictment.

4.7.2 **Threats to cause criminal damage**

Section 2 of the Criminal Damage Act 1971 states that it is an offence for a person who without lawful excuse, makes to another a threat, intending that the other would fear it would be carried out, to destroy or damage:

(a) any property belonging to that other or a third person; or
(b) his/her own property in way which s/he knows is likely to endanger the life of that other or a third person.

The threat can relate to a third party but the conduct that is threatened must refer to damage and the extent of the threatened damage must constitute an offence under s 1 of the Criminal Damage Act 1971. A stated intention to destroy or damage the property can be communicated in any way, for example email, text message, fax, letter or phone call—and it could be an 'idle threat': there need be no intention to actually carry it out.

This offence is triable either way and the penalty is six months' imprisonment and/or a fine if tried summarily, and ten years' imprisonment on indictment.

4.7.3 **Possessing an article with intent to cause criminal damage**

Section 3 of the Criminal Damage Act 1971 states that it is an offence for a person to have anything in his/her custody or under his/her control intending without lawful excuse to use it or cause or permit another to use it to destroy or damage:

(a) any property belonging to some other person; or
(b) his/her own or the user's property in a way which s/he knows is likely to endanger the life of some other person.

For the purposes of this offence, 'anything' is not defined but should take its everyday meaning. In order to have custody of such an article, a person must be able to have access to it and be able to use or guard it. Control, on the other hand, suggests a degree of authority in relation to where the article is located.

This offence is triable either way. The penalty is six months' imprisonment and/or a fine not exceeding the statutory maximum if tried summarily, and ten years' imprisonment on indictment.

TEST BOX 9

Time to check how much you remember.

1. What are the three offences in the Criminal Damage Act 1971?
2. What 'lawful excuse' might someone offer?
3. How might threats to cause criminal damage be conveyed?
4. What might the penalty be on indictment of threats to cause criminal damage?

4.8 **(LPG4_1_01) Drug Awareness**

Several different types of controlled drugs are widely in public use and some are 'recreational drugs', so detection of them is often linked to the 'night-time economy'. It is an important part of a police officer's role to recognise both the drugs and the effects that they have on those under their influence (see Table 4.3 overleaf).

Many people who commit criminal offences do so under the influence of drugs, or in order to fund their habit, so you will often deal with drugs and drugs-users in the course of your duty. Drugs come in many different forms: pills, powders, liquids and resins. Your first thought therefore when finding substances which may be controlled drugs, should be to suspect that it *is* a controlled drug and use your common sense. Be prepared to use your personal protection equipment. Remember that a person under the influence of drugs may be aggressive or unpredictable. Treat **any drugs suspect with caution**, leaving yourself a good space to react to any form of aggression. Ensure that you watch carefully so as not to give the suspect any opportunity to discard drugs or paraphernalia. **Wearing gloves** when you conduct a search under the Misuse of Drugs Act is vital, as serious injury and contamination from equipment used by drugs-users is a real possibility.

Table 4.3: Illegal and proscribed drugs

Class A

Drug	Street name	Effects	Paraphernalia
Heroin A powerful painkiller derived from opium Brown powder smoked or injected following preparation	H, Brown, Horse, Skag, Smack, Dark	* Slows down body functions * Reduces physical and psychological pain * Most users get a rush or buzz * A small dose of heroin gives the user a feeling of warmth and well-being * Bigger doses can make the user sleepy and very relaxed * Highly addictive	Scored tinfoil, syringes and needles, scored spoons, ligatures, citric acid or lemon juice
Cocaine A powerful stimulant White powder usually sniffed	Coke, Charlie, C, White, Percy, Snow, Sniff	* Feeling on top of the world * Feeling confident * Some get over-confident, arrogant and aggressive and end up taking very careless risks * Body temperature raised * Heart beats faster	Small mirrors, razors, straws, small squares of paper or clingfilm
Crack cocaine. A powerful stimulant A 'rock' form of cocaine prepared and smoked	Crack, Wash, Pebbles, Rocks, Stones	* Acts faster that snorted cocaine and is more addictive * Feeling on top of the world * Feeling confident * Some get over-confident, arrogant and aggressive and end up taking very careless risks * Body temperature raised * Heart beats faster	

Drug	Street name	Effects	Paraphernalia
Ecstasy A stimulant also known by its chemical name, MDMA. Associated with clubbing; usually comes as pills	E, Brownies, Cowies, Crystal, Dolphins, Mandy, MDMA, Pills, XTC	* Stimulants taken to keep users awake and alert * Makes people feel in tune with their surroundings—sounds and colours are more intense * Feel great love for the people around them * Feel chatty: chats which don't make sense to others * Sometimes feelings of anxiety, panic attacks and confusion * Overheating of the body	Small self-sealing plastic bags

CLASS B

Drug	Street name	Effects	Paraphernalia
Cannabis The most widely used illegal drug in Britain Cannabis is made from the cannabis plant. The active chemical in it is tetrahydrocannabinol (THC for short)	Dope, Draw, Ganja, Grass, Hash, Hashish, Herb, Marijuana, Pot, Puff, Skunk, Weed	Usually… * Chilled out * Relaxed and happy * Feeling sick * Giggles or is talkative * Hunger pangs: munchies But can be… * Hallucinations * Anxiety and paranoia	Small containers, cigarette papers, grinders

(continued)

Table 4.3: Continued

Drug	Street name	Effects	Paraphernalia
Amphetamines A stimulant used to keep awake A white powder with small lumps	Speed, Amphet, Base, Billy, Dexies, Paste, Phet, Sulph, Whizz	* Makes people feel wide awake, excited and chatty * Gives users energy to do things for hours without getting tired * It can make people overactive, agitated or even acutely psychotic	Small self-sealing plastic bags

CLASS C

Drug	Street name	Effects	Paraphernalia
Tranquilisers Drugs used to treat anxiety and insomnia. They are prescription-only medicines that can normally only be prescribed following a consultation with a doctor	Jellies, Benzos, Eggs, Vallies, Moggies, Rohypnol	* Depresses the nervous system and 'slows' the brain and body down * Relief of tension and anxiety—helping the user feel calm and relaxed * Help with insomnia * Dependence—some people getting very reliant on their use, on stopping they get nasty withdrawal symptoms, including decreased concentration, tremors, nausea, vomiting, headaches, anxiety, panics and depression	

TEST BOX 10

Let's find out what you can remember about drugs.

1. When might you find 'recreational drugs'?
2. What is 'skag'?
3. What are the common effects of taking ecstasy?
4. What is the active chemical in cannabis?
5. What paraphernalia might you find among cocaine users?
6. What behaviour might you anticipate from a suspect drugs-user?
7. What risk assessments should you make?

4.9 **(LPG1_2_02) Section 1 PACE 1984**

Sections 1 and 2 of the **Police And Criminal Evidence (PACE) Act** 1984 give you the power to stop, search and detain individuals and vehicles. The PACE Act 1984 Codes of Practice safeguard the rights of an individual while you carry out such a search.

4.9.1 **Grounds for 'stop, search and detain'**

Section 1(3) of the PACE Act 1984 states that you do not have the power to search unless you have **reasonable grounds** for suspecting that you will find stolen or prohibited articles. Reasonable grounds for suspicion depend on the circumstances in each case (see Code A, para 2.2), but the following factors can all be considered:

- a suspect's behaviour, for example trying to hide something
- accurate and current intelligence or information and/or
- reliable information that members of a particular group habitually carry prohibited articles.

Reasonable grounds do *not* include personal factors, such as ethnicity, age, appearance or previous convictions (either alone, or in combination with each other, or with any other factor). You must never generalise or stereotype groups of people as being more likely to take part in criminal activity, nor should a person's religion or belief-system contribute to forming grounds for reasonable suspicion.

If you discover an article which you have reasonable grounds to suspect to be stolen or prohibited, you can seize it (s 1(6), PACE Act 1984).

4.9.2 **Appropriate locations for 'stop, search and detain'**

Section 1(1) of the PACE Act 1984 states that you may search:

(a) in any place to which...the public or any section of the public has access, on payment or otherwise, as of right, or by virtue of express or implied permission;

(b) in any other place to which people have ready access at the time when [you propose] to exercise the power, but which is not a dwelling.

The public have a **right** to use roads and footpaths and other public areas during opening hours. They have **express permission** to enter cinemas, theatres or football grounds having paid an entrance fee and they can remain there until that particular entertainment is over, when permission to be there ends. There is an **implied permission** for persons to enter buildings to carry out business transactions with the owners, and even to use a footpath to a dwelling-house for the purposes of paying a lawful call upon the householder. That implied permission remains until withdrawn by the householder or the owner of the business premises. Places to which the public has **ready access** include places such as a private field if that field is regularly used by trespassers, or a garden if it is accessible by jumping over a low wall.

This power can never be used to search inside a place of residence (a dwelling). If the search is to be carried out on land attached to a dwelling (including a garden or yard), you cannot search any person who lives in the dwelling or any other person who has the resident's permission to be on the attached land. The same principles apply to searching vehicles; you cannot search a vehicle located on land attached to a dwelling if the person who lives in the dwelling has permitted the vehicle to be on that land.

You must carry out the search at or 'nearby' the place where the person or vehicle was first detained. Code A, para 3.4, note 6 defines 'nearby' as 'within a reasonable travelling distance', but gives no indication of actual distance. Without any further guidance from case law, the term should be interpreted relatively cautiously.

4.9.3 **Who or what can be 'stopped, searched and detained'?**

Having made sure that you first of all satisfy the requirements listed in the previous paragraph concerning the location, under s 1(2)(a) of the PACE Act 1984 you can search any person, vehicle or anything which is in or on a vehicle.

4.9.4 **Items you may search for under 'stop, search and detain'**

Section 1 of the PACE Act 1984 can only be used for searching for stolen or prohibited articles. Stolen articles include any article which you have reasonable grounds for suspecting to be stolen. Here is more detail about prohibited articles:

Table 4.4: Prohibited articles

Prohibited article	Description
Offensive weapons	Includes any article made, intended or adapted for causing injury to a person (see 4.9.9.5), for use either by the person having it with him/her or by someone else
Bladed or sharply pointed articles	Includes any article which is bladed or sharply pointed, but excludes a small folding pocket-knife (see 4.9.9.2)
Any articles used in the course of or in connection with certain criminal offences	Includes any article made, intended or adapted for use (by either the person having it with him/her or by someone else) in the course of or in connection to any: • burglary (see 4.5), for example screwdriver, gloves • theft (see 4.5), for example pliers, large bag • taking a conveyance (see 4.6), for example master keys • fraud, for example false identity documents • criminal damage (see 4.7), for example spray cans
Fireworks	Only includes fireworks possessed in contravention of a prohibition imposed by any of the firework regulations

4.9.5 Requirements regarding the search of persons and vehicles

You must take reasonable steps to provide information to the person to be searched (or to the person in charge of the vehicle to be searched), and this can be best remembered by the use of a mnemonic.

GO WISELY

G Grounds of the suspicion justifying the search

O Object/purpose of search

W Warrant card (if you are not in uniform or if requested by the person)

I Identity of the officer performing the search

S Station to which the officer is attached

E Entitlement to a copy of the search record

L Legal power used

Y You are detained for the purposes of a search

After searching an unattended vehicle or anything in or on it, you must leave a record of the search inside the vehicle. However, if the vehicle has not been opened (see Code A, para 4.8), or it is not reasonable or practical to leave the record inside without causing damage (see s 2(7), PACE Act 1984), the record should be attached to the outside of the vehicle.

4.9.6 **Conducting the search**

When searching persons:

- You must seek the **cooperation** of the person to be searched. Reasonable force may be used as a last resort (under s 117, PACE Act 1984), but only after your attempts to search have been met with resistance (see Code A, para 3.2)
- You must keep the search **relevant**: the extent of the search must relate to the object you are searching for, and if the suspicion relates to a certain pocket, then only that pocket can be searched (see Code A, para 3.3)
- You cannot search a member of the **opposite sex** if it involves removal of more than outer coat, jacket, gloves, headgear or footwear, and you cannot be present at such a search, unless the person being searched specifically requests it (see Code A, para 3.6)
- You cannot require any person to remove any **clothing** in public other than an outer coat, jacket and gloves
- You can place your hands inside the **pockets** of outer clothing and feel round the inside of collars, socks and shoes (see Code A, para 3.5)
- You can search a person's **hair** as well, but only if this does not require the removal of headgear (see Code A, para 3.5)
- You can carry out a **more thorough search**, for example requiring the removal of a T-shirt, but it must be undertaken out of public view, for example in a police van or police station if it is nearby (see Code A, para 3.6)
- You do not have to be in uniform to carry out such a search
- You may detain a person or vehicle for the purpose of such a search, but the length of time the person or vehicle is detained must be reasonable and kept to a minimum (Code A, para 3.3).

4.9.7 **Recording a search**

You must make a **record** of the search at the time unless it is impossible to do so, for example in serious public order situations (see Code A, paras 4.1 and 4.2). In such cases, you should make a record as soon as possible afterwards.

4.9.8 **Documents to be provided to the person**

You must give either a full copy of the record or an 'electronic receipt' (printed) to the person you have searched unless it is impracticable to do so.

If you provide an electronic receipt you must inform the person that it is an alternative to a copy of the full record, and explain how a full record may be accessed (see Code A, para 4.2A). If, for technical reasons, it is not possible to provide either a full copy of the record or an electronic receipt (for example, because you have no access to either a printer or a paper-based version of the form), or you have to leave urgently, you must still provide some form of receipt.

This 'receipt' (a business card, for example) must include your name, a unique reference number, the power used and information on how to obtain a full copy of the search record (see Code A, para 4.10B and note 21).

TEST BOX 11

Now a 'knowledge check' on PACE Act 1984.

1. What does PACE stand for?
2. What does it do?
3. What are the Codes for?
4. Can you stop someone on the grounds of appearance?
5. Where does PACE not apply?
6. What can you search for?
7. What does the mnemonic GO WISELY tell you?
8. What must you think about when searching someone?
9. What must you do on conclusion of a search?

4.9.9 (LPG1_2_03) Related offences

Here we cover several different types of offence associated with crime prevention:

- **Possession of an article with a blade or point** under s 139(1) of the Criminal Justice Act 1988
- **Possession of an offensive weapon in a public place** under s 1(1) of the Prevention of Crime Act 1953
- **Possession of an offensive weapon or article with a blade or point on school premises** under s 139A of the Criminal Justice Act 1988
- **Manufacturing, selling or hiring offensive weapons** under s 141(1) of the Criminal Justice Act 1988
- **Going equipped** under s 25(1) of the Theft Act 1968.

4.9.9.1 Possession of an article with a blade or point

Section 139 of the Criminal Justice Act 1988 states that it is an offence for a person to have with him/her in a public place, an article which has a blade or is sharply pointed.

4.9.9.2 The definition of 'bladed' and 'sharply pointed' articles

The definition of **bladed** includes any kind of article with a blade, for example a kitchen knife, scissors, a craft knife, a pocket-knife, a dagger, a scalpel or any other article which has been given a cutting edge or blade. Pocket-knives with a blade less than 7.62 cm long which cannot be locked in the open position are not classed as bladed under this legislation.

The definition of **sharply pointed** includes any kind of article with a point, for example a needle, geometry compasses, a bradawl or any other article which has been given a sharp point.

A court must decide whether or not an article has a blade or is sharply pointed, so the prosecution must be able to prove that the article fits this description.

4.9.9.3 Defences for having bladed or sharply pointed articles

There may be a good reason for a person having a bladed or sharply pointed article in their possession, such as a carpet layer carrying a specialist knife for cutting carpet at work. But neither general self-defence nor ignorance nor forgetfulness are suitable defences; see the descriptions in Table 4.5.

This offence is triable either way: summarily: six months' imprisonment and/or a fine and on indictment: four years' imprisonment and/or a fine.

4.9.9.4 Possession of an offensive weapon in a public place

Section 1 of the Prevention of Crime Act 1953 states that it is an offence for any person without lawful authority or reasonable excuse, the proof of which shall lie on him/her, to have with him/her in any public place, any offensive weapon.

Table 4.5: Other grounds for defence (s 139 of the Criminal Justice Act 1988)

Defence	Example
Lawful authority	The lawful authority may not stay with the person continuously. For example, as a Special Constable, you have the lawful authority to have with you a bladed or sharply pointed article after seizure and before placing it into a special property store. Members of the Armed Forces also have lawful authority to carry articles such as bayonets whilst on duty, but if such an article was carried off duty they might be liable to prosecution
For use at work	A joiner uses wood chisels with very sharp cutting edges during the course of his/her work and might need to carry them in a bag while moving between jobs in the street. S/he would, however, not be able to use this claim if s/he had a chisel in a night club whilst socialising
Religious reasons	Genuine followers of the Sikh religion carry kirpans (a small rigid knife) for religious reasons
Part of any national costume	Whilst wearing national costume, some Scots carry a skean dhu (a small dagger, tucked in the top of a sock). However, this defence could not be used if the person was carrying the knife but was not wearing national costume

4.9.9.5 Definition of an offensive weapon

An offensive weapon (s 1(4)) is any article made, adapted or intended for causing injury:

1. A **made** article includes any article which has been made or manufactured with the intention of causing injury to people, for example a flick knife. These are offensive weapons; the courts need no proof of their intended use, but do require proof that the defendant had no reasonable excuse for possessing such an item
2. An **adapted** article includes any article which has been modified in some way with the intention of causing injury, for example a broken bottle with sharp edges. A jury decides whether or not articles have been specifically **adapted** to be offensive weapons
3. An **intended** article includes any article in the suspect's possession with which s/he intends to cause injury. The precise nature of the article is not important: it is what the suspect intends to do with it. A pillow could become an offensive weapon if it can be proved that the suspect intended to use it to cause injury to an elderly relative. Once again, gathering evidence through interview is important here.

Of course, some items that may be classed as offensive weapons might have innocent uses, and the person would therefore have a reasonable excuse for carrying such an item. An example might be a Forestry Commission Ranger carrying an axe along a woodland path. If the Ranger were to walk down the High Street of a town carrying the axe, the possession is not so reasonable.

4.9.9.6 Reasonable and unreasonable excuses

A person **might** have a reasonable excuse if s/he fears for his/her safety: for example, a security guard who fears attack while picking up or dropping off money at a bank. Other reasonable excuses include having an **innocent reason**, such as a chef carrying knives.

Unreasonable excuses include:

- **Forgetfulness**—a person might not have a reasonable excuse if s/he has forgotten s/he has an offensive weapon with him/her
- **Ignorance**—a person might not have a reasonable excuse just because s/he does not know the true identity of the item, for example not knowing that an antique but functioning swordstick is not a walking stick
- **General self-defence**—a person does *not* have reasonable excuse to have an offensive weapon with him/her generally for self-defence, *'just in case'* s/he is attacked. This is an excuse that Special Constables hear all the time. Be sure you know the law on this, as it is possible that confiscation could prevent escalation of violence.

In any prosecution, the burden of proving a reasonable excuse for possession of an offensive weapon lies with the defendant: if the defendant can persuade the court to consider the likelihood that s/he had a reasonable excuse that could be enough for a Not Guilty verdict.

This offence is triable either way: summarily: six months' imprisonment and/or a fine; or on indictment: four years' imprisonment and/or a fine.

4.9.9.7 **Weapons on school premises**

The Criminal Justice Act 1988 states that it is an offence for any person to have with him/her on school premises an offensive weapon (s 139A(2)) or a bladed or sharply pointed article (s 139A(1)). School premises include land used for the purposes of a 'school', including open land such as playing fields or playgrounds (s 139A(6)), and a 'school' is also defined by s 14(5) of the Further and Higher Education Act 1992 as an educational institution providing primary and secondary education. Further and higher educational establishments (eg FE colleges or universities) are not covered by this Act.

The classification of these offences and powers of search are the same as for possessing an offensive weapon in a public place (see 4.9.9.5). A police officer does not have to be in uniform to enter school premises if s/he suspects an offence under this section is being or has been committed.

Reasonable force may be used to secure an entry. If offensive weapons, or bladed or sharply pointed articles (4.9.9.2), are found, they can be seized (s 139B, Criminal Justice Act 1988).

4.10 **Going Equipped**

Section 25 of the Theft Act 1968 states that it is an offence for a person when not at his/her place of abode, to have with him/her any article for use in the course of or in connection with any burglary or theft.

Place of abode: where someone lives and would normally include the garage and garden of a house but ultimately it will be for the court to decide.

Has with him/her: knowledge of the existence of the article and having physical control over it. However, the article does not necessarily need to be on the suspect's person.

Any article: not defined in legislation but has an everyday meaning. The articles which can be used in a theft or burglary are unlimited.

The offence is not committed simply by the suspect being in possession of the articles. In order to commit the offence of going equipped, the suspect must have possession of the articles and be on his/her way to carry out a theft or burglary (see *R v Ellames* [1974] 3 All ER 130). The offence cannot be committed when coming away from the crime.

This offence is triable either way. The penalty is six months' imprisonment and/or a fine if tried summarily, or three years' imprisonment on indictment.

TEST BOX 12

A knowledge check now on offensive weapons:

1. Give three examples of a 'bladed article'.
2. Give an example of a 'sharply pointed article'.
3. Give an example of a defence to possession of a bladed or sharply pointed article.
4. Define an 'offensive weapon'.
5. What is 'going equipped'?

4.11 **(LPG1_3_16) Drunk in a Public Place/Drunk and Disorderly**

Here we cover two types of offence associated with drunkenness:

- Drunk and incapable in a public place under s 12 of the Licensing Act 1872
- Drunk and disorderly under s 91 of the Criminal Justice Act 1967.

4.11.1 **Drunk in a public place**

Section 12 of the Licensing Act 1872 states that it is an offence for a person to be found drunk on any highway or in any public place or licensed premises; drunk in charge on any highway or other public place of any carriage, horse, cattle or steam engine, or who is drunk when in possession of any loaded firearms.

Highway: roads, bridges, carriageways, cart ways, horse ways, bridleways, footways, causeways, church ways and pavements.

Public places: any place to which the public have or are permitted to have access, whether on payment or otherwise, building or not.

Carriages: include vehicles and bicycles.

Firearm: includes an air weapon but not a ball-bearing gun.

4.11.2 **Signs and symptoms of drunkenness**

The terms 'drunk' and 'drunkenness' are not defined in law, but the *Oxford Reference Dictionary* (1996) is blunt and to the point: **drunk** is defined as '*rendered incapable through alcohol*'. The general rule that the 'lay' opinion of a witness is inadmissible does not apply in this particular context: a competent witness may give evidence that, in his/her opinion, a person was drunk (*R v Davies* [1962] 1 WLR 1111). A competent witness is a person who understands questions put to them and gives answers that can be understood. As a Special Constable, you can therefore state, as a competent witness, your opinion whether a particular person was drunk. You should also be able to give the facts on which your opinion is based, such as:

- he was unsteady on his feet
- her eyes were glazed
- his speech was slurred or
- you could smell intoxicating liquor on her breath.

The court itself must decide whether or not a suspect was drunk.

4.11.3 **Drunk and disorderly**

The precise meaning of the term 'disorderly behaviour' is not defined by statute but its everyday meaning is 'unruly or offensive behaviour'. Under s 91(1) of the Criminal Justice Act 1967, it is an offence for any drunk person to display such behaviour in any highway, public place or licensed premises.

Both of the drunkenness offences are triable summarily and the penalty is one month's imprisonment or a fine. They are also penalty offences for the purposes of s 1 of the Criminal Justice and Police Act 2001 (PND).

TEST BOX 13

What do you know about dealing with a drunk?

1. Which legislation defines the offence of being drunk on a highway or public place?
2. Define 'drunk'.
3. What indicators are there of drunkenness?
4. What does 'drunk and disorderly' mean?

4.12 **(LPG1_3_23) Firearms Awareness**

Each police force has highly trained and visible Firearms Units which will work on planned firearms operations and spontaneous incidents:

- Spontaneous incidents which arise suddenly and without warning
- Pre-planned-incidents where police have time to prepare a response.

The decision to deploy armed officers in the United Kingdom is still one that is taken at the highest level (usually chief officer) and only under strict criteria which are detailed in the *ACPO Manual of Guidance on the Management, Command and Deployment of Armed Officers* (2011) as:

where the officer authorising the deployment has reason to suppose that officers may have to protect themselves or others from a person who:

- is in possession of or has immediate access to, a firearm or other potentially lethal weapon, or

- is otherwise so dangerous that the deployment of armed officers is considered to be appropriate;
- as an operational contingency in a specific operation (based on the threat assessment); or
- for the destruction of animals which are dangerous or are suffering unnecessarily.

As a Special Constable in the course of your duty it is possible that you may be the first on the scene of an incident which may involve the criminal use of firearms. Your main priorities will always be the safety of the victim, the public, the police and even the suspect. Remember that a firearms incident which results in a shooting will be subject to the highest level of scrutiny (usually by the Independent Police Complaints Commission, IPCC) into every decision made at every level, *including yours as a first responder.*

4.12.1 **Responsibilities of unarmed officers attending firearms incidents**

- **Stay safe**—think about your own and the public's safety
- **See**—what is happening and where
- **Tell**—communicate, describe incident/type of weapon and any information gathered from the scene or from witnesses
- **Act**—stay safe, update, observe/contain
  - Use cover—keep in view if possible to do so safely
  - Safe approach
  - Look after others
  - Gather intelligence—numbers, direction, casualties, weapons, actions of offender
  - Communication—location, type of incident, update
  - First aid
  - Handling weapons—if you do not know what you are doing, leave well alone
  - Crime scene—safety will always be the priority but if you can identify any firearm or ballistic item (cartridge case, wadding, 'chalice' etc) or mark, leave it in situ and point it out to investigators/CSIs.

A good initial response and update to the firearms teams arriving will assist greatly with their tactical objectives at a firearms incident which will be to:

- Identify offender(s), intelligence background including previous history, access to and knowledge of firearms
- Locate—precise location
- Contain the offender physically, technically or visually
- Neutralise, arrest or lethal option.

4.12.2 **Firearms handed in/surrendered/found in course of normal duties**

Firearms come in many shapes and sizes and you may encounter firearms which may be handed to you. If you do not have expertise in handling firearms, leave well alone and contact an authorised firearms officer to make the weapon safe.

Firearms handed in or surrendered will be sent to the Force Armourer and details will be sent to the National Ballistics Intelligence Service (NABIS) which may require to examine the firearm.

The following diagram shows the definition of a firearm.

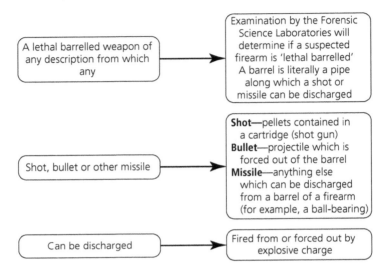

Firearms are classified into the following categories:

- Shotguns
- Air weapons
- Section 1 Firearms—covers everything other than shotguns and air weapons and imitation firearms
- Prohibited weapons—in general automatic weapons and handguns.

TEST BOX 14

What do you need to know about firearms?

1. What two instances involve attendance by firearms officers?

2. Who authorises deployment of firearms officers?

3. What are the criteria for deployment?

4. If you are first officer attending a firearms incident, how can you help the firearms team?

5. Define a firearm.

4.13 (LPG1_4_01) Arrest and Detention

Here we cover arrest and later detention at a police station:

- **Constable only power of arrest without warrant** under s 24 of the PACE Act 1984
- **Other persons' powers of arrest without warrant** under s 24A of the PACE Act 1984
- **Information to be given on arrest** under s 28 of the PACE Act 1984
- **Use of force** under s 24A of the PACE Act 1984 and s 3 of the Criminal Law Act 1967
- **'De-arresting' and further arrest whilst in custody** under ss 30 and 31 of the PACE Act 1984
- **Searching a person on arrest** under s 32 of the PACE Act 1984
- **Role and responsibilities of and towards a Custody Officer** under the PACE Codes of Practice
- **Powers and duties in relation to searching of detained persons** under s 54 of the PACE Act 1984.

4.13.1 Constable only power of arrest without warrant (s 24, PACE 1984)

In the course of your duties whilst on Supervised or Independent Patrol, you may need to arrest without a warrant someone who you suspect of committing a criminal offence. Apart from the power to arrest for a breach of the peace (see **5.3**), and specific powers of arrest from other legislation, you also have a statutory power of arrest without a warrant that derives from s 24 of the PACE Act 1984. Using this power, you may arrest a person whether you are in uniform or not, but only if certain criteria are met.

4.13.2 The two conditions for an arrest to be lawful

The two conditions for an arrest to be lawful are:

1. that a person is about to commit an offence, or is in the act of committing an offence, or that there are reasonable grounds to suspect that a person is involved, or has attempted to be involved in the commission of an offence and
2. that there are reasonable grounds for believing that the person's arrest is necessary.

You must not arrest a person solely because of his/her involvement, or suspicion of involvement, in a criminal offence. You must make an arrest **only if it is necessary**. The reasons for which an arrest may be necessary are specified in s 24(5) of the PACE Act 1984 and its Code G, para 2.9.

Before we look further at the power of arrest, it is important that you understand the term 'reasonable grounds to suspect', as it is a central component part of the power.

4.13.3 Reasonable grounds to suspect

Although words such as 'suspicion', 'grounds' and 'belief' are in common use, they have particular meanings within the law.

129

Definition of reasonable grounds to suspect

Whether or not something is **reasonable** is a conclusion that one or more people reach in agreement as a result of personal experience or understanding. **Grounds** for something include a reason or argument for a thought to exist. To **suspect** something is to think that it is probably true, although you are not certain. To **believe** something is a stronger and more concrete conclusion.

Therefore, in order to decide whether you have 'reasonable grounds to suspect', consider the offence, the component parts of that offence and whether or not a like-minded person would draw the same conclusion as you about the suspect and the offence. For example, did the person have the means, the opportunity, the motive, the presence of mind and the incentive to commit the offence?

Note, however, that **an arrest can never be justified simply on the basis of obeying the orders of your supervisors or managers** (O'Hara (AP) v CC of the RUC (1997) 1 Cr App R 447). Equally, it is insufficient for you to infer that your supervisors or managers had reasonable grounds for suspicion (see Commissioner of Police of the Metropolis v Mohamed Raissi (2008) EWCA Civ 1237). To justify an arrest, you must have been given sufficient information by a supervisor or manager to generate **your own** reasonable grounds to suspect that it was necessary to arrest that person: (see (1) Sonia Raissi (2) Mohamed Raissi v Commissioner of Police of the Metropolis (2007) EWHC 2842 (QB)).

4.13.3.1 Involvement in the commission of a criminal offence

The first condition for an arrest to be lawful is that you know, or have reasonable grounds to suspect, that a criminal offence is in the process of being committed (or is about to be committed). This is shown in Table 4.6.

You may also arrest someone on suspicion of committing an offence on an earlier occasion, but you must be certain that it is **necessary** to arrest the suspect, and have clear **reasons** in mind (see 4.13.2).

In these circumstances, you may arrest:

- **anyone who is guilty of the offence** and/or
- **anyone who you have reasonable grounds for suspecting to be guilty**.

4.13.4 **Reasons that make an arrest necessary**

A Special Constable would decide on the basis of each particular situation:

- what action to take when first in contact with the suspect—for example, when to caution, search, or use personal safety equipment and
- whether to arrest, report for summons, grant street bail, issue a fixed penalty notice or take any other action.

Table 4.6: Circumstances in which you can know, or have reasonable grounds to suspect, that a criminal offence is in the process of being committed (or is about to be committed) under the PACE Act 1984

Level of involvement	Example
A person is **about to commit** an offence	You are on duty, not in uniform, in an electrical store when you see a woman, not a member of the shop staff, walk up to a display of iPods, select one and put it under her coat. You see her walk towards the entry/exit of the shop, making no attempt to pay for the item. You stop her as she is about to leave the shop, as she is about to commit an offence. If it is **necessary**, you may arrest her (see 4.13.2)
A person is **in the act of committing** an offence	You are on duty, not in uniform, in an electrical store when you see a man walk up to a display of DAB radios, cut a security link, pick up a radio and walk towards the door of the shop past the pay-points, without paying for the radio. The store alarm is activated and the man continues to walk out of the shop. You decide the man is stealing the radio and stop him just outside the shop as he is in the act of committing the theft of the radio. If it is **necessary**, you may arrest him (see 4.13.2)
You have **reasonable grounds** for **suspecting** a person to be **about to commit** an offence	You are on duty, not in uniform, in an electrical store when you see a man walk up to a display of mobile phones. You see him take a metal cutter out of his pocket. He then reaches out towards the security chain of the mobile and appears to be about to cut the chain when he is disturbed. He puts the tool back in his pocket and walks away. A few seconds later he returns to the display of mobiles, takes out the same tool, places the cutter on the security chain and sets off the alarm. You walk up to the man having decided you have reasonable grounds for suspecting he is about to commit an offence. If it is **necessary**, you may arrest him (see 4.13.2)
You have **reasonable grounds** for **suspecting** a person **to be** committing an offence	You are standing outside a store that sells electrical goods when you see a person just inside the store near the doorway, carrying an unpacked, new DVD player underneath his arm with the lead and plug dragging behind. He also has a rucksack on his back. You see him use a tool to cut away the security tag from the DVD player and put the player in his rucksack. The person then walks towards the door as if to leave the store. You possess 'reasonable grounds for suspecting' that he has been found to be in the process of committing an offence of theft of a DVD player. If it is **necessary**, you may arrest him or her (see 4.13.2)

In 4.13.2.4, we explained that there are two conditions which need to be satisfied before an arrest should be made. The first concerns the existence of an offence, and this is discussed in Table 4.6. The second condition is that one or more of a number of **reasons** make the arrest **necessary**. The possible reasons are set out in the PACE Act 1984, Code G, para 2.9 (Code G is available at <http://www.homeoffice.gov.uk/publications/police/operational-policing/pace-codes/>).

An arrest is deemed to be necessary if one or more of the following reasons apply.

4.13.5 **To obtain someone's name or address**

You must always explain, if the person refuses to provide his/her name or address, that it may lead to his/her arrest. Remember, this is not a power to arrest a person who simply refuses to give you his/her name or address. Instead, this is just one of several reasons that make a person's arrest necessary in particular circumstances. You may arrest someone in a situation where:

1. *You do not know and cannot readily ascertain the person's name or address*: do not just ask him/her for his/her name and address once, or in a manner that lacks confidence. Make it clear to him/her that you need his/her name and address, and explain that you suspect that s/he has committed an offence and that you require his/her name and address in order that the process of investigation can be followed

2. *You have reasonable grounds for doubting whether a name or address given by the person is real*: you must have a logical reason for not believing that the name or address s/he gave you is correct, for example:

   ○ s/he cannot give you anything which identifies him/her with the name or address (for example, a driving licence with a photograph)
   ○ you suspect s/he is using the name or address of a close relative with the same details (which are therefore false)
   ○ there is no record of the name or address s/he provided in the voters' register or telephone directory
   ○ you suspect his/her name or address is fictitious because it is the name or address of a famous person or character.

Code D of the PACE Act 1984 Codes of Practice provides more detailed information about the definition of a satisfactory address (Code D is available at <http://www.homeoffice.gov.uk/publications/police/operational-policing/pace-codes/>).

4.13.6 **To prevent injury, damage, indecency or obstruction**

A reason for arresting someone could be to prevent the person:

• *causing physical injury to another person*: for example, if you were investigating an offence of throwing fireworks in a street or public place under s 80 of the Explosives Act 1875, you might reach the conclusion that the suspect could harm him/herself or somebody else

- *suffering physical injury*: for example, if you were investigating a person for an offence of being a pedestrian on the carriageway of a motorway under s 17(4) of the Road Traffic Regulation Act 1984, you might decide that the suspect could suffer physical injury him/herself from passing vehicles
- *causing loss of or damage to property*: for example, if you were investigating someone for the offence of 'interference with a motor vehicle or trailer' under s 9 of the Criminal Attempts Act 1981, you might conclude that the suspect caused damage to a vehicle during the interference
- *committing an offence against public decency*: for example, if you were investigating a person for an offence of using obscene language under the Town Police Clauses Act 1847, you might decide that the suspect was committing an offence against public decency (however, this legislation can only be used when the acts are committed in the presence of members of the public who cannot avoid the suspect)
- *causing unlawful obstruction of the highway:* for example, if you were investigating a person for an offence of wilful obstruction of the highway under s 137 of the Highways Act 1980 and the suspect was stopping or slowing vehicular traffic on the highway, you might conclude that the person should be removed.

4.13.7 **To protect a child or other vulnerable person**

If you were investigating a person for any offence and you suspected that the suspect was putting the health and safety of a vulnerable person or child at risk as a result of his/her conduct, you might arrest the person.

4.13.8 **To allow the prompt and effective investigation of the offence or of the conduct**

There may be many reasons why you could feel that an investigation might be jeopardised if you did not arrest the suspect, such as grounds to believe that the person:

- has made false statements (for example, dates of birth, denials of disqualification from driving)
- has made statements which cannot be readily verified (for example, ownership of property for which s/he has no records, such as vehicle registration documents)
- has presented false evidence (for example, forged driving licence)
- might steal or destroy evidence (for example, disposing of stolen property from a burglary)
- might make contact with fellow suspects or conspirators (for example, using a mobile phone to warn an associate)
- might intimidate, threaten or make contact with witnesses (for example, in cases where the identities of the suspect and victim are known to each other).

Other instances might include an arrest in connection with an **indictable** offence where there is an operational need to:

- enter and search any premises occupied or controlled by the person being considered for arrest: if you do not arrest him/her, you will not be able to use s 18 of the PACE Act 1984
- search the person: if you do not arrest him/her, you will not be able to use s 32 of the PACE Act 1984 (see 4.9) to search and seize property
- prevent contact with others: if you do not arrest him/her, you will not be able to seek the authority to delay the right of the detained person to have someone informed of his/her detention
- take fingerprints, footwear impressions, samples or photographs of the suspect: if you do not arrest him/her, you will not be able to obtain forensic evidence from the suspect
- test him/her for drugs, thereby ensuring compliance with statutory drug-testing requirements: if you do not arrest the person, you will not be able to use s 63B of the PACE Act 1984 to obtain samples from the suspect to ascertain whether s/he has taken a Class A drug.

4.13.9 **To prevent the disappearance of the person in question**

This may arise if there are reasonable grounds for believing that if the person is not arrested, s/he will fail to attend court: for example, there is currently a warrant for the arrest of the person for failing to appear at court and s/he has now committed another offence.

4.13.10 **Other persons' power of arrest without warrant (s 24A, PACE Act 1984)**

Section 24A(1) of the PACE Act 1984 states that a person other than a constable may arrest without a warrant (a) anyone who is in the act of committing an indictable offence or (b) anyone whom s/he has reasonable grounds for suspecting (see 4.9.4) to be committing an indictable offence.

Where an indictable offence has been committed, a person other than a constable may arrest without a warrant (a) anyone who is guilty of the offence or (b) anyone whom s/he has reasonable grounds for suspecting to be guilty of it (s 24A(2)).

However, both these powers of arrest are only exercisable if (a) the person making the arrest has reasonable grounds for believing (see 4.9.4) that for any of the following four reasons mentioned it is necessary to arrest the person in question and (b) it appears to the person making the arrest that it is not reasonably practicable for a constable to make it instead (s 24A(3)).

The four reasons that make an arrest necessary are:

(a) causing physical injury to him/herself or any other person;
(b) suffering physical injury;

(c) causing loss of or damage to property; or

(d) making off before a constable can assume responsibility for him/her (s 24A(4)).

4.13.11 Information to be given on arrest

Section 28 of the PACE Act 1984 states that:

. . . an arrest is not lawful unless at the time or as soon as practicable [you] inform the person they are under arrest (s 28(1)) . . .	Although it is recommended, it is not necessary to say words such as 'I arrest you' for an arrest to be lawful. Code C 10.3 states the suspect must be informed at the time or as soon as practicable that he/she is under arrest and Code C Note 10B states the suspect must be given sufficient information to enable him/her to understand that he/she has been deprived of his/her liberty.
. . . when [you] arrest a person, [you] must still inform him/her that he/she is under arrest even though that fact is obvious . . .	Do not think that making the most obvious actions alone will be enough, for example placing your hand on the shoulder of the suspect and preventing him/her from going anywhere after you have just seen him/her seriously injure a person. It will not be sufficient! You must still apply s 28(1) above.
. . . an arrest is not lawful unless at the time or as soon as practicable [you] inform the person of the grounds for the arrest.	There is no need for technical or precise language providing the suspect knows why he/she has been arrested. There is no need to refer to the power of arrest but the reason must be the correct reason, otherwise it is unlawful. Also, the information given must be sufficient for the suspect to respond. The suspect must be informed at the time or as soon as practicable of the grounds for the arrest, Code C 10.3. The suspect must be given sufficient information to enable him/her to understand the reason for the arrest (Code C Note 10B). However, you are not required to inform the suspect of the grounds for the arrest if it was not reasonably practicable to do so (s 28(5)), for example because he/she escaped from you before you could give the information.

According to Code G, para 2 of the PACE Act 1984 Codes of Practice, you are required to inform the arrested person about the circumstances surrounding his/her involvement, suspected involvement or attempted involvement in the commission of a criminal offence, and the reason(s) why the arrest is necessary (see 4.9.4).

4.13.12 **Use of force to arrest a person**

You may need to use force to arrest a person, but the amount of force you use must be **reasonable**. Two pieces of legislation will help you here: s 3 of the Criminal Law Act 1967 and s 117 of the PACE Act 1984.

Section 3(1) of the Criminal Law Act 1967 states that:

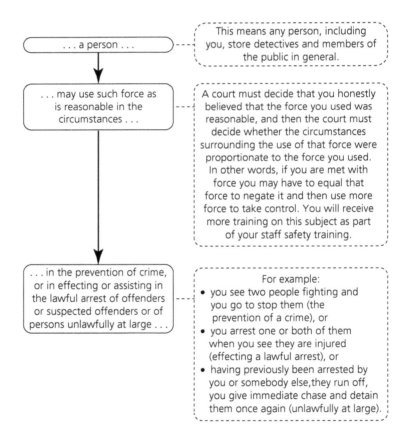

Section 117 of the PACE Act 1984 states that where any part of the PACE Act 1984:

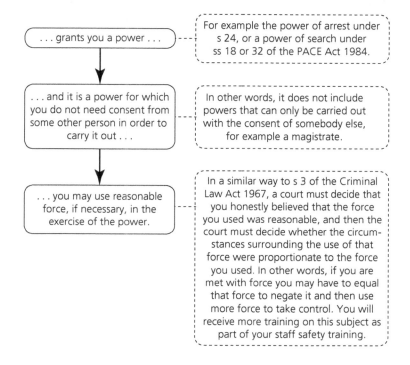

... grants you a power ...

> For example the power of arrest under s 24, or a power of search under ss 18 or 32 of the PACE Act 1984.

... and it is a power for which you do not need consent from some other person in order to carry it out ...

> In other words, it does not include powers that can only be carried out with the consent of somebody else, for example a magistrate.

... you may use reasonable force, if necessary, in the exercise of the power.

> In a similar way to s 3 of the Criminal Law Act 1967, a court must decide that you honestly believed that the force you used was reasonable, and then the court must decide whether the circumstances surrounding the use of that force were proportionate to the force you used. In other words, if you are met with force you may have to equal that force to negate it and then use more force to take control. You will receive more training on this subject as part of your staff safety training.

4.13.13 **What to do immediately after an arrest**

Do not forget to caution the suspect (see 5.6 and the PACE Act 1984, Code G, para 3.4). Then, unless it is impracticable to do so, record in your pocket notebook (PNB):

- the nature and circumstances of the offence leading to the arrest
- the reason or reasons why the arrest was necessary
- the fact that you gave a caution and
- anything said by the person at the time of arrest.

4.13.14 **Searching suspects and premises upon arrest**

The powers of search under s 32 of the PACE Act 1984 can only be used at the time of an arrest when you have reasonable grounds for believing that the suspect might have concealed anything for which a search is permitted (see 4.9.4). Similarly, you may not search premises unless you have reasonable grounds for believing that there is evidence for which a search is permitted (see 4.9.4) and the suspect has been arrested for an indictable offence.

Section 32(1) of the PACE Act 1984 states that you can search any person who has been arrested elsewhere than at a police station if you have reasonable grounds for believing that the arrested person may present a danger to him/herself or others. This is *not* a power to search everybody after arrest: you must have reasonable grounds for believing that the person to be searched might have concealed on his/her person anything that could be used to effect an escape or which might provide evidence of an offence:

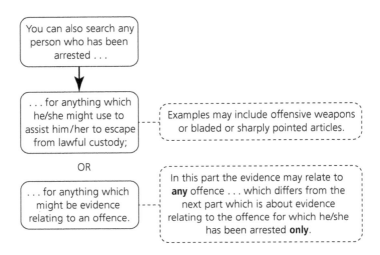

When using these powers to search a person, you only have a power to search to the extent required to find the item you are seeking. You cannot require the person being searched to remove any clothing in public other than an outer coat, jacket or gloves, but you may search a person's mouth.

Under s 32(2)(b) of the PACE Act 1984, you may search premises, but only if the offence for which the person has been arrested is an indictable offence. Further details about your powers in this instance are in the *Police Operational Handbook* edited by Ian Bridges (2006), pp 659–61.

4.13.15 **Seizing items**

You can **seize** (take into police possession) anything you find on the person or premises as a result of searching (under s 32), apart from items protected by legal privilege—for example, letters from the suspect's legal representative (ss 19, 32(8) and 32(9), PACE Act 1984).

4.13.16 **'De-arresting' and further arrest whilst in custody under ss 30 and 31 of the PACE Act 1984**

A person who has been arrested must be taken to a police station (s 30(1) and Code C, para 11.1A) without delay. The only exception (s 30(10)) is if a delay could:

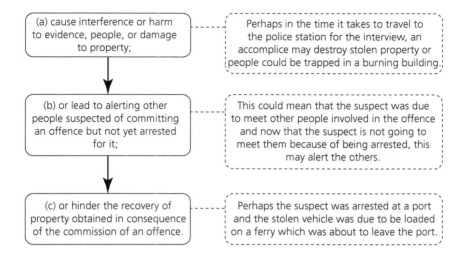

Any discussion of the alleged offence on the way to the police station should be avoided. This is because any questioning of a person regarding his/her involvement or suspected involvement in a criminal offence is considered to be an interview, and interviews must be carried out under caution in a suitable place (Code C, para 11.1A).

However, if the suspect freely provides information, then follow the guidelines in relation to significant statements and relevant comments (see 5.6).

4.13.17 'De-arresting' a suspect

Any person arrested in a place other than at a police station must be released if there are no longer any grounds for keeping him/her under arrest (s 30(7), PACE Act 1984). An example of this could be when a suspect initially refuses to provide his/her name but then provides it on the way to the police station. A record must be made of such a release in your PNB (4.14) explaining the circumstances, and why the reasons for keeping him/her under arrest no longer exist.

4.13.18 The suspect has committed further offences

After the arrest and taking the suspect to the police station, it might become apparent that the suspect has committed further offences. You have to decide whether to arrest the person again, for the further offences(s). You will need to reflect as follows: if the person had committed only the further offences and was not at a police station, would there be a need to arrest him/her? If the answer is 'yes' then you should arrest the person for the further offences (s 31, PACE Act 1984). All the procedures related to any arrest must be carried out in full for this second arrest (such as giving the grounds for the arrest and cautioning the suspect appropriately).

4.13.19 **Role and responsibilities of and towards a custody officer**

When an arrested person reaches the boundary of a police station, s/he should be taken before a custody officer as soon as practicable after arrival (Code C, para 2.1A). The time that the arrested person arrived at the police station is relevant because s/he can only be kept in custody for 24 hours after arrival. The arrival time is referred to as the 'relevant time' (s 41(2), PACE Act 1984). You should make a note of this time in your PNB to provide continuity of evidence between time of arrest, arrival at the police station and subsequent authorisation and detention by the custody officer.

4.13.20 **The custody officer**

The custody officer's main duty is to ensure that any person in police detention is treated according to the PACE Act 1984 and the Codes of Practice, and that such treatment is recorded on a custody record. A custody officer will usually be a police officer of at least the rank of sergeant, but this role is sometimes provided by a police support employee designated as a staff custody officer.

When an arrested suspect is taken to the custody suite, the custody officer must be informed of the relevant circumstances of the arrest, the suspect's involvement in the commission of a criminal offence and the reason(s) why the arrest was necessary. This is obligatory under s 24 of the PACE Act 1984 and Code G, para 2.2. You should then stay with the suspect during the initial stages of the custody process.

4.13.21 **Searching the detainee**

The custody officer has the power to search detainees, though s/he may ask you to carry out the search instead, perhaps so that s/he can observe (if appropriate). The custody officer will decide the extent to which the search will be made (s 54(6), PACE Act 1984) but the search must not be intimate (it must not involve the physical examination of orifices other than the mouth). The search must be carried out by a Special Constable or regular police officer of the same sex as the detainee (s 54(7)).

A **strip search** can be authorised, but only if it is necessary to remove an article which the detainee would not be allowed to keep (Code C, Annex A10), and if it is reasonably considered that the detainee has concealed such an article. A strip search must be carried out:

- by an officer of the same sex
- in an area away from other people
- in a safe place with at least two other people present, and
- with regard to sensitivity.

The following should also be noted:

- to assist with the search, the detainee can be required to lift his/her arms and stand with his/her legs apart
- if anything is found the detainee should be asked to hand it over and
- the strip search should be carried out as quickly as possible.

4.13.22 **Items found during a search**

All or any of the items found during a search may be recorded on the custody record. Clothes and effects can only be seized (s 54(3)) if the custody officer believes the detainee would use them to:

- harm him/herself
- damage property
- interfere with evidence
- assist in escape or
- when there are reasonable grounds for believing such items may be evidence relating to an offence.

4.13.23 **The detainee's rights after arrest**

If the custody officer decides to detain the arrested person, s/he must inform the detainee of certain rights, which continue throughout the detention (PACE Act 1984, Code C, para 3.1). The suspect's rights are:

1. to have someone informed of his/her arrest
2. to consult privately with a solicitor and receive free legal advice and
3. to consult the PACE Act 1984 Codes of Practice.

The detainee must be given two written notices (Code C, para 3.2). The first notice sets out:

- the three rights noted earlier
- the arrangements for obtaining legal advice
- the right to a copy of the custody record and
- an explanation of the caution, for example what it means to him/her (see 5.6).

The second notice sets out the detainee's entitlements while in custody, for example the provision of food and drink, access to toilets, and so on.

The detainee will be asked to sign the custody record to confirm his/her decision about legal advice and whether to inform someone of his/her arrest (Code C, para 3.5). The custody officer will also determine and record (on the custody record) whether the detainee requires:

- medical attention, for example as a result of an injury or lack of medication
- an appropriate adult, for example the parent or guardian for a juvenile or a relative or guardian for a mentally vulnerable person
- help to check documentation, for example clarification of any of the rights or
- an interpreter, for example for detainees who cannot speak English or detainees with speech or hearing impairments.

The custody officer will also carry out an assessment of the detainee to determine whether s/he will be a risk to him/herself or to others. Such assessment will include a check of the PNC, and consultation with the arresting officer and appropriate health-care professionals, for example custody nurses (Code C, para 3.6).

4.13.24 **The detainee's right to inform someone of the arrest**

The detainee may have one friend, relative or interested person informed of his/her whereabouts as soon as practicable (s 56, PACE Act 1984 and Code C, para 5.1). If the attempt fails, the detainee can suggest two other people to be contacted, to try to ensure that at least one person knows the detainee's whereabouts. At the discretion of the custody officer or the officer in charge of the investigation, further attempts can be made to contact other people until the information has been conveyed to one person. In the case of a juvenile, the person responsible for his/her welfare must be informed of his/her detention.

The detainee should be given writing materials if requested, and be allowed to telephone one person (in addition to the person informed as noted in the previous paragraph) for a reasonable time.

4.13.25 **Delaying the detainee's right to contact**

The right to contact people and to legal advice can be delayed if the offence involved is an indictable offence or if it is believed that the communication is likely to lead to:

- interference with or harm to evidence or other people
- alerting other people who are suspected of committing an indictable offence, but not yet arrested or
- hindrance to the recovery of property.

Such a delay must be authorised by an officer of at least the rank of inspector, and the delay must not be for more than 36 hours (s 56, PACE Act 1984 and Code C, Annex B). Delaying a detainee's right to legal advice (Code C, Annex B) is very rare, and must be authorised by an officer of the rank of superintendent or above.

TEST BOX 15

This has been a very large section; correspondingly our test of what you can remember is longer than usual:

1. What two conditions must be met for an arrest to be lawful?
2. Where will you find specific reasons for arrest?
3. Define what is meant by 'reasonable'.
4. Can someone order you to arrest someone else?
5. When might you arrest 'preventively' (to stop someone doing something)?
6. Which two pieces of legislation assist you in deciding to use force to arrest someone?
7. What two things must you do immediately after an arrest?
8. What legislation allows you to search someone arrested who is not at a police station?
9. Why should you avoid questioning the person arrested on the way to the police station?
10. Which part of the PACE Act 1984 makes it obligatory for you to take a suspect to a custody officer once you reach the police station?
11. When is a strip search justified?
12. What are the parameters (conditions applying) to a strip search?
13. What are a detainee's rights after arrest?

4.14 **(LPG1_4_03) Documentation (PNB)**

Very soon after joining your police force as a Special Constable you will be issued with a pocket notebook (commonly referred to as a 'PNB'). No doubt at the same time you will be given instructions on force policy concerning the keeping and use of the PNB, its surrender, the issuing of new PNBs and so on. However, there are a number of fundamental aspects of the PNB common to virtually all police forces:

- It notes the start and finish time of each period of duty
- It is used to keep a contemporaneous account (unless impossible) of information collected during an incident: for example, a statement made by a suspect or a description given by a witness
- It should note clearly where you have consulted with another police officer (for example, your assessor whilst on Supervised Patrol) in the writing of an entry
- It may be used to increase the extent and accuracy of recall in court
- There is a need to ensure that the language you employ in writing the notebook is clear, factually based, and does not employ exclusionary language.

4.14.1 **How to use the PNB**

Although it may appear on the surface rather trivial, the importance of your PNB cannot be overemphasised. Your force places obligations upon you to record matters within it and, if you use it to give evidence, the courts have the opportunity to examine it. Therefore, rules have been established in relation to its completion and if these rules are not followed then the correctness or even the authenticity of the entries will be questioned.

Top ten hints for using a PNB

1. Carry it at all times on duty
2. Use it to record evidence (not your opinion, except in the case of drunkenness!)
3. It is a supervisor's responsibility to issue you with a new one when needed
4. Always apply the general rules (see the following paragraph)
5. It often contains other useful information
6. You may refer to it while giving evidence
7. Remember, it is police property
8. Use it for drawing diagrams as well as writing
9. On duty, do not use additional pieces of paper either to supplement your PNB, or as an alternative
10. Don't lose it!

Image 4.1 (p 145) which depicts a page from a PNB, outlines **general rules** that you should apply to its completion.

4.14.2 **Example of a PNB entry**

Image 4.2 (p 146-7) is an example of a typical PNB entry.

4.14.3 **Summary of the rules**

PNB rules can be summarised by a mnemonic commonly used in police training.

No ELBOWS(S)

E no Erasures

L no Leaves torn out/Lines missed

B no Blank spaces

O no Overwriting

W no Writing between lines

S no Spare pages

(S) but Statements should be recorded in 'direct speech'

Image 4.1

	01

Write the day, date, and year at the beginning of entries for each day and underline them

	DO NOT LEAVE SPACES
	If you do leave a space, then ——— draw ——— a ——— line to ———
	indicate nothing further can be added. ———————————
	Always make the pocket book entries in black ink. ———————
	Make all entries legible. ———————————————
WRITE	Write in the pocket book at the same time as the event happens. If the ———
THE	circumstances make it impossible to do so at the time, then do it as soon as ———
TIME	practicable after the event, in which case always give a reason for not doing so,
IN THIS	eg: 'Whilst using officer safety techniques, I was unable to make any entries'.
COLUMN	Each entry should include the time and name the location where the notes ———
USING	were made.———————————————————
THE	Write your entries in a single line of writing on the lines of the pages of the ———
24 HR	book ONLY, not anywhere else in the book (except when you make drawings, in
CLOCK	which case, draw across the page).———————————
	Use every line and page of the pocket notebook. ———————
	Do NOT overwrite errors. ——————————————
	Do NOT erase or obliterate errors. ————————————
	If you do make a mistake, cross it out with a single line, so it can still be ———
	read, then put your initials beside the deletion, and then write down ———
	the word(s) you wish to use straight after the mistake I.N.I.T.I.A.L.S. ———
	If you accidentally turn over two pages by mistake and leave some blank pages,
	draw a diagonal line across the blank pages and write 'omitted in error' across
	the page. —————————————————————
	Do NOT tear out or remove any of the pages or parts of the pages. ———
	Write all SURNAMES in BLOCK CAPITALS. ——————————
	Write down the names and addresses of victims, suspects and witnesses. ———
	Write down all identifying features such as serial numbers of property, ———
	including vehicles or documents, e.g. the registration numbers of vehicles. ———
	If you write down what a person says to you 'Then do so in direct speech!' and
	make sure that you record the conversation verbatim or word for word. ———

Image 4.2

	01
	Wednesday 16th January (0000)

	Duty 0600–1600 ———— Patrol ZZ 10 ————
	Refreshment time 0900 and 1400————
0545	Briefing at ZZ————
0550	Collected keys for ZZ 10 patrol vehicle index number ZZ 00 ZZZ ————
0600	Checked vehicle seats and feet areas for property—no trace of any property ————
0605	Commenced patrol ————
0610	At the time stated on the date above, I was alone on mobile patrol in uniform ————
	travelling in an easterly direction along Sheerbury Road, Ramstone, ————
	approximately 50 metres east of the junction with Applebreaux Road, when I
	saw a Fordover motor vehicle, index number YY 00 ZZZ being driven in the ————
	same direction approximately 20 metres in front of me. There was a clear ————
	unobstructed view of this vehicle. I caused the vehicle to stop in Sheerbury ————
	Road, 20 metres west of the junction with Applebreaux Road and spoke to the ————
	driver who was the sole occupant of the car. The driver identified him/herself ————
	to me as First Middle LASTNAME, born 00/00/00 address 101 Hernegate ————
	Road, Ramstone, Kentshire. ————
Q	'May I see your driving Licence and insurance for this vehicle please?' ————
R	'Haven't got my insurance with me, but here is my driving licence'. ————
	Driving licence details LASTN0000FM9ZZZ ————
Q	'As a result of what you have just told me, I suspect you of failing to produce or
	not having a certificate of insurance for this vehicle.' I cautioned Mr(s) ————
	LASTNAME and said s/he was not under arrest and free to leave at any time.
Q	'Where is your insurance certificate right now?' ————
R	'It's at home, I think. It's been a while since I last saw it.' ————
Q	'What is the name of your insurance company?' ————
R	'I can't remember that either.' ————
Q	'How much did you pay for the insurance?' ————
R	'Again, sorry, can't remember.' ————
Q	'How long have you owned this vehicle?' ————
R	'About a month.' ————
	PNC CRO check no trace LASTNAME. PNC vehicle check LASTNAME RO at ————
	address given. Voter's register check confirmed LASTNAME living at address ————
	I completed an HO/RT/1 form. ————

Q	'As you haven't been able to produce your insurance to me now, please produce
	your certificate of insurance and this form at a police station within 7 days ———
	Have you got any questions for me, and do you understand what you have to ———
	do?' LASTNAME gave no reply. ———
Q	'I have been making a record of our conversation, would you please read these
	notes I have made, and if you agree they are a true record of what we have ———
	said, would you please sign my notes to that effect?' ———
	This is a true record. FM Lastname ———
Q	'As you have been unable to produce your certificate of insurance to me here, I
	am going to report you for the offence of failing to produce or not having a ———
	certificate of insurance for this vehicle.' I cautioned LASTNAME and there was
	no reply. These notes were made at the time between 0610 and 0630. ———
	CL Underwood PC 118118 ———
0630	Resumed patrol. ———
0900	Refs ZZ ———
0945	Resumed patrol. ———

TEST BOX 16

A short knowledge check on the PNB:

1. What is common to most police forces in using a PNB?
2. Name three of the 'top ten hints'.
3. What mnemonic might help you remember the importance of filling in your PNB properly?

4.15 **(LPG1_4_07) Police Communications**

As a Special Constable you will have access to data and information which you will need to complete your role. Failure to treat information correctly could lead to misconduct procedures or criminal charges. Access to data and the protection of that data is covered by two Acts of Parliament and the Police 'Codes of Conduct' (a common and familiar name in policing, but now known as **Professional Standards**, see 3.2).

4.15.1 **Potential offences**

Computer Misuse Act 1990: this Act introduced criminal offences which could apply to police officers accessing information *when not in the course of their duty*, such as carrying out checks on neighbours and friends or obtaining the registration details of a vehicle one of them might be about to purchase.

- Unauthorised access to computer material, punishable by six months' imprisonment or a fine

- Unauthorised access with intent to commit or facilitate commission of further offences, punishable by six months' imprisonment/maximum fine on summary conviction or five years' imprisonment/fine on indictment.

Data Protection Act 1998: legislation requires all police forces which hold and use personal information to ensure that it is only used correctly. The Chief Constable has a duty to ensure that all officers accessing data do so lawfully and only when relevant.

All personal data held by police services must be:

- processed fairly and lawfully
- processed for a lawful purpose
- adequate and relevant for purpose
- no personal data may be kept for longer than necessary.

Police 'Professional Standards' serve as a reminder about how important it is to treat information correctly:

Confidentiality

All information which comes into the possession of the police should be treated as confidential. It should not be used for personal benefit and nor should it be divulged to other parties except in the proper course of police duty. Similarly, officers should respect, as confidential, information about force policy and operations unless authorised to disclose it in the course of their duties.

4.15.2 **The Police National Computer (PNC)**

The PNC holds details of people, vehicles, crimes and property that can be electronically accessed by the police and other criminal justice agencies. It is a national information system, widely used, and allows officers to search for:

- **People**—enables the search of the names database to identify suspects through the use of gathered information such as physical description and personal features. Includes reports to identify a wanted or missing person and warning signs for suspects
- **Vehicles**—enables users to search the vehicles database by search criteria such as registration, postcode and colour details. Includes reports such as stolen vehicles and no insurance held
- **Property**—search for items which are lost and found such as firearms, trailers, marine, plant and animals.

When completing a person check over the radio system, a set format is used to access the information and allow an operator to input the information in the correct order to get the best and most accurate result, you will need to know and use the **NASCH** format:

Name—person's name: family name/surname first, followed by first name and any middle names, spelling all names using the phonetic alphabet

Age/date of birth—age can be estimated or given; a full date of birth will give a more accurate result

Sex—PNC recognises Male, Female or Unknown

Colour—identity codes should be used to indicate ethnicity of the subject: ICI—White European; IC2—Dark European; IC3—African/Afro-Caribbean; IC4—Asian; IC5—Oriental; IC6—Arab

Height—metric or feet and inches.

4.15.3 The phonetic alphabet is in use by all police services

Table 4.7: The phonetic alphabet

A	Alpha	J	Juliet	S	Sierra
B	Bravo	K	Kilo	T	Tango
C	Charlie	L	Lima	U	Uniform
D	Delta	M	Mike	V	Victor
E	Echo	N	November	W	Whisky
F	Foxtrot	O	Oscar	X	X-ray
G	Golf	P	Papa	Y	Yankee
H	Hotel	Q	Quebec	Z	Zulu
I	India	R	Romeo		

4.16 (LPG1_4_08) Powers of Entry

The PACE Act 1984 provides you with a power to enter premises in which you believe a person you are seeking to arrest is located, or to save life.

4.16.1 Entering premises to arrest

There are a number of situations in which you have the power to enter premises in order to arrest a person, such as having a relevant warrant or in order to arrest for certain offences.

As to the scope of such an entry and search, s 17 of the PACE Act 1984 states that:

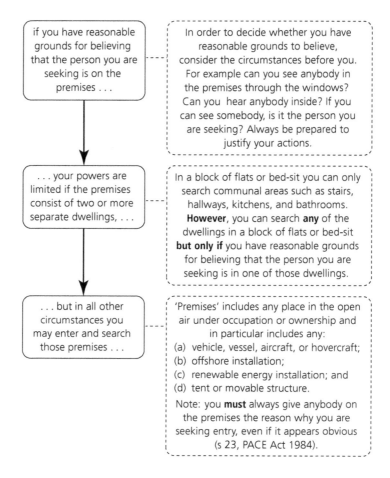

if you have reasonable grounds for believing that the person you are seeking is on the premises . . .

In order to decide whether you have reasonable grounds to believe, consider the circumstances before you. For example can you see anybody in the premises through the windows? Can you hear anybody inside? If you can see somebody, is it the person you are seeking? Always be prepared to justify your actions.

. . . your powers are limited if the premises consist of two or more separate dwellings, . . .

In a block of flats or bed-sit you can only search communal areas such as stairs, hallways, kitchens, and bathrooms. **However**, you can search **any** of the dwellings in a block of flats or bed-sit **but only if** you have reasonable grounds for believing that the person you are seeking is in one of those dwellings.

. . . but in all other circumstances you may enter and search those premises . . .

'Premises' includes any place in the open air under occupation or ownership and in particular includes any:
(a) vehicle, vessel, aircraft, or hovercraft;
(b) offshore installation;
(c) renewable energy installation; and
(d) tent or movable structure.
Note: you **must** always give anybody on the premises the reason why you are seeking entry, even if it appears obvious (s 23, PACE Act 1984).

4.16.2 **Entering premises to arrest on warrant**

You may enter to arrest a person and search those premises under the execution of the following warrants:

- An **arrest warrant** issued in connection with or arising out of criminal proceedings: Home Office Circular 88/1985, para 8, states that this section 'is deliberately widely drawn and the words "in connection with" enable a constable to enter and search premises for the purpose among other things of executing a warrant for the arrest of a person for non-payment of a fine'
- A **warrant of commitment** (that is, for commitment to prison): this goes further than a default warrant (which orders an offender to appear before a court to explain the reasons for non-payment of a fine). A warrant of commitment requires the offender to be taken straight to prison unless the money stated in it is paid, and is issued under s 76 of the Magistrates' Courts Act 1980 (for failure to pay fines).

4.16.3 **Entering premises to arrest for specified offences**

You may also search and enter premises in order to arrest a person for any indictable offence (this includes either-way and indictable-only offences), and also for certain non-indictable offences shown in Table 4.8.

Table 4.8: Circumstances in which you may search and enter premises to arrest a person under the PACE Act 1984

Non-indictable offence for which you can use the power of entry to arrest	Explanation
s 163 of the Road Traffic Act 1988	This legislation requires a person driving a mechanically propelled vehicle or riding a cycle on a road to stop if you require him/her to do so. Failing to stop is an offence. Note that you can only use this power when you are in uniform
s 4 of the Road Traffic Act 1988	This is an offence of driving or being in charge of a mechanically propelled vehicle on a road or other public place when unfit through drink or drugs (see 5.9)
s 27 of the Transport and Works Act 1992	This offence may be committed by certain staff operating the railways and other guided transport systems when they are under the influence of drink or drugs
s 6, 7, 8 or 10 of the Criminal Law Act 1977	These offences include using violence to secure entry (s 6), trespassing with a weapon of offence (s 8), and entering and remaining on premises (s 7), also known as 'squatting'. Note that you can only use this power when you are in uniform
s 4 of the Public Order Act 1986	The result of the suspect's conduct in this offence is to bring about a feeling of fear or provoke a reaction of violence in the victim or recipient (note that this power of entry does not extend to s 4A of the same Act)
s 61 of the Animal Health Act 1981	This offence relates to the control of rabies and sets out a power for you to arrest any person you have reasonable cause to suspect to be committing (or to have committed) an offence in relation to bringing animals into the UK
ss 4, 5, 6(1) and (2), 7 and 8(1) and (2) of the Animal Welfare Act 2006	These are offences relating to the prevention of harm to animals

4.16.4 **Entering premises to arrest for other specified circumstances**

You also have a power of entry to arrest anyone whom you are immediately **pursuing**. This could include a person who had escaped from you having just been arrested, as well as a patient who has escaped from involuntary custody at a psychiatric unit. Note, however, that the chase must be under circumstances of 'hot pursuit', for example the person must have only just escaped from lawful custody or a hospital; it cannot be used after a period of days or weeks.

You also have the power of entry to arrest anyone who is liable to be **detained** in a prison, remand centre, young offenders' institution or secure training centre. Section 32(1A) of the Children and Young Persons Act 1969 gives you a power to arrest a **child** who is absent from care, but only if the child is in care after having been remanded or committed to local authority accommodation (s 23(1) of the same Act).

4.16.5 **Searching premises for a suspect**

The power of entry to arrest under s 17 of the PACE Act 1984 permits you to search premises in order to find the person to be arrested, but does not allow you to search for anything else unless you have other justifications for searching (s 17(4), PACE Act 1984).

4.16.6 **Entering premises to save life and property**

Section 17(1)(e) of the PACE Act 1984 gives you the power to enter premises 'to save human life and limb' and also to prevent serious damage to property. Under subsection (e) you can enter and search:

- even if you do not have reasonable grounds for believing any person is on the premises and
- all the flats within a block of flats and not just one of them.

(Note that s 17(1)(e) does not give you power of entry in order to arrest a person.)

In the case of *Mandy Baker v CPS* [2009] EWHC 299 (Admin), it was further decided that you can enter and search under subsection (e):

- without seeking the permission of the occupant (otherwise this might be self-defeating)
- to save someone from him/herself as well as from a third party
- without having to give an occupant a reason for using the power of entry if it is impossible, impracticable or undesirable to do so but
- only to the extent that was reasonably required to satisfy the objective for using the power of entry. For example, if the reason was the danger to life or limb posed by a knife, then the powers available would relate only to a search for that knife (s 17(4), PACE Act 1984).

4.16.7 **Power of entry and breach of the peace**

Nothing in s 17(6) of the PACE Act 1984 affects any power of entry to deal with or prevent a breach of the peace. You are entitled to enter either private or public premises in order to make an arrest for a breach of the peace or to prevent a breach of the peace. However, you should *always* make sure that the circumstance you are faced with really constitutes a breach of the peace (see 5.3).

TEST BOX 17

1. Which law makes it illegal for you to access the PNC for private use?
2. How should people's personal data be treated in the police service?
3. What might you find on the PNC?
4. What is NASCH?
5. Spell AMEX (the name of a football stadium) phonetically.
6. What warrants permit entry to premises to arrest?
7. What legislation allows you to stop a vehicle?
8. When might you enter premises and arrest or search without a warrant?
9. What did *Mandy Baker v Crown Prosecution Service* [2009] EWHC 299 (Admin) determine?

4.17 **(LPG1_4_11) Summons and Warrants**

There are three ways in which an offender can be brought before a court:

- By a summons issued by the court which orders a person to attend court
- By warrant which directs a constable (or another specified person) to arrest or carry out a specific action
- By arrest without warrant.

A **summons**—summary offences are usually dealt with by the magistrate at the magistrates' court.

There are a number of ways of getting an offender/suspect to appear before a relevant criminal court. The lower level of offences on the statue books in the United Kingdom are known as summary offences, these include offences which you will deal with during the course of your duty as a Special Constable, offences such as driving without insurance, taking a vehicle without the owner's consent ('twocking') and common assault.

Reporting an offender for summons—reporting an offender for summons is the process by which an offender gets to court without being arrested, the offender will be ordered by a summons produced either by the court or a Criminal Justice Unit (CJU) to attend a notified court at a specified time and date to answer the alleged offences. In order to allow the court to issue a summons, an officer must ensure that essential information and evidence of the offence is gathered and recorded. The details required to allow a summons report to be completed need to include:

- Details of the offence, including the location, date and time of the offence
- Full name
- Date of birth
- Address including post code
- For driving offences a driver number will be helpful
- If possible, obtaining a national insurance number will help to speed up the court process.

All details that are obtained should be checked and confirmed to ensure accuracy on your behalf and honesty in the suspect's account. Reasonable steps to be taken should include PNC and local database checks and a voters' register check; remember that doubt could lead to an arrest becoming necessary if you feel unable to clarify the information or you doubt the details given (s 24(5), PACE Act 1984).

The evidence relating to the offence will need to be gathered in a PNB and must be detailed enough to provide evidence in the event of a suspect pleading not guilty. Points which need to be included:

- Cautions given and compliance with PACE
- Any direct questions following caution regarding the offence
- Any replies to questions relating to the offence including any defences
- Visual evidence seen, heard, felt, etc (for example, damage, injuries or paper-work shown)
- Officer pointing out the offence to suspect
- Reporting for summons—recorded in direct speech: 'I am reporting you for the offence of...'
- Caution of the suspect using the 'Now' caution
- Offer of the notes in PNB to suspect to sign and acknowledge a true record of the interaction.

4.17.1 **Service of a summons**

A summons report and statement will be produced by an officer and sent for a decision as to whether to prosecute. A summons will be generated by the court or CJU and, generally, will be posted to the address provided on the summons report; this will be considered as 'served'. A summons can also on occasions be served by police officers handing it to the suspect in person or by leaving it at their last known or usual place of abode.

4.17.2 **Types of warrant**

The two types of warrants that will mostly concern Special Constables will be:

- A commitment warrant
- An arrest warrant.

Both of which will be issued by the court and indicate a specific function which the court requires an officer to carry out, the grounds for the arrest will be stated in the warrant.

A **commitment warrant**: issued by the court usually for non-payment of fines—the offender will have been through the court system, been found guilty and fined then failed to pay the resulting fines. The court will direct that the offender is arrested and taken straight to prison for a specified number of days which will be relevant to the fines outstanding unless the fine is paid immediately. An officer would know of the existence of a commitment warrant when completing a person check on the PNC where it will show as a 'marker'.

An **arrest warrant**: issued by the court when an offender has failed to appear at the court following charging, bail or to answer a summons in the following circumstances:

- **Non-appearance**—a warrant issued for the non-appearance of a suspect at the court following the service of a summons or an adjourned trial. The court may, if the accused fails to appear at court, issue a warrant. The warrant will remain in force until it is either executed or withdrawn by the court. An officer would know of the existence of such a warrant when completing a person check on the PNC where it will show as a 'marker'.

EXECUTION—the arresting officer does not have to have the warrant in his/her possession at the time of its execution, but it must, if requested by the arrested person, be shown to him/her as soon as practicable. Once executed, the warrant must be endorsed by the officer and the PNC updated in order to cancel the arrest warrant.

- **Failure to surrender to bail**—a warrant issued by the court for the arrest of any person who, having been released on bail with a duty to surrender to the custody of the court at a specified time on a specified date, fails to do so or, having surrendered as required, s/he leaves without the court's permission (s 7, Bail Act 1976).

EXECUTION—the warrant does not need to be with the officer in order to be executed. If there is a 'no bail endorsement' on the warrant, the prisoner must be brought before a magistrate as soon as practicable after his/her arrest. Once executed, the warrant must be endorsed by the officer and the PNC updated in order to cancel the arrest warrant.

An officer would know of the existence of an arrest warrant when completing a person check on the PNC where it will show as a 'marker'.

TEST BOX 18

Summons

1. Name three ways in which an offender can be brought before a court.
2. What details do you need to complete a summons report?
3. When reporting someone for summons, what should be in your PNB entry?

Further Reading

ACPO, *Manual of Guidance on the Management, Command and Deployment of Armed Officers*, 3rd edn. (2011, London: ACPO)

Bridges, I (ed.), *Police Operational Handbook* (2006, Oxford: Oxford University Press), pp 659–661

PACE Codes are available at <http://www.homeoffice.gov.uk/publications/police/operational-policing/pace-codes/>

Powers and Duties

5.1 **(LPG4_4_01) Police Officer Statement**

For the purposes of presenting evidence before a court, any witness, including those in the police 'family', writes down his/her evidence in the form of a **statement**. This form is 11th in a series of approximately 20 forms contained in a prosecution document called the **Manual of Guidance** used to build case files. It is consequently often referred to as an 'MG11'. It is also called a 'section nine statement' because under s 9 of the **Criminal Justice Act 1967**, a person's evidence can be read out in court from such a statement if s/he has not been called as a witness.

5.2 **Completing the Duty Statement**

The following has been designed in sections to help you to understand the requirements of completing a duty statement.

KEY POINT

Some of what follows is adapted from an unpublished document 'A Guide to Form MG11, General Rules for Completion' by Kent Police, reproduced by kind permission of the Chief Constable.

The unique reference number (URN) at the top of the first page on the right will be generated by your own Criminal Justice Department or office.

Always include your full name with your surname (family name) in capitals. If you usually write in capitals, then underline your surname (family name).

Always give your occupation as a Special Constable and add your collar/badge/SC number.

RESTRICTED (when complete)   MG11

WITNESS STATEMENT

(CJ Act 1967, s.9; MC Act 1980, ss.5A(3) (a) and 5B; MC Rules 1981, r.70)

URN [| | | |]

Statement of:...*Jo Britton MATTHEWS*..

Age if under 18: (if over 18 insert 'over 18') *over 18* Occupation: *Special Constable 999999*

Always complete the 'number of pages' section on completion of the statement.

Always sign the declaration and take seriously the content of the warning each time you make a statement.

Always date the statement. Retain each statement you make subsequently which relates to the same investigation and reveal them to the Public Prosecution Service. Never destroy previously completed statements.

This statement (consisting of 4 page(s) each signed by me) is true to the best of my knowledge and belief and I make it knowing that, if it is tendered in evidence, I shall be liable to prosecution if I have wilfully stated anything in it, which I know to be false, or do not believe to be true.

Signature:........*Jo Matthews SC 999999*.................. Date:........*14th January 2010*...........

Always begin all statements with the **time**, **day**, **date**, **location**, **SC status** (foot patrol or mobile patrol) and details of any other persons **present** (normally other colleagues). Always use the 24-hour clock when making reference to timings to lessen confusion. Do not use the phrase 'At *approximately ....hours ...*', as a Special Constable, you should be specific and use 'At...*hours ...*'.

If your evidence has been visually recorded, the box must be ticked accordingly. Do not start your statement with the words '*I am the above named person ...*'. It is not necessary to include your name, title, number or station at the start of the main body of text as this is clearly displayed in the first box. Always write statements in chronological order.

Tick if witness evidence is visually recorded ☐ *(supply witness details on rear)*

At 0855 hours on Monday 14th January 2010 I was on foot patrol in uniform on the north pavement of Cotton Lane, 15 yards east of the south entrance to the Precinct, Tonchester. There I saw a member of the public who identified herself to me as Pat OLDFIELD

Always record relevant conversation in 'direct speech' (what the person actually said).

Mrs OLDFIELD said to me 'Excuse me, I have just walked through the Precinct and seen a bloke spray painting the wall outside a shop called "Buy One Get One Free". ' I said to Mrs OLDFIELD, 'Please give me a description of this person.' She replied 'Well, he's white, around 20 years old, stocky build, and his hair is a right mess 'cos it is a mass of dark bushy hair, round face, wearing glasses, clean shaven, approx. 5'8" tall, wearing a black top with a hood and some of those baggy jeans and dirty white trainers'.

> I asked, 'What exactly did you see him do?' Mrs OLDFIELD replied, 'As I walked past,
> he was spraying a symbol on the wall outside the shop, it looked foreign to me. He was using
> a spray can, must have got it from the car superstore 'cos it's the same colour as my old car,
> "British Racing Green", it's even metallic. The spray can he was using ran out and he threw
> it in a rubbish bin nearby. Here it is, you take it.' I then took possession of a 'British Racing
> Green' spray can from Mrs OLDFIELD, exhibit labelled and marked PO/1.

Use your senses to evidence what it is that you saw, smelled, touched, tasted or heard. Be definite. Instead of saying 'I noticed', say 'I saw'. If you are unsure of a detail, then say so, as this will inform the reader that you have at least considered the point even if you are unable to give succinct details. Set the scene so that the reader can form a mental picture of the layout of the area.

> At 0900 hours the same day, I entered the Precinct via the south entrance. The Precinct is a
> shopping area between Daniell Street in the north east and Cotton Lane in the south,
> bordered east and west by The High and London Road. As I entered the Precinct, I saw a
> white male, 20 years, stocky build, a mass of dark bushy hair, round face, wearing glasses,
> clean shaven, approx. 5'8" tall spraying the wall of 'Buy One Get One Free' with a spray
> can on the western side of the walkway approx. 15 yards south of the exit to Daniell Street.

Always include the identification points, highlighted by the case of 'Turnbull'. Fully describe how it was you were able (or unable) to see the suspect so clearly:

> I had the suspect under observation for 30 seconds. It was this amount of time as I looked
> at my watch when I first saw the suspect and again when I made contact with him.
> The distance between me and the suspect was approx. 25 metres. I know this because when
> I started to walk towards the suspect I counted 25 steps. I could clearly see the suspect as the
> Precinct has a glass roof and the sun was shining through. There were no obstructions between
> me and the suspect; there were no shoppers at the time as the shops were shut. I have not
> seen the suspect before nor did I know his identity. I remembered the suspect easily because
> he had a mass of dark bushy hair. There was no time lapse between me seeing the suspect
> and finally introducing myself, as I had him under constant observation for 30 seconds.
> I made one and only recording of the description of the suspect as there was no break.

When setting out your statement, make use of paragraphs, but do not leave a blank line in between. You do not need to 'rule off' an incomplete line as you would do in your PNB.

160

> I walked up to the suspect and could clearly see that he had a scar over the left eye.
> I said to him, 'Excuse me, my name is SC Jo MATTHEWS and I have just seen you spraying
> this wall with a spray can.' The suspect replied, 'What are you doing here? You lot never come
> round here. What if I am?— It's my tag, nobody's ever stopped me before. I'm quite proud
> of it actually, do you like it? Do you want to me to put me tag on your nice white
> shirt? . . . only joking!'

Always use proper grammar and sentence construction. Avoid abbreviations and the use of police jargon. Write in plain English, so that everyone can understand what you mean.

Surnames/family names should be written in capitals. If you write entirely in capitals, then <u>underline</u> them. This applies to all names written in a statement to avoid ambiguity and misunderstanding by the reader.

> The suspect identified himself to me as Toni STALYBRIDGE, born 06/04/88,
> address 24, Morgan Street, Tonchester. I could clearly see the graffiti which were 33cm wide
> and 20cm tall on the outside of the 'Buy One Get One Free' shop. There were three symbols in
> total, all in 'British Racing Green'. There were no other painting marks on what was otherwise
> a clean wall made of bricks and mortar measuring 2 metres in length and 1 metre in height,
> below the front window of the shop. When I arrived, the sprayed symbols were still wet and
> I could clearly smell the odour of cellulose paint.

There is no requirement to record the caution in full; however, replies after caution should be recorded in direct speech.

> I said to STALYBRIDGE 'It is an offence to damage the wall of this shop with paint from
> a spray can.' I cautioned him and he replied, 'Yeah go on, get it over and done with.'
> At 0902 hours the same day, I had said to STALYBRIDGE, 'Earlier, when I first walked up to
> you outside this shop, you said to me ,' What are you doing here? You lot never come
> round here. What if I am? - It's my tag, nobody's ever stopped me before. I'm quite proud
> of it actually, do you like it? Do you want to me to put me tag on your nice white shirt? . . .
> Only joking!" STALYBRIDGE replied, 'Yeah it's true, I did say all that.'

Ensure that you correctly spell the names of places and people. Consider the effect on your credibility if important evidence, such as a location or a person's name, is spelled wrongly.

Take pride and care in the completion of your statement to avoid errors. Any errors you do make in the text should be corrected by striking through with one line. This should then be initialled in the margin. You **must never** over-write a mistake or use correction fluid.

Always write in black ink.

Pages should be held together by use of a paper clip and not stapled.

> I then said to STALYBRIDGE 'I am reporting you and you may be prosecuted for the offence of causing criminal damage.' I cautioned him and he replied, 'Yeah, I understand, you've got a job to do.' At 0910 hours the same day, the interview was terminated. STALYBRIDGE read the record of the interview and signed my pocket note book as correct. At 0915 hours the same day, I attended the security room at the Precinct. There I saw a person who identified herself to me as Gamme Ubelele NANATANGA. At that time I took possession of a CCTV video tape from Ms NANATANGA exhibit labelled and marked GUN/1.
> Jo Matthews SC 999999 14.01.10

After the last word of the statement and at the bottom of the first and subsequent pages, sign your name (including your SC number) and date.

There is no need for anybody to witness your signature (this is for witness statements only).

> Signature. Jo Matthews SC 999999 .... Signature witnessed by
> ....

At the top of each subsequent page print your name.

In the top right-hand corner of each page write the page number.

> Continuation of Statement of: Jo Britton MATTHEWS   Page No 2 of X

Do not put your home address or home telephone number on the rear of an MG11 because of the potential consequences if a defendant obtained these details. Record your force address in the **'Home address'** section in CAPITAL letters. Endorse the **'Home telephone number'** section as 'N/A'. Include the telephone number of your police station in the **'Work telephone number'** section. The **'Preferred means of contact** ...' section should be endorsed as 'N/A'. Delete **'Male/Female'** as appropriate. Include your **'Date and place of birth'**. Complete the **'Former name'** section if you have one or endorse as 'N/A'. Your **'height'** must be included. The **'Identity Code'** section must be completed with your ethnic appearance code. The **'Dates of witness availability'** section does not have to be completed. Your statement should be accompanied by a completed MG10 which records your availability status.

RESTRICTED-FOR POLICE AND PROSECUTION ONLY (when complete)

Witness contact details

Home address: ..*c/o TONCHESTER CENTRAL POLICE STATION, HIGHSTREET,*..........

................*TONCHESTER, TONFORD*.......................... Postcode: ....*T01 9TF*.........

Home telephone No: *N/A*   Work telephone No: ...*01 1212999*..........

Mobile/Pager No:..............*N/A*.............. E-mail address: ......*SC999999@999.uk*.......

Preferred means of contact: ....*N/A*..............................

~~Male~~/Female (delete as applicable) Date and place of birth: ....*25.04.1980 W1*.....

Former name: ....*N/A*.............. Height:...*5' 8'*....... Ethnicity Code: ....

Dates of witness non-availability:

The Victim Personal Statement does not apply to you (unless you are a victim) when you are making a duty statement. It applies to a witness.

The *'Statement taken by ...'* section should be endorsed as 'N/A'. This is for you when you take a statement from a witness, the time and location of statement completion should be recorded in your PNB.

Statement taken by (print name): *N/A*....................... Station: ....

Time and place statement taken:

All this may seem complicated, but with practice it will become a straightforward exercise. Don't let it become routine and **always take seriously the making of a duty statement**.

TEST BOX 19

This is a brief knowledge-check of the Duty Statement.

1. What is an 'MG11'?

2. What must you *always* do when making a Duty Statement?

3. What should begin all statements?

4. What is 'direct speech'?
5. What constitutes evidence?
6. How do you correct a mistake in a duty statement?
7. Why don't you put your home address and home telephone number on a Duty Statement?

5.3 **(LPG4_4_02) Counter-Terrorism (CT)**

Terrorism in the United Kingdom is an important but uncommon element in core policing skills. Each police area will have its own CT policies, often classified as 'Restricted' documents, that you will need to become familiar with. You will also need to be well versed in which local places are considered to be at greater risk of a terror attack. These are often places such as busy shopping centres and well-known landmarks referred to simply as 'Crowded Places'; those areas which by virtue of their crowd density may be liable to terrorist attack (for example, shopping centres, sporting stadia, concert venues, pubs and bars or transport centres, bus and railway stations).

More detail about the United Kingdom strategy to counter terrorism, CONTEST, can be found via the Home Office website. The United Kingdom's strategy aims to link all agencies and interested parties together in order to reduce the risk here and overseas from terrorism.

KEY POINT

CONTEST is organised around four principal streams of work:

Pursue: to stop terrorist attacks

Prevent: to stop people from becoming terrorists or supporting terrorism. (This is the area where police officers working within their neighbourhoods will be able to contribute most to the CONTEST Strategy, through engaging with members of all communities and feeding intelligence in through appropriate channels)

Protect: to strengthen our protection against terrorist attack

Prepare: where an attack cannot be stopped, to mitigate its impact.

5.3.1 **Threat levels**

The Home Office also categorises and publishes on behalf of CT agencies, various levels of threat regarding terrorism. The assessment is more sophisticated than the old familiar 'traffic light' warning categories, which did not have gradations of, for example, imminence and likelihood. The national threat levels now indicate how likely it is that there will be a terrorist attack in the United Kingdom or against its citizens or interests abroad.

There are five levels of threat, which are listed here from the highest to the lowest:

> **Levels of terrorist threat in UK**
>
> **Critical**—an attack is expected imminently
> **Severe**—an attack is highly likely
> **Substantial**—an attack is a strong possibility
> **Moderate**—an attack is possible but not likely
> **Low**—an attack is unlikely.

The current assessed threat (2013) to the United Kingdom from international terrorism is graded as **Substantial**—this means that a terrorist attack is a strong possibility. We must not forget that there are other kinds of terrorism too, from local specific targeting by animal rights activists through to Irish republican/nationalist terrorism with the 'Real IRA' and 'Continuity IRA', which, somewhat forlornly, continue the struggle in Northern Ireland against the police (PSNI), local political targets and the remnants of the British Armed Forces. The example of Anders Breivik in Oslo in 2011, who bombed and shot 77 adults and children reminds us that there are toxic elements on the right wing which could attempt, as he did, a 'spectacular' against immigrants or ethnic minority communities. Often, the police will be the first on the scene of any terrorist attack, and you should ensure that you are conversant with your ('Restricted') force contingency planning and local practices.

5.4 **(LPG1_5_01) Breach of the Peace**

There is some considerable debate concerning 'Breach of the Peace'; both in its meaning and whether it should still be dealt with by the Special Constabulary as a police matter. Part of the reason for this debate is that the law surrounding a breach of the peace is somewhat unusual: it is neither a criminal offence nor part of statute law. It is part of the common law, however, and case law has set a precedent in defining its meaning. The case of *R v Howell* [1981] 3 All ER 383, provides a definition of the meaning of breach of the peace:

Definition of breach of the peace

A breach of the peace is committed whenever harm is done, or is likely to be done to a person, or, in his presence to his property, or, whenever a person is in fear of being harmed through an assault, affray, riot or other disturbance.

Any person committing a breach of the peace can be arrested by any other person, and this includes you as a Special Constable, on or off duty but only in certain circumstances: (1) where a breach of the peace is committed by the person arrested in the presence of the person making the arrest; or (2) where the person making the arrest reasonably believes that such a breach will be committed in the immediate future by the person whom s/he has arrested, although no breach has occurred at that stage; or (3) where a breach of the peace has been committed by the person arrested and the person making the arrest reasonably believes that a renewal of it is threatened.

Having been arrested, individuals can be detained until there is no likelihood of a breach of the peace happening again. Alternatively, a Special Constable can 'lay a complaint upon' a person and bring him/her before a criminal court. (A 'complaint' is similar to a charge.) Breach of the peace is unique. You must always identify the all-important ingredient of **harm** and compare the actual circumstances with the definition. Then check that the breach took place in your presence, or that the threat or its renewal is both real and imminent. A common law power of entry exists to make an arrest for a breach of the peace or to prevent a breach of the peace.

5.5 **(LPG1_5_06) Lost and Found Property**

This section does not constitute part of the criminal law (unless theft is involved); nonetheless you will become familiar with lost and found property as part of your daily duties.

5.5.1 **Found property**

Most people still consider the police to have a responsibility to deal with both lost and found property. On occasions when on duty, you will be handed items of found property and will need to be aware of how to deal with property, recording details of it accurately and storing items correctly if an owner cannot be immediately located. A person who finds property is not legally bound to hand it to the police or report such finding, only to take steps to find the owner to avoid committing an offence of theft. People may hand property to the police if they have been unable immediately to locate the owner. If the owner cannot be traced, the 'finder' may have a claim on the property. An officer will never have a personal claim on any property that s/he finds either on or off duty.

If an item of found property is handed to police, the requirements in respect of lost property are simply to keep accurate records and take reasonable steps to identify the owner.

If found property is handed to you on duty, your pocket notebook (PNB) should be used to record the following details:

- Where and when property was found
- A detailed description of the property

- Details of the finder
- Location of property if retained by the finder—in some cases this is possible but not in the case of dangerous items or drugs.

Police stations all have property stores and databases to record lost and found property which should be completed at the earliest opportunity and property stored correctly—a decision to leave or place found property in a locker at the end of a shift rather than spending a few minutes completing the necessary paperwork will lead to unnecessary delay in tracing an owner and possibly to a misconduct investigation for the officer failing to deal correctly with the property.

5.5.2 **Lost property**

Lost property is simpler to deal with and your PNB should be used to record the following:

- Name and address of owner
- Where and circumstances of the loss
- Detailed description of lost property.

A database will be used to record lost property at the station and must be completed at the earliest opportunity to maximise the possibility of matching found and lost property.

If the property reported as lost is hazardous, dangerous or of high value or of interest to the public (such as firearms or drugs), a supervisor should be advised so that s/he can consider any further actions needed to protect the public or manage media attention.

5.6 **(LPG1_7_09) Discretion**

The use of discretion in policing has been subject to many debates and the concept of the use of discretion by a police officer has been defined as follows:

Definition of discretion

- Freedom of judgement and action
- Authority to decide and choose
- Selecting the best course of action, having considered all the facts and all the alternatives available.

The proper use of discretion is recognised as a necessary policing skill and although it is difficult to teach (a bit like trying to teach common sense), it is a skill which an officer needs to acquire and use wisely. Our experience suggests that knowing when and when not to exercise discretion is very often the result of having done the job for a while. The use of discretion is not about interpreting legislation but more about considering the options available to resolve a situation; for example, considering a VDRS (A Vehicle Defect Rectification Scheme, remember?) against a fixed penalty for a traffic offence or issuing a penalty notice for shoplifting instead of making an arrest.

Many factors will affect your decision and in some matters, such as domestic abuse, there will be guidance issued by way of policy to assist but in other matters it will be a decision made purely by the officer on the spot at the time; you, in other words. The decisions made need to be recorded in your PNB and should withstand scrutiny from supervisors and the public alike. You should be consistent: allowing a bad day or your prejudices to affect your decision is *not* discretion and should not feature in your decision-making. Indeed, Special Constables should not enforce the law mechanically and must use discretion to ensure that prosecutions are in the public interest as well as lawfully justified.

5.7 (LPG1_7_20) Cautions, Significant Statements and Unsolicited Comments

These components from the PACE Codes are very important, and you should ensure that you know when to use the Caution, and that **you thoroughly understand** the difference between and how to respond to 'significant' statements and 'unsolicited comments'.

5.7.1 Cautions

From the moment you start dealing with anybody you suspect of having committed an offence, you must remember that s/he has the right to **a formal warning** or **caution** at certain points during the investigative process (Code C, para 10, PACE Act 1984 Codes of Practice).

The type of caution given depends on the stage of the investigation. The caution may be given:

- at the very beginning of an investigation, when s/he is first arrested and interviewed, or interviewed without having been arrested. In this case use the **when questioned** caution (see later) or
- at the end of the investigation, before s/he goes to court (whether arrested or not), as a result of charge or reporting the suspect. This is the **'now'** caution, and is his/her last chance to have what s/he says recorded before going to court.

5.7.2 The three parts to a caution

There are three parts to a caution (Code C, para 10.5):

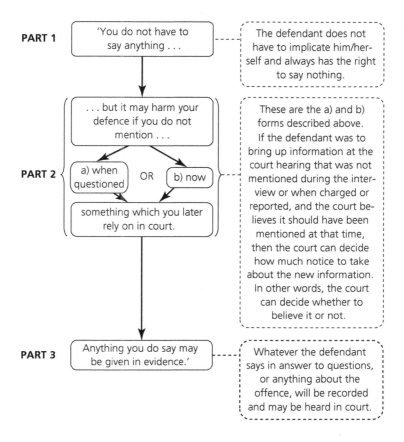

PART 1 — 'You do not have to say anything . . .'
The defendant does not have to implicate him/her-self and always has the right to say nothing.

PART 2 — . . . but it may harm your defence if you do not mention . . . a) when questioned OR b) now — something which you later rely on in court.
These are the a) and b) forms described above. If the defendant was to bring up information at the court hearing that was not mentioned during the interview or when charged or reported, and the court believes it should have been mentioned at that time, then the court can decide how much notice to take about the new information. In other words, the court can decide whether to believe it or not.

PART 3 — Anything you do say may be given in evidence.'
Whatever the defendant says in answer to questions, or anything about the offence, will be recorded and may be heard in court.

5.7.3 **When to caution a suspect**

If you have arrested your suspect, you must caution him/her at the time of the arrest unless:

- it is impossible for you to do so because of his/her condition or behaviour: for example, where s/he is unconscious, drunk or fighting (Code C, para 10.4 and Code G, para 3.4) or
- the suspect has already been cautioned before s/he was arrested, because s/he was suspected of committing an offence (Code C, para 10.4 and Code G, para 3.4).

The correct time to give a caution was explained succinctly in *R v Nelson and Rose* [1998] 2 Crim App R 399:

The appropriate time to administer the caution . . . is when, on an objective test, there are grounds for suspicion, falling short of evidence which would support a *prima facie* case of guilt, not simply that an offence has been committed, but committed by the person who is being questioned.

After giving the 'when questioned' caution to a person who is not under arrest, s/he must be told that s/he (1) is not under arrest and (2) is free to leave (Code C, para 10.2). This is often referred to as **'caution + 2'**. A person attending a police station voluntarily must also be told that s/he (1) is not under arrest, (2) is not obliged to remain at the station and (3) if s/he remains at the station s/he may obtain free and independent legal advice if required. This is often referred to as **'caution + 3'**.

5.7.4 **Is a caution required?**

If you have not arrested your suspect, and your questions are for other purposes (Code C, para 10.1), *you do not need to use a caution*. Examples of such situations are:

- when you ask for a driver's name and date of birth under the Road Traffic Act 1988 (see Code C, para 10.9)
- when you ask for a person's identity or the identity of the owner of a vehicle
- when you ask a suspect to read and sign records of interviews and other comments (see Code C, para 11 and Note 11E)
- whilst you carry out a search using an appropriate power and at the same time following the PACE Codes of Practice.

5.7.5 **Other times when a caution is needed**

You need to use a caution when informing someone that s/he may be prosecuted for an offence: for example, when:

- you **charge** (a charge is a written accusation) a detained person with an offence or inform a person that s/he may be **prosecuted** (reported for an offence). At this stage, use the word '*now*' in part 2 of the caution in 5.7.2 (see Code C, para 16.2)
- you inform a person not under arrest that s/he may be prosecuted for an offence. At this stage, use the word '*now*' (as 5.7.2). This is not a requirement within the Codes of Practice, *but* if the 'now' caution is not given at this point, the court cannot draw its own conclusions if the defendant subsequently provides new information at the hearing. The court might be more likely to believe the new information (see Code C, Note 10G). Our advice is therefore to use the 'now' caution after informing a person that s/he may be prosecuted.

5.7.6 **Recording a caution**

Always write down in your PNB (or on a record of the interview) when you give a caution. You must also record whether it was the '*when questioned*' or the '*now*' version (see Code C, para 10.13). There is no need to write out the caution in full in your PNB. Something like 'the subject was cautioned, using the "when questioned" formula, at 1855', would do.

5.7.7 **Understanding the caution**

The caution is a necessary warning that must be given to a person to protect his/her rights and keep him/her informed of the consequences of what s/he says during an investigation. This can only be done if you yourself have a thorough understanding of the *'when questioned'*, *'now'* and *'restricted'* variants of the caution, so that you can convey the shades of meaning to the suspect. The suspect can be made more aware of the importance of a caution if you are yourself aware of its significance.

5.7.8 **Unsolicited comments by suspects**

Following a decision to arrest a suspect, he/she must not be interviewed about the relevant offences except at a police station (Code C, para 11.1). An interview is defined as the 'questioning of a person regarding his/her involvement in a criminal offence'. So what should an officer do when a suspect who has been arrested suddenly says something that applies to the offence in question or to another offence? After all, the comments may contain information that could be used in evidence. Such utterances are referred to as 'unsolicited' or voluntary comments. The procedures for recording unsolicited comments (and their possible subsequent use in a court hearing) are provided in the Codes of Practice. Unsolicited (or voluntary) comments are of two types: **relevant comments** and **significant statements**.

A **relevant comment** includes anything which might be relevant to the offence (Code C, para 11.13 and Note 11E), for example 'That other person you've arrested, it was them that did it, you'll see, just ask them you've been talking to, they'll back me up, you'll see!'

A **significant statement** includes anything which could be used in evidence against the suspect (Code C, para 11.4A). The term derives from Part III of the Criminal Justice and Public Order Act 1994:

KEY POINT

Legal clarification: A significant statement or silence
A significant statement or silence is one which appears capable of being used in evidence against the suspect, in particular a direct admission of guilt, or a failure or refusal to answer a question or to answer it satisfactorily which may give rise to an inference.

It may be part of a relevant comment but it must have been made in the presence and hearing of a police officer (or other police staff member); for example, 'I wish

I never done it now, but I lost it, the knife was on the table and I just kept stabbing, stabbing and stabbing!'

5.7.9 **Recording unsolicited comments**

All such comments made by the suspects should be recorded in a PNB entry noting when the comment was made, signed by the police officer. When practicable, the suspect should be asked to read it and to check whether it is a true record of what was said. If the suspect agrees that it is a true record, he/she should endorse the record with the words 'I agree that this is a correct record of what was said' and then sign (Code C, Note 11E). If the suspect does not agree with the record, the details of any disagreement should be recorded in a PNB entry. The suspect should then read the record and sign that it accurately reflects his/her disagreement. A refusal to sign should also be recorded (Code C, Note 11E).

TEST BOX 20

We have had a number of brief sections in this part. This is a knowledge check on all of them.

1. What is unusual about 'breach of the peace'?
2. Define a breach of the peace.
3. Name two of the 4 Ps.
4. Name two of the CT alert states.
5. If you are handed 'found property', what should you record in your PNB?
6. Define 'discretion'.
7. What legislation gives suspects the right to be cautioned?
8. What is the 'caution + 2'?
9. What is the difference between a **significant statement** and a **relevant comment**?

5.8 **(LPG4_7_01) Types of Interview and Communication Techniques**

As a Special Constable you will be required to interview different categories of people in the course of your duties.

Definition of interview

An interview is defined as a conversation with a purpose.

You will be required to interview witnesses, victims and suspects for low-level offences.

A victim will provide information and evidence in the form of a statement or with physical evidence and is the person who has been harmed by the crime. The victim you deal with may be vulnerable, upset, angry or confused (or a combination of all of these) and will need to be treated according to his/her needs. When faced with vulnerable or intimidated victims or witnesses, it is important that you seek guidance before beginning an interview.

A witness is defined as someone who sees, knows or touches something and can give evidence in person by oral or written deposition or by affidavit. A witness must be legally competent to testify.

A suspect will be the person whom police will need to interview under caution and interview in accordance with Code C of PACE.

A suspect interview is defined in the PACE Codes of Practice as:

Definition of suspect interview

The questioning of a person regarding his/her involvement or suspected involvement in a criminal offence or offences which, by virtue of para 10.1 of Code C PACE, is required to be carried out under caution.

It is important that you know when a caution must be delivered in order to ensure that comments and statements can be used in evidence. The usual place for a suspect interview is in the police station.

Your initial response to all types of interview can be very important and can decide how future interactions take place. Whilst it may be stressful, it is important that you remain calm and in control and do not allow the emotions of the situation to affect your judgement or responses. This may be particularly the case involving children or other vulnerable people, such as the elderly.

There are some key principles which apply to all types of interview. Home Office Circular 2/1992 provided the following:

Seven principles of investigative interviewing

1. The role of investigative interviewing is to obtain accurate and reliable information from suspects, witnesses and victims in order to discover the truth about matters under police investigation.
2. Investigative interviewing should be approached with an open mind.
3. Information obtained from the person who is being interviewed should always be tested against what the interviewing officer already knows or what can be reasonably established. When questioning anyone, a police officer must act fairly in the circumstances of each individual case.

---

4. The police officer is not bound to accept the first answer given. Questioning is not unfair merely because it is persistent. Even when the suspect exercises the right of silence, the police still have a right to put questions.

5. When conducting an interview, police officers are free to ask questions in order to establish the truth: except for interviews with child victims of sexual or violent offences which are to be used in criminal proceeding, they [the police] are not constrained by the rules applied to lawyers in court.

6. Vulnerable people, whether victims, witnesses or suspects must be treated with particular consideration at all times. The interviewing of victims, witnesses or suspects is an everyday part of the police role.

7. The interview is the formal means by which vital information and evidence is obtained in relation to incidents. This requires specific skills to obtain this information and evidence in a way which conforms to the laws of the land.

(Adapted from HOC/2/1992; our additions)

5.9 Professionalising the Investigative Process (PIP)

The aim of PIP is to develop professional investigators at four different levels, so that they will be able to conduct investigations to a national standard based on recognised good practice. Each level is aimed at different roles within the police service and training is relevant to the skills required. Special Constables do not attain PIP accreditation during initial training but some forces are offering training at PIP level 1 to 'operational' Special Constables (that is, those who have attained Independent Patrol status and who are routinely deployed to incidents requiring an investigative capability). It is important that you understand what is involved in a professional investigation, which is why we consider it here.

PIP Level 1 is for patrol officers and allows for investigation into volume crime.

PIP Level 2 is for dedicated Investigator/CID Officers whose role includes substantive investigation into more serious/complex offences and will include those investigating road traffic deaths.

Although you will not initially be PIP-accredited, you will interview witnesses and victims routinely and an understanding of a number of different types of question (and the appropriate time to use them) will help you to get an accurate and factual account from a witness or victim:

Open questions are useful in getting witnesses to give information, they often begin with the words: **W**ho, **W**hat, **W**hen, **W**here, **W**hy and **H**ow (5WsH). Such questions are difficult to answer with a simple yes or no, and will tend to elicit a more detailed response with facts and information ('Who did you see standing by the window?').

A closed question is a question that requires a yes or no answer; they are useful for confirming facts ('Were you standing here?') but should be used in moderation.

A leading question is a type of question which can prompt the respondent to answer in a particular way ('You lost your temper, didn't you, and that's why you stabbed him, isn't it?') and should almost always be avoided.

TEST BOX 21

A quick résumé of interviewing for this knowledge check:

1. Who might you be required to interview?
2. What applies to police interviews with suspects?
3. Why might your role in initial interviewing be important?
4. What principle is established at No 3 in the Seven Principles?
5. What does PIP mean?
6. What are 'open' questions?
7. What is a leading question?

5.10 (LPG1_8_04) Drink Drive, Powers of Entry and Hospital Procedure

How does a Special Constable decide when a driving (or any other) offence has been committed, and when can s/he decide to intervene in the lives of other citizens? The answer to both questions is: when you have '*due cause*'. For this reason, you must not administer random breath tests or other preliminary tests; you must not arbitrarily stop a driver simply because you feel like it.

You can only test a driver if:

- you have reason to suspect that s/he might be under the influence of alcohol or drugs or
- a moving traffic offence has been committed or
- the vehicle has been involved in an accident.

See Table 5.1:

Table 5.1: Scenarios for testing for drink/drugs-driving offences

General scenario	Example
A collision	A vehicle runs into the back of another vehicle at a junction
A moving traffic offence	A driver crosses against a red traffic light

Table 5.1: Continued

General scenario	Example
Inappropriate style of driving	A dumper truck has stalled at some traffic lights and the driver has failed to restart the engine. His speech is slurred when he attempts to respond to your questions
Vehicle stopped for another reason, and then you become suspicious	You stop a vehicle under s 163 Road Traffic Act 1988 to carry out a test and inspection of the vehicle for roadworthiness. There are beer cans on the seat, the driver has a sleepy grin on his face, and his breath smells of alcohol
Other information about drink/drug consumption	A witness observes a group of people consuming alcohol in a pub. They stagger into the adjacent car park and, after some shouting and laughter, squeeze into a small car, which moves off with a jerk. The witness then contacts the police and supplies the registration number of the car

The level of alcohol or drugs in a driver's blood is not always easy to judge. If you are suspicious that alcohol or other drugs may be present, a **preliminary test** is administered at the roadside in order to confirm your suspicions. The best known of these tests is the 'breath test' for alcohol. The results of such a test *only provide grounds for suspicion* that the proportion of alcohol in the person's breath or blood exceeds the prescribed limit (an offence under s 5 of the Road Traffic Act 1988).

There are two main driving offences relating to driving while under the influence of alcohol or other drugs, and these are both covered under the Road Traffic Act 1988:

- driving or attempting to drive or being in charge of a **mechanically propelled vehicle** while **unfit to drive** through drink or drugs (s 4, Road Traffic Act 1988) and
- driving or attempting to drive or being in charge of a **motor vehicle** with **alcohol in excess of the prescribed limit** (s 5, Road Traffic Act 1988).

The key difference between these two offences is that, for a s 4 offence, the prosecution has to prove that the suspect's ability to drive was actually impaired, whereas for s 5 offences a high blood-, breath- or urine-alcohol level is the only evidence required.

5.10.1 Definitions of key terms from the relevant legislation

Sections 4(2) and 5(1)(b) of the Road Traffic Act 1988 refer to a person being **in charge** of a vehicle. In order to decide if a person is in charge of a vehicle the court is likely to consider the following:

- Was the person in question the most recent driver?
- How long ago had s/he been driving the vehicle?

- Where was the person found, in relation to the vehicle?
- Did s/he have the keys?

It may be necessary to negate defences in relation to being 'in charge'.

5.10.1.1 Unfit to drive through drink or drugs

Section 4 of the Road Traffic Act 1988 states that a person commits an offence when driving or attempting to drive (s 4(1)) or is in charge (s 4(2)) of a mechanically propelled vehicle on a road or other public place whilst unfit to drive through drink or drugs. *Remember, there is no need to administer a preliminary test for breath-alcohol levels or for drug consumption before arresting a driver for this offence.*

The suspect's level of impairment and ability to drive properly is assessed by a police medical practitioner at a police station through an evidential test. Specimens of breath, blood or urine may also be taken for other evidential tests, particularly to prove the presence of drugs in the body (which would imply impairment). In addition, even though a suspect has been arrested for a s 4 offence s/he may eventually be charged with an offence under s 5, depending on the results of evidential tests measuring the level of alcohol in the body. Section 4 can also be used if the driver is over the limit for alcohol but the vehicle involved is not a motor vehicle.

There is no power of arrest for a s 4 offence under the Road Traffic Act 1988. Instead, use your s 24 PACE powers of arrest if the circumstances are appropriate, such as suspicion that the offence is being committed and the arrest is therefore necessary for a prompt and effective investigation of the offence (see 4.13). Offences under s 4 of the Road Traffic Act 1988 are triable summarily and the penalties are:

1. for **driving** and **attempting to drive** whilst unfit due to drink or drugs (s 4(1)):
   - six months' imprisonment and/or a fine
   - obligatory disqualification
2. for being **in charge** of a vehicle whilst unfit due to drink or drugs (s 4(2)):
   - three months' imprisonment and/or a fine
   - discretionary disqualification.

5.10.1.2 Blood-alcohol in excess of the prescribed limit

For this offence (under s 5, Road Traffic Act 1988), the evidence required is a blood, breath or urine evidential test result showing that the level of alcohol in the driver's body was above the prescribed limit. Section 5(1) of the Road Traffic Act 1988 states that it is an offence for a person to: (a) drive or attempt to drive a motor vehicle on a road or other public place, or (b) is in charge of a motor vehicle on a road or other public place, after consuming so much alcohol that the proportion of it in his breath, blood or urine exceeds the prescribed limit.

The prescribed limits are shown in Table 5.2 below. Note the units: micrograms (µg), milligrams (mg) and millilitres (ml).

Table 5.2: Prescribed blood-alcohol limits for drink-driving offences

Type of sample	Amount of alcohol per 100 millilitres	
Breath	35 micrograms	A good way to help memorise
Blood	80 milligrams	these figures is to remember that all the digits in each measurement
Urine	107 milligrams	add up to 8

These offences are triable summarily and the penalties are as noted earlier for the s 4 offence.

5.10.2 Preliminary tests

Preliminary tests are also called 'roadside tests' and are covered in ss 6A, 6B and 6C of the Road Traffic Act 1988. *They are only used for drivers of motor vehicles* (and not mechanically propelled vehicles). Preliminary tests are used to find out if it is **likely** that a drugs- or alcohol-related driving offence has been committed.

The three main types of preliminary test are:

- a **preliminary breath** test to indicate whether the proportion of alcohol in the breath or blood is likely to exceed the prescribed limit (s 6A, Road Traffic Act 1988)
- a **preliminary impairment** test of whether a person is unfit to drive (whether due to drink or drugs). This is done by observing the person's performance during a set of tasks or observing his/her physical state. You can only carry out such a test if you are approved for that purpose by the chief officer of the police force to which you belong (s 6B, Road Traffic Act 1988) and
- a **preliminary drug** test to indicate the presence of drugs in a person's body. A specimen of sweat or saliva is obtained and tested with an approved device (s 6C, Road Traffic Act 1988).

If you state a requirement for a person to take part in a preliminary test, you do not need to be in uniform. However, the **Special Constable actually administering a preliminary test must be in uniform** (except after an accident). You will need to complete a Home Office statistical return form after administering a preliminary test.

In some situations it might not be clear who was driving, so you should first clarify who was in the vehicle at the time of the accident; witnesses may be able to help on this matter. However, remember that you only have to 'reasonably believe' that a person was driving a vehicle at the time of the accident, and therefore if no one admits to being the driver, you can test more than one person from the same vehicle.

5.10.2.1 Preliminary breath tests

There are currently two styles of preliminary breath-test devices approved by the Secretary of State:

- **electronic devices** include models such as the Lion Alcolmeter, the Alcosensor IV, the Draeger Alert, and the Draeger Alcotest 7410 and
- **others** (such as Alcotest 80 and R80A and the Alcolyser) are not electronic and involve the inflation of a bag.

All of these devices test air that has come from deep within the lungs. It is most important that you follow the manufacturer's instructions as well as force policy when using these devices.

You must say to the suspect (when you are requesting a specimen of breath):

> I suspect that you are driving a motor vehicle on a road under the influence of alcohol. I require you to provide a specimen of breath for a breath test here. Failure to do so may make you liable to arrest and prosecution.

You must also ask the person when s/he last drank alcohol or smoked; if the person has been drinking or smoking recently, you must comply with the manufacturer's instructions to wait a period of minutes before administering the test (as recent smoking of a cigarette or cigar can 'mask' the measurement of alcohol content). To carry out the test, you should ask the driver to take a deep breath and to blow into the machine in one continuous breath until requested to stop. Tell the person the result of the test.

A positive result from a preliminary breath test directly justifies arrest: you must tell the suspect that s/he is under arrest (s 6D(1), Road Traffic Act 1988) on **suspicion** that the proportion of alcohol in his/her breath or blood exceeds the prescribed limit. You should then caution him/her and conduct an evidential breath test. A patient in a hospital must not be arrested (s 6D(3)).

5.10.2.2 What to do after a preliminary test

If the results of a preliminary breath test are negative but you still suspect the driver of being under the influence of drugs:

1. consider administering a preliminary impairment or drugs test if you are qualified and have the apparatus available or
2. consider arresting the driver on suspicion of the s 4 offence of driving whilst unfit, using your s 24 PACE powers of arrest.

If no other offences have been committed, then the driver is free to leave.

Figure 5.1 overleaf summarises the actions that should be taken in relation to other outcomes from preliminary tests:

Figure 5.1: Summary of actions that should be taken in relation to other outcomes from preliminary tests

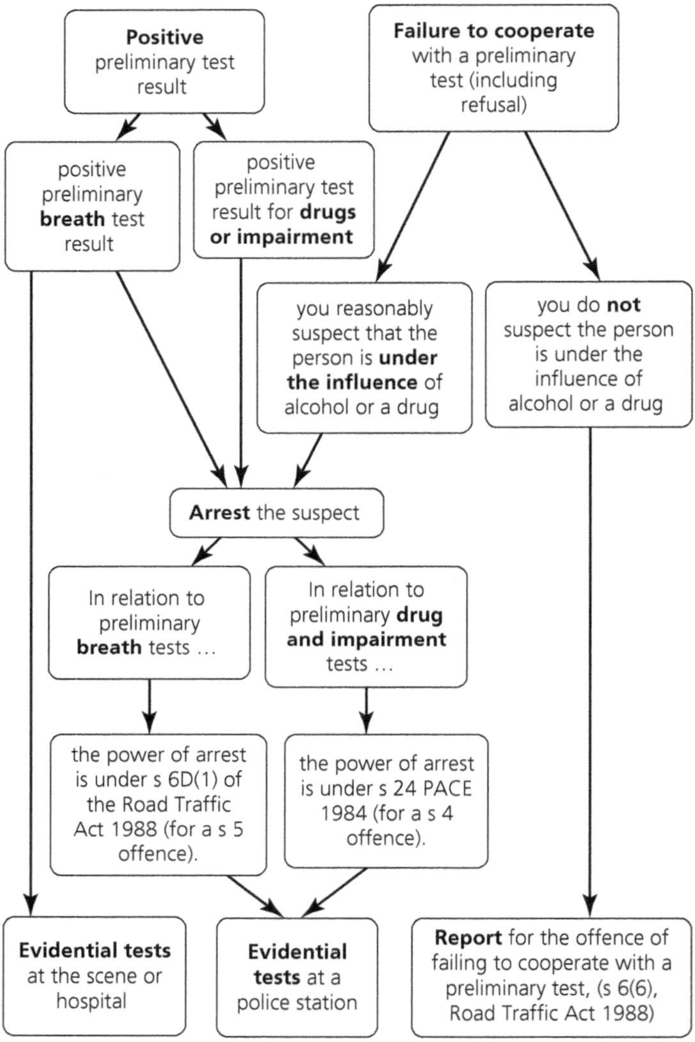

You have the **power of entry** in order to arrest a person who has provided a positive preliminary test and has been involved in an injury accident. This power is given under s 6 of the Road Traffic Act 1988.

5.10.2.3 Evidential tests

The results of these tests (for drugs, alcohol and impairment) can be used as evidence in a court. The tests are usually carried out at a police station (or hospital if the suspect is a hospital patient) but some may also be conducted at the roadside.

We don't have the space to go into the details of taking evidential tests (breath, blood or urine). Look at the *Police Operational Handbook* (Bridges, 2006: 527–40), sections 10.10 and 10.11.

5.10.3 **Hospital procedure**

Here we consider situations where a driver has been admitted to hospital after an accident. This is covered under s 9 of the Road Traffic Act 1988. A hospital is defined by the Act to mean an institution which provides medical or surgical treatment for in-patients or out-patients. The term 'patient' is not defined and will be a question of fact for the court to decide, but generally speaking a patient is a person who is currently on hospital grounds receiving, or waiting to receive, medical treatment.

Before a requirement is made or any test carried out on the patient, the medical practitioner (usually a doctor) in immediate charge of his/her case must be notified of the proposals for tests. The procedures must be explained and the doctor must be given the opportunity to object (s 9(1), Road Traffic Act 1988), as the welfare of a patient is of primary importance. A further complicating factor is that the suspect might receive drugs as part of his/her medical treatment, and these could interfere with the accuracy of the police investigation alcohol and drugs tests.

5.10.3.1 **Obtaining samples from a hospital patient**

The regulations governing such procedures are given in s 9(1) of the Road Traffic Act 1988. Before making any requirements, the relevant medical practitioner must be notified. A general description of preliminary and evidential tests is given in 5.10.2.

Preliminary tests in a hospital can only be requested and carried out if the doctor agrees, and s/he will object if the process is prejudicial to the care or treatment of the patient. If the doctor does not object, the patient can be asked to cooperate with a preliminary test. If the result of the test is negative, the patient must be told that no further action will be taken with regard to tests for alcohol. If s/he does not cooperate and refuses to have the test, s/he should be reported for an offence under s 6(6) of the Road Traffic Act 1988. Note that a person who is a patient in hospital cannot be arrested for failing to cooperate with a preliminary test (s 6D(3)).

Evidential tests will be carried out if the result of the preliminary test is positive (or the patient fails to complete the test). The outline procedure is shown in Figure 5.2, overleaf.

For a blood test, a police medical practitioner must take the specimen of blood. If this is not possible then another medical practitioner may be asked (this is very rare), but s/he should not have a responsibility for the clinical care of the patient.

An unconscious patient is not able to take part in a breath test and so a blood sample will be required and, once again, the relevant medical practitioner must

Figure 5.2: Evidential procedure in a hospital

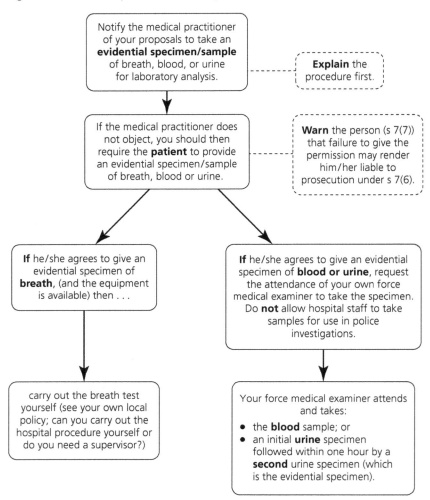

Notify the medical practitioner of your proposals to take an **evidential specimen/sample** of breath, blood, or urine for laboratory analysis.

Explain the procedure first.

If the medical practitioner does not object, you should then require the **patient** to provide an evidential specimen/sample of breath, blood or urine.

Warn the person (s 7(7)) that failure to give the permission may render him/her liable to prosecution under s 7(6).

If he/she agrees to give an evidential specimen of **breath**, (and the equipment is available) then . . .

If he/she agrees to give an evidential specimen of **blood or urine**, request the attendance of your own force medical examiner to take the specimen. Do **not** allow hospital staff to take samples for use in police investigations.

carry out the breath test yourself (see your own local policy; can you carry out the hospital procedure yourself or do you need a supervisor?)

Your force medical examiner attends and takes:
- the **blood** sample; or
- an initial **urine** specimen followed within one hour by a **second** urine specimen (which is the evidential specimen).

be notified (see the previous section and s 9(1A), Road Traffic Act 1988). Consent cannot be given by an unconscious patient, so in such circumstances it is lawful for a medical practitioner to obtain a specimen of blood (s 7A(3)). However, this must not be subjected to a laboratory analysis until the patient comes round and gives permission (s 7A(4)). It is an offence to refuse such permission (s 7A(6)).

TEST BOX 22

These are some questions for you to test your knowledge of 'Drink Drive, Powers of Entry and Hospital Procedure' (LPG1_8_04).

1. Under which three circumstances can you decide to test a driver for drink or drugs?
2. What sections of which Act relate to administering a 'preliminary test'?
3. What facts might determine if someone is 'in charge' of a vehicle?
4. What is the 'evidential test' and who administers it, and where?
5. What units are used to measure prescribed blood/alcohol limits?
6. What is an easy way to remember the figures?
7. 'Preliminary tests' are also known as what?
8. What are the three 'preliminary' tests that may be administered?
9. What should you say to the suspect when administering a preliminary breath test?
10. How do you test an unconscious hospital patient?

5.11 **(LPG1_8_05) Road Traffic Collisions and Driver Obligations: s 170 of the Road Traffic Act 1988**

The meaning of 'accident' has not been defined by statute and remains a question of fact for the courts to decide. However, in *R v Morris* [1972] RTR 201 'accident' was held to be 'an unintended occurrence which has an adverse physical result'. If the accident meets certain criteria, then the driver has to provide particular information to other people or, failing that, report the incident to the police (s 170(1), Road Traffic Act 1988). The criteria for a 'section 170 accident' are **the location of the accident**, **the vehicle** and **the result**.

The **location** of the vehicle at the time of the accident is important. It must have been on a road or other public place such as hospital grounds, household garage blocks or motorway service areas. If the vehicle leaves the road or other public place and ends up in a private dwelling, or grounds adjacent to the road or public place, an accident to which s 170 of the Road Traffic Act 1988 applies has still occurred. If a collision takes place at any location other than a road maintained at public expense, evidence will be required to prove that it is a public place. (This evidence could relate to the frequency of use, by whom and under what circumstances.)

The **vehicle** must be mechanically propelled, in other words the vehicle is powered by a motor (driven by electricity, petrol, diesel or other fuel). The meaning is not defined by any Act of Parliament, so whether a particular vehicle is a mechanically propelled vehicle is therefore a question of fact for a court to decide. The type of vehicle would include those intended or adapted for use off-road (for example, dumper trucks and off-road motorcycles). The collision must be due to the presence of the mechanically propelled vehicle on a road or other public place.

The **damage** must be to another vehicle such as a bicycle, or to property such as a road sign, garden wall or certain animals. The damage can be to private property, but the vehicle must have been travelling along a road or other public place immediately before the incident. Damage does not have to be permanent or beyond repair, but the physical appearance must have been altered in some way. The following animals (but no others) are classed as property: horse, cattle, ass, mule, pig, sheep, goat or dog.

The **injury** must be to another person other than the driver of the vehicle, for example passengers, pedestrians or people in other vehicles. Injury includes shock as well as actual bodily harm. If the only injury or damage caused is to the driver or his/her vehicle itself (or an animal in or on it), it is not an accident for the purposes of s 170 of the Road Traffic Act 1988.

5.11.1 Providing information and documents after a s 170 accident

After a s 170 accident the drivers must stop and remain at the scene for as long as necessary to provide information to others (s 170(2), Road Traffic Act 1988). Failing to stop at an accident is a serious offence and is committed even if the person reports the accident to the police at a later time.

At the scene, a driver must provide particulars to anyone who has reasonable grounds for needing the information, such as the driver or rider of any other vehicle involved, the passengers in any of the vehicles, property owners, pedestrians or their representatives. The driver must provide:

* his/her name and address
* the name and address of the vehicle's owner and
* the identification marks of the vehicle (for example, the vehicle registration number).

Failing to stop or report an accident is an offence under s 170(4) of the Road Traffic Act 1988. This offence is triable summarily, the penalty is six months' imprisonment and/or a fine and the offender may also be disqualified.

If the driver cannot or does not provide the relevant information to anyone who has reasonable grounds for it at the time of the accident, then s/he must 'report' the accident and provide the relevant information to the police. This must be done as soon as reasonably practicable and certainly within 24 hours (s 170(3) and (6), Road Traffic Act 1988). S/he must report in person to a constable or police station; it is not sufficient to telephone, or send a fax or email, nor should the driver just wait for the police to make contact. It is a matter for a court to decide what is 'reasonably practicable' for the particular circumstances.

A certificate of insurance must be produced by the driver where personal injury is caused to a person other than him/herself (an 'injury accident'). The certificate should be shown to a police officer and any person having reasonable grounds for requiring it to be produced, for example the injured person (s 170(5)). If this is not possible at the time, the driver must report the accident to the police and produce the insurance as soon as is reasonably practicable and, in any case, within 24 hours (s 170(6)). Failing to produce proof of insurance after an injury accident is a summary offence under s 170(7) of the Road Traffic Act 1988 and the penalty is a fine.

TEST BOX 23

A brief knowledge check on road traffic collisions:

1. What is an 'accident'?
2. Which four aspects are important in dealing with a road traffic collision?
3. What animals are classed as 'property'?
4. What must a driver provide on request?
5. Which law provides the charge for failing to stop for an accident?

5.12 **(LPG1_8_06) Fixed Penalty Procedure**

The fixed penalty system for motoring offences (Pt III, Road Traffic Offenders Act 1988) provides offenders with the opportunity to pay a fixed fine instead of going to court. A Fixed Penalty Notice (FPN) can only be issued to the person actually committing the offence or driving the vehicle involved: a FPN cannot be used for people who cause or permit an offence. In some circumstances, a FPN can be issued by leaving the documents on the vehicle without the need for the driver to be present, such as a parking ticket affixed to a car's windscreen.

If the FPN is not accepted by the driver, there is no further action to be taken on the street, and the driver will have to be reported and prosecuted. A fine for a FPN must be paid within 28 days (to the Central Ticket Office in the area). If the fine is not paid within this time, it will be increased by 50 per cent and be recovered by the courts.

There are two kinds of FPN:

1. **Non-endorsable fixed penalty notices (NEFPN)**, for offences which do not add penalty points to an offender's driving licence, such as offences relating to:
   o parking
   o seat belts
   o vehicle lighting
2. **Endorsable fixed penalty notices (EFPN)**, for offences which add penalty points to an offender's driving licence. Such offences include:
   o contravening a red traffic light
   o failing to observe a stop sign and
   o driving a vehicle with defective tyres.

5.12.1 **Issuing a non-endorsable fixed penalty notice**

When you are in uniform and you have reasonable grounds to believe that a person is committing or has committed a fixed penalty offence, you may issue that person with a NEFPN in respect of that offence (s 54, Road Traffic Offenders Act 1988). If the driver is present you should:

1. Point out the offence
2. Caution the driver using 'when questioned' and satisfy Code C, para 10.2 (explaining to the suspect that s/he is not under arrest and does not have to remain with you, sometimes referred to as 'caution + 2')
3. Question the driver and allow the driver to ask questions (in relation to the offence(s))
4. Check that the driver wishes to proceed with a NEFPN
5. Complete and issue the NEFPN
6. Report the driver or owner for the offence
7. Use the 'now' caution.

If the driver is not present and the offence relates only to the vehicle, you may attach a NEFPN to a stationary vehicle (s 62(1)). Note that it is an offence to remove or interfere with any FPN fixed to a vehicle.

5.12.2 **Endorsable fixed penalty notice**

Where the penalty for the offence is obligatory endorsement, s 54 of the Road Traffic Offenders Act 1988 states that you may only issue an EFPN if:

- the driver produces a licence and its counterpart for inspection and surrender
- you are satisfied on inspecting the licence and its counterpart that the driver would not be liable to disqualification and
- the driver accepts an EFPN.

The procedure for issuing an EFPN is the same as that for a NEFPN, except for the procedures described in the following section.

5.12.3 **The significance of the driver's licence**

If the driving licence contains fewer than 12 points and the driver accepts an EFPN then:

- ask the driver to surrender the licence and provide a receipt to the driver
- issue a FPN and explain to the driver that s/he needs to pay within the specified time or face an increased fine (as for NEFPN; see 5.12.2).

If the licence contains more than 12 points an EFPN cannot be issued: **you must report the driver for prosecution**. If the driver does not have a driving licence available, you should issue a provisional EFPN and instruct him/her to produce the licence for inspection at a police station (of his/her choice) within seven days.

5.13 **(LPG1_8_07) HORT/1 Process and Completion**

If a person drives a motor vehicle on a road then s/he needs to comply with various pieces of legislation in relation to the documentation that is legally required to keep the vehicle roadworthy. A police officer/vehicle examiner (and in some cases PCSOs) have powers under the Road Traffic Act 1988 to stop vehicles and require production of certain documents in order to check that drivers are complying with the requirements placed on them. The following parts of the Road Traffic Act 1988 detail your powers to stop vehicles and demand production of documents:

Section 163 of the Road Traffic Act 1988 requires that any person

- driving a mechanically propelled vehicle
- or riding a pedal cycle
- must stop on being required to by an officer in uniform.

It is an offence to fail to stop on so being required.

A constable has a power to enter property under s 17(1) of the PACE Act 1984 in connection with this offence.

Section 164 of the Road Traffic Act 1988 gives you the power to require of:

- a **driver or the supervisor** of a learner driver
- a person you have reasonable cause to believe was the driver at the **time of an accident**
- a person you believe to have committed an **offence** related to a motor vehicle on a road
- or a person supervising a learner at the **time of an accident or a suspected offence** being committed by the learner driver
- to produce to you their driving licence for your inspection.

Section 165 of the Road Traffic Act 1988 is the similar power relating to production of an insurance certificate and test certificate, again you can require the

- person **driving** a motor vehicle
- person who you have reasonable cause to believe **was driving when an accident** occurred
- person you have reasonable cause to believe to have **committed an offence** in relation to the use of the motor vehicle.

But note with this section there is no power in relation to a **supervisor of a learner driver** to produce to you his/her certificate of insurance and test certificate for your inspection.

Legislation requires that a person must produce the documents required by a police officer at the time that the requirement is made, however legislation does not require a driver to have the documents in his/her possession. In order to get around this, if the driver is unable to produce the documents at the time s/he may elect to produce them at a police station of his/her choice within seven days of the requirement being made. An officer making the requirement will complete a form HORT/1 and may require the person to produce his/her driving licence and paper counterpart, test certificate, certificate of insurance and the vehicle registration document.

5.14 (LPG1_8_08) Driving Licences, Test Certificates and Insurance

It is inevitable that you will investigate and detect a number of offences relating to driving licences in the course of your Special Constable's duties. This section explains the paperwork required legally to drive, and your powers to inspect driving licences and counterparts.

5.14.1 Driving licences

Anyone driving a motor vehicle or motorcycle on a road must have a driving licence in order to comply with legislation. A learner driver must have a provisional licence and must comply with the conditions of that licence.

For a motor car, a provisional licence holder:

- Must be accompanied and supervised by a qualified driver—over 21 years and a licence held for three years
- Have L plates displayed to the front and back of the vehicle.

For a motorcycle, the provisional licence holder:

- Must have L plates to be displayed to the front and back of the vehicle
- Must not carry passengers, with or without a side car
- Must have completed Compulsory Basic Training (CBT) before riding on a road.

Table 5.3: Categories of licence

Category	Description	Minimum Age
P	Mopeds with an engine size up to 50 cc and a maximum speed of up to 50 km/h	16 years
A1	Light motorcycles with an engine size of up to 125 cc and a power output of up to 11 kW (14.6 bhp)	17 years
A	Medium-sized motorcycles up to 25 kW (33 bhp) and a power to weight ratio of up to 0.16 kW/kg	17 years
B Cars and light vans	Motor vehicles with a maximum authorised mass (MAM) of up to 3,500 kg, no more than eight passenger seats, with or without a trailer, weighing no more than 750 kg (in common language: a car)	17 years

Table 5.3: Continued

Category	Description	Minimum Age
C1 Medium-sized vehicles	Vehicles weighing between 3,500 kg and 7,500 kg, with or without a trailer, weighing no more than 750 kg	18 years
D1 Minibuses	Vehicles with a minimum of nine and a maximum of 16 passenger seats, with or without a trailer, weighing no more than 750 kg	21 years
F	Agricultural tractors	17 years
G	Road rollers	21 years
H	Tracked vehicles	21 years
K	Mowing machine or vehicle controlled by a pedestrian	16 years

There are exceptions to the age requirements mainly related to disability or to membership of HM Forces.

A driving licence contains a large amount of information and if produced must be examined carefully, as a number of offences could be exposed. A driving licence contains the following information:

- The type of licence held—provisional or full
- Name and address of the holder
- Date of birth of the holder
- Date of issue and expiry
- A driver number
- Photo
- Holder's signature
- List of categories/classes of vehicle which the driver is entitled to drive
- List of endorsements.

(See also 5.15 below.)

The driving licence offences which you are most likely to deal with are:

- Driving a motor vehicle on a road otherwise than in accordance with a licence. A number of ways that this offence is committed include failing to comply with the conditions of a provisional licence (no L plates) to driving without the necessary licence, for example driving an HGV vehicle on a standard car licence
- Failing to sign the licence in ink
- Failing to notify change of address.

5.14.2 **Certificate of insurance**

All users of motor vehicles and motorcycles are required by law to have a minimum third party insurance cover. This will cover damage or injuries to third parties (that is, not the driver but anyone else including passengers). If a driver is insured, s/he will have a certificate containing:

- a certificate number
- the policy holder's name
- the vehicle(s) which are covered
- permitted drivers
- commencement and expiry dates
- limitations as to the use of the vehicle—generally social, domestic and pleasure purposes.

There are a number of offences which can be committed in relation to insurance and the certificate produced should be examined carefully to ensure that it covers:

- that person
- to drive that vehicle
- at that time.

The components of the insurance offence are shown in the following diagram.

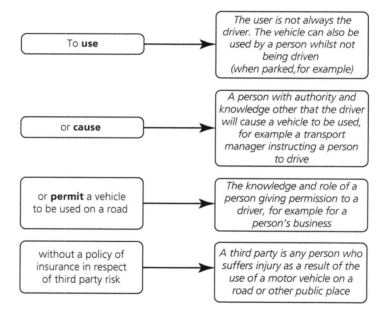

5.14.3 **Power to seize vehicles driven without licence or insurance**

This power applies only to a police officer in uniform under s 165A of the Road Traffic Act 1988.

A constable in uniform can seize a motor vehicle on the spot for:

- Failing to produce a driving licence with reasonable grounds for **believing** that the vehicle was being driven other than in accordance with a licence.

The constable must be in uniform and have required a person to produce his/her licence and its counterpart for examination. The person has failed to produce his/her licence and its counterpart and the constable has reasonable grounds for **believing** that the motor vehicle is or was being driven in contravention of s 87(1) of the Road Traffic Act 1988.

- Failing to produce insurance with reasonable grounds for **believing** that there is no insurance in place.

The constable must be uniform and have required a person to produce evidence that a motor vehicle is not or was not being driven with no insurance in respect of a third party risk and that the person has failed to produce such evidence and the constable has reasonable grounds for **believing** that the vehicle is or was being driven without insurance.

- A vehicle failing to stop when requested by an officer in uniform, with reasonable grounds for **believing** the vehicle was driven otherwise than in accordance with a licence or without insurance.

The constable must be uniform and have required a person driving a motor vehicle to stop. The person has failed to stop or failed to stop for long enough for the officer to make reasonable enquiries and that the officer has reasonable grounds for believing that the vehicle is or was being driven with no insurance and/or otherwise than in accordance with a licence.

Note: reasonable grounds to believe a driver is uninsured or unlicensed, has to be more than mere suspicion. Where a driver is unable to produce insurance or driving licence or it is unclear whether such documentation exists, all possible databases (PNC and local) must be searched for the information required. The aim of these powers is the removal of vehicles from the road where the driver is uninsured or unlicensed, not as a punishment for the driver. Consideration must be given to the human rights implications of seizing a vehicle and the duty of care that may arise with persons left without transport. Many forces allow **only authorised officers** to seize a vehicle under this legislation.

5.14.4 **Test certificates**

A test certificate (MOT) is issued annually and is valid for 12 months. Categories of vehicle which require an MOT after the third anniversary of their registration, details of which will be found on a registration document for the vehicle, are:

- Passenger goods with up to eight passenger seats (family cars)
- Rigid goods motor cars (small vans)
- Dual purpose vehicle (pick-up trucks)
- Motorcycles
- Motor caravans.

Some vehicles require testing earlier because of the amount of use they have. The following classes of vehicle require testing 12 months after initial registration:

- Taxis licensed for hire
- Ambulances
- Passenger vehicles with more than eight seats.

5.14.4.1 Offence

To use, cause or permit a vehicle to be used on a road without a test certificate. Within the legislation there are two exemptions which should always be covered by questioning in a PNB before reporting a person for this offence:

- Vehicles travelling to a pre-arranged MOT test
- Vehicles that have failed an MOT and are being delivered to be broken up for scrap or for work to be completed.

5.15 Driving Licences: Decoding the Information

Driving licences have two parts: the **photocard** and the **counterpart**. Photocard full licences are pink, but provisional licences are green. The driver number contains 'coded' information about the driver:

Table 5.4: How to interpret the driver number

The driver number is:	**GARDN 605109C99LY**
The first five characters are the first five of the surname:	**GARDN**
The first and last digits are derived from the year of birth:	605109 shows the year of birth is 19**69**
The second and third digits represent the month of birth and the gender of the licence holder:	605109 shows that the person was born in May and is male. For females, 5 is added to the second digit so for a female born in May the number would be 655109. For females born in the months of October, November and December, the second digit becomes 6
The fourth and fifth digits show the day of birth:	605109 shows that the date of birth was the 10th of the month
The first two characters of the final cluster represent the initials:	C (if there is only one initial, 9 is used in place of a second initial)
The middle number of the final cluster is computer-generated, in order to avoid duplicate records:	9 (can be any digit between 0 and 9)
The final two letters are also computer-generated:	LY in this case

Full details concerning the driving licence, including the meaning of the various symbols and codes, may be found at the DVLA website: <http://www.dvla.gov.uk>.

5.15.1.1 **The photocard**

Figure 5.3 describes the main features of the front of the photocard. The reverse of the photocard contains the information shown in Figure 5.4 (overleaf).

Figure 5.3 Driving licence photocard—front

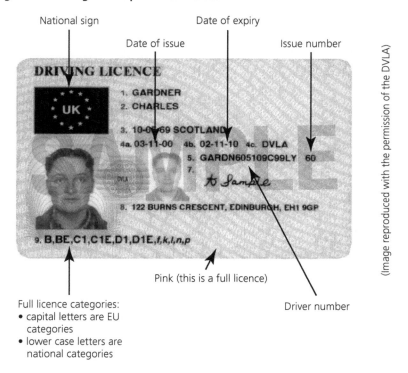

(Image reproduced with the permission of the DVLA)

5.15.1.2 **The counterpart**

The counterpart is a paper document (see Figure 5.5, p 195) showing additional information, such as the vehicle categories the holder is entitled to drive provisionally, the entitlement history (superseded categories), and any endorsements. It is green and pink for both full and provisional licences.

Figure 5.4 Driving licence photocard—reverse

Vehicle categories as listed on the
front of the photocard, with
pictograms for clarity.

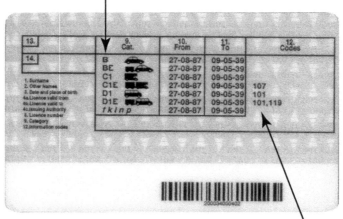

(Image reproduced with the permission of the DVLA)

Information codes showing restrictions applying
to the adjoining category. For example,
101 means that the licence holder
cannot drive that category of vehicle
for hire or reward.

5.15.2 Requiring to see a driver's licence

Under s 164(1) of the Road Traffic Act 1988 you may require a person to produce his/her driving licence. This applies to any person:

(a) **driving** a motor vehicle on a road
(b) whom you have reasonable cause to believe to have been driving a motor vehicle involved in an **accident** on a road
(c) whom you have reasonable cause to believe to have **committed an offence** in relation to the use of a motor vehicle on a road or
(d) supervising a provisional licence holder in any of the three previous circumstances.

A failure to produce the licence is an offence unless the driver produces it within specified time limits.

5.15.2.1 Requiring a person to state his/her date of birth

Under s 164(2) of the Road Traffic Act 1988 you may require a person to state his/her date of birth if s/he:

- has failed to produce his/her licence
- has produced a licence that is unsatisfactory (for example, it seems to have been altered or if it contains information you suspect to be incorrect) or
- is the supervisor of a learner driver at the time of an accident or an offence, and you have reason to suspect that s/he (the supervisor) is under 21 years of age.

Figure 5.5 Driving licence counterpart

List of categories for which the holder
is entitled to drive provisionally

The issue number on the counterpart
will be followed by a letter

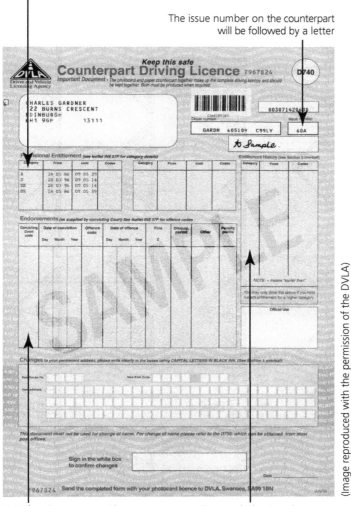

(Image reproduced with the permission of the DVLA)

List of endorsements with
dates and codes

Superseded categories
of vehicles

5.15.3 Offences relating to failing to produce a licence

Under s 164 of the Road Traffic Act 1988 it is an offence for a person to fail to:

- produce his/her licence and its counterpart or
- produce his/her certificate of completion of a motorcyclist's training course (CBT) or
- state his/her date of birth.

Under s 164(8) of the Road Traffic Act 1988 it will be a *defence* for that person to produce the relevant licence either:

- within **seven days** in person at a police station (specified by her/him at the time of the request)
- as soon as **reasonably practicable** or
- at a **later time** if s/he can prove it was not reasonably practicable to do so before the day on which written charge proceedings were commenced.

It will be a question of fact for the court to decide when is 'as soon as is reasonably practicable', given the circumstances of the case.

5.16 (LPG1_8_14) Vehicle Defect Rectification Scheme (VDRS)

Drivers in possession of a vehicle found to be in an unsuitable condition can be given the opportunity to join the VDRS, which is a way of dealing with certain minor vehicle defects without the need to prosecute or to issue a FPN.

The advantages of this scheme include:

- the vehicle defects are rectified, which contributes to road safety
- the offender does not have to go to court
- better police and public relations.

When you consider using the VDRS you must:

- check your own force policy in relation to what defects and for how many the VDRS can be used
- point out the offence to the person responsible for the vehicle
- inform him/her that no further action will be taken if s/he agrees to participate in the scheme
- inform the driver that VDRS is voluntary.

If the driver declines to participate in the VDRS, you should then proceed with a FPN, or report the driver for the offence.

5.17 **(LPG4_8_01) Construction and Use**

Here we cover several different types of offences relating to the condition and maintenance of:

- Tyres
- Exhausts and silencers
- Wipers and washers
- Lights.

5.17.1 **Offences relating to the condition and maintenance of tyres**

The component parts of a tyre profile are shown in the diagram.

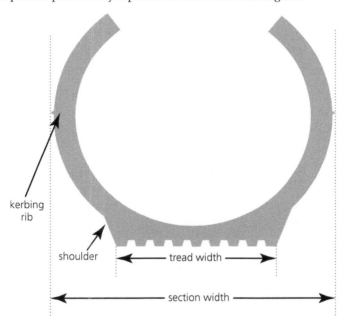

For use as evidence, all the identifying codes and features on the wall of a tyre should be noted, including serial numbers and characters relating to the type of tyre. Full details of the meaning of the letters and number refers can be found at <http://www.blackcircles.com/general/sidewall>.

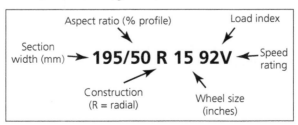

5.17.2 **Regulations relating to the condition and maintenance of tyres**

Regulation 27 of the Road Vehicle Construction and Use Regulations 1986 describes a range of tyre problems relating to tyre condition and the circumstances in which they are being used. These regulations only apply to vehicles and trailers used on roads with pneumatic (inflatable) tyres. Some types of vehicle or circumstances are not subject to the regulations. A summary of the regulations and the exemptions is shown in Table 5.5.

Table 5.5

Regulations in relation to the condition and maintenance of tyres

Regulations	Exemptions
The **type** of tyre must be:	
• the correct type for the vehicle, including taking into account the type of tyres fitted to the other wheels • the correct type for the road conditions or purpose	• Agricultural motor vehicles which have a maximum speed of 20 mph
The tyre must not be **damaged** in the following ways:	
• cuts in excess of 25 mm or 10 per cent of the section width of the tyre (whichever is the greater), measured in any direction on the outside of the tyre, and deep enough to reach the ply or cord • lumps, bulges or tears caused by separation or partial failure of its structure • exposed ply or cord	• Agricultural trailers or trailed appliances • Broken-down vehicles or vehicle en route for breaking up or being towed at a maximum speed of 20 mph
The tyre must be inflated to the correct **pressure** for the purpose	
The tyre must not be so **worn** that the base of any groove which showed in the original tread pattern of the tyre is not clearly visible	• Cars (and other passenger vehicles carrying no more than eight passengers), but see the note at the end of this section • Light goods vehicles and trailers
The tyre must be correctly **maintained** so it is fit for the use to which the vehicle or trailer is being put, and must not have defects which might cause damage to the road surface or persons in the vehicle or road	No exemptions

A 'bald' tyre is when part of the original tread has been worn below the minimum tread depth (see the following paragraph) for the vehicle class. The position of worn patches is significant. Worn patches on the central three-quarters of the tread width **do** matter, but worn patches on the outer eighth of each side of the tread width **do not** matter unless they are associated with cuts or deeper wear. (Furthermore, the tyres for some vehicles, such as motorcycles, are manufactured with no grooves or tread on the outer eighths of the tread width.)

To calculate the width of the central three-quarters of the tread width, see the diagram showing a new unworn tyre.

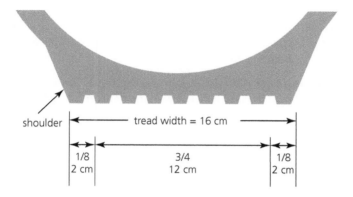

To calculate the central three-quarters of the tread width, using the measurements from the tyre in the diagram:

1. Measure the breadth of the tyre in contact with the road (total width = 16 cms)
2. Obtain the width of the central three-quarters of the tyre by dividing the total width by 4, then multiplying by 3 (16 cm/4 = 4 cm, and then 4 cm × 3 = 12 cm)
3. Obtain the width of each of the two outer eighths of the tyre by dividing the total width by 8 (16 cm/8 = 2 cm)
4. Check that your calculations are correct by adding the value for the central three-quarters to twice the value for the outer eighth (12 cm + 2 cm + 2 cm = 16 cm, hence correct).

For **cars,** light **goods vehicles and trailers**, if any groove or tread is less than 1.6 mm deep in the central three-quarters anywhere round the tyre, an offence is committed. Note, therefore, that the outer areas can therefore be bald. The 1.6 mm rule does not apply to agricultural vehicles, or to any vehicle which has broken down, is en route for breaking up or is being towed at a maximum speed of 20 mph.

For other types of vehicle (such as motorcycles, larger passenger vehicles and larger goods vehicles) the groove depth over the central three-quarters of the tread must be at least 1.0 mm.

5.17.3 **Vehicle components**

Exhausts and silencers: exhaust systems and silencers must be maintained in good working order, and must not be altered to increase the noise made by escaping exhaust gases (reg 54).

- Motorcycle exhausts must be the correct type (only for a moped or motorcycle first used after 1 January 1985, reg 579A(1) or (4)). The silencer should be either the original fitted by the manufacturer or an approved British Standard replacement. (A motorcycle should not be used on a road if its exhaust is marked 'not for road use' or similar.)
- Vehicle emissions must not contain any smoke, visible vapour, grit, sparks, ashes, cinders or oily substance that causes (or is likely to cause) damage to property or injury or danger to other road users (reg 61). Police forces sometimes have instruments to test vehicle emissions.

Wipers and washers: the wipers and washers (those that are required to be fitted) must be maintained in efficient working order and be properly adjusted (reg 34).

Lights on vehicles: the following information relates in part to the Road Vehicles Lighting Regulations 1989.

There is a possibility of underestimating the importance of lights on vehicles when placed alongside other demands on your time, particularly when compared with incidents involving violent criminal activity. However, the position, style, maintenance and colour of vehicle lights are all very important for road safety. Your many Special Constabulary responsibilities include identifying vehicles with lights that are not working properly, testing and inspecting lights and bringing the faults to the attention of the owner and/or driver. Drivers are also expected to employ their lights with consideration for other road users; you can offer advice to drivers about how they use their vehicles' lights—for example, lights should not be used in a way that causes undue dazzle or discomfort to other persons using the road.

Obligatory lights: on the **front of a car**, the following lights are obligatory:

- front position lights ('side lights')
- dipped-beam headlights
- main-beam headlights and
- direction indicators.

On the **back of a car**, the following are obligatory:

- rear position lights
- direction indicators
- rear stop (brake) lights
- rear fog light
- rear registration-plate lamp
- rear reflector (not strictly a light, but obligatory).

A 'hazard warning signal device' to operate the direction indicator lights on the front and back of the car is also obligatory. Hazard warning signalling uses the same lamps as the direction indicators. It is controlled by a switching device that makes all the direction indicators flash at the same time. It operates automatically in some vehicles when the driver brakes hard. It should only be used:

- when the vehicle is stationary to alert other road users of the obstruction or
- on a motorway or dual carriageway to warn drivers behind of an obstruction ahead or
- by the driver of a bus to summon help or
- by the driver of a bus when children under 16 are getting on or off.

The switch for this device must be in reach of the driver. The switch button surface often has a small triangle which will be illuminated when the hazard warning lights are switched on.

Dipped-beam headlamps are powerful white lights at the front of the car. They illuminate the road ahead but should shine downwards and to the left to avoid dazzling drivers of oncoming vehicles. The headlights are often switched on with two clicks of the lights switch. They must be lit when the car is being driven during hours of darkness, except on a 30-mph road with street lighting or if the vehicle's fog lights are illuminated. They should also be used during the day in seriously reduced visibility. The headlights do not need to be illuminated if the car is being towed.

Sunrise, sunset, lighting-up times and hours of darkness: to establish when position lamps or sidelights must be illuminated, published sunrise and sunset times may be consulted. Times can be found in diaries, the internet or local publications such as newspapers, and databases accessible by your Control Room.

Remember: **S**unset and **S**unrise for **S**idelights

For the purposes of finding out when dipped headlights must be used, hours of darkness can be calculated by adding 30 minutes to sunset time and taking away 30 minutes from sunrise time, in other words half an hour after sunset and half an hour before sunrise.

Remember: Hours of **D**arkness for **D**ipped headlights

5.17.4 **Fog lamps**

Front fog lamps are obligatory and if in use (in seriously reduced visibility), there is usually no need to use the main-beam headlights. Rear fog lamps, on the other hand, are optional and consequently they do not have to be maintained. They are very bright red and are operated by an independent switch that will only work when the headlights are illuminated. They should be used only if visibility is reduced and do not need to be used when the car is towing a trailer. Rule 226 of the Highway Code considers that, in general terms, visibility is seriously reduced 'when you cannot see for more than 100 metres (328 feet)'. Fog lamps must not be used in such a way that they cause undue dazzle or discomfort to other road users.

TEST BOX 24

This knowledge check covers sections 5.11 to 5.16.

1. What is the difference between NEFPN and EFPN?
2. What does s 163A of the Road Traffic Act allow a police officer in uniform to do?
3. How old must you be to drive vehicles of Category F?
4. What information does a driving licence contain?
5. What is the minimum permissible insurance cover?
6. Which kinds of vehicle need MOT-type testing more frequently than 12 monthly?
7. What is the VDRS?
8. What constitutes a 'bald tyre'?
9. In addition to functioning lights and reflectors, what other device is obligatory on a vehicle?
10. When is visibility 'seriously reduced'?

5.18 Racially or Religiously Aggravated Offences

The term 'racially or religiously aggravated' is defined by s 28 of the Crime and Disorder Act 1998. In everyday Special Constabulary language, certain offences, such as 'a s 29 assault', can be **aggravated** (regarded as made more serious through additional action, such as carrying an offensive weapon, and hence carrying a heavier sentence on conviction) by being motivated, at least in part, by racial or religious factors.

The following categories of offence can be racially or religiously aggravated:

- assaults (s 29)
- criminal damage (s 30)
- public order offences (s 31) and
- harassment (s 32).

In the absence of racial or religious aggravation, such an offence is sometimes referred to as a 'basic offence' in order to distinguish it from the aggravated form of the offence.

Definition of racially or religiously aggravated

The definition is provided in s 28(1) of the Crime and Disorder Act 1998. An offence becomes racially or religiously aggravated for the purposes of ss 29 to 32 if the offender:

(a) ...demonstrates...hostility (on racial or religious grounds), or

(b) ...is motivated...by hostility (on racial or religious grounds).

It is easier to prove that an aggravated offence has been committed if hostility has actually been demonstrated through the suspect's behaviour.

For s 28(1)(a), the offender demonstrates hostility if:

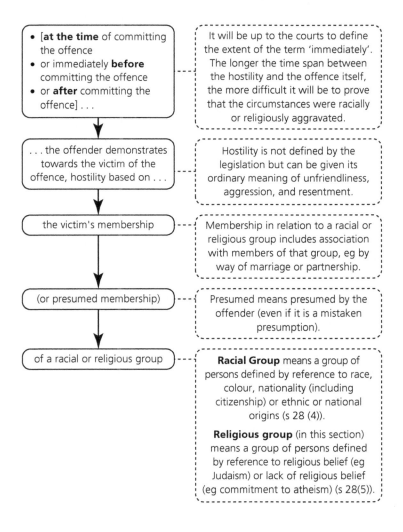

5.18.1 **Racially or religiously aggravated assaults**

Under s 29(1) of the Crime and Disorder Act 1998, the following types of assault as a basic offence can be racially or religiously aggravated (Table 5.6).

Table 5.6: Racially or religiously aggravated assaults (s 29(1), Crime and Disorder Act 1998)

Basic offence	Notes
Any offence under s 20 of the Offences Against the Person Act 1861	Includes malicious wounding or grievous bodily harm, but excludes s 18 'with intent'
Any offence under s 47 of the Offences Against the Person Act 1861	See 4.2 on occasioning actual bodily harm
Common assault	See 4.2 on unlawful personal violence

The motivation for the basic offence must be taken into account—it must be racially motivated or based on hostility to race or religion.

Aggravated versions of the offences under ss 20 and 47 of the Offences against the Person Act 1861 (offences under s 29(1), Crime and Disorder Act 1998) are triable either way:

- summarily: six months' imprisonment and/or a fine
- on indictment: seven years' imprisonment and/or a fine.

Aggravated common assault offences are triable either way:

- summarily: six months' imprisonment and/or a fine
- on indictment: two years' imprisonment and/or a fine.

5.18.2 **Racially or religiously aggravated public order offences**

Section 31 of the Crime and Disorder Act 1998 covers offences that are aggravated forms of basic public order offences. Table 5.7 shows the basic public order offences that may be racially or religiously aggravated, and also identifies the corresponding subsections of the Crime and Disorder Act 1998 for the aggravated forms of the offences.

Table 5.7: Racially or religiously aggravated public order offences (s 31, Crime and Disorder Act 1998)

Basic offence	Aggravated offence
Fear or provocation of violence: s 4 of the Public Order Act 1986	s 31(1)(a) of the Crime and Disorder Act 1998
Intentional harassment, alarm or distress: s 4A of the Public Order Act 1986	s 31(1)(b) of the Crime and Disorder Act 1998
Causing harassment, alarm or distress (see *Norwood v DPP* [2003] EWHC 1564): s 5 of the Public Order Act 1986	s 31(1)(c) of the Crime and Disorder Act 1998

TEST BOX 25

Racially or religiously aggravated offences

1. Where is 'racially and religiously aggravated' defined?
2. What can be racially or religiously aggravated?
3. How is hostility demonstrated?
4. What penalty might result from summary conviction under s 29(1) of the Crime and Disorder Act?
5. What constitute racially or religiously aggravated public order offences?

Further Reading

Bridges, I, *Blackstone's Police Operational Handbook* (2006, Oxford: Oxford University Press)

Home Office, Circular 2/1992 (1992, London: Home Office)

Kent Police, 'A Guide to Form MG11, General Rules for Completion' (2002, updated 2003, unpublished, on file with contributor Robert Underwood)

Practical Operational Activities: Crime Scene Management

6.1 **Introduction**

This chapter brings together the activities in active police operations that you may sometimes be called upon to do when you are 'first officer attending' a crime scene. This chapter gives some explanations and contexts for police operational activity and complements what has gone before. Let's begin with the crime scene and what you should do.

6.1.1 **The Golden Hour: priorities at a crime scene**

Many of you will be familiar with the 'Golden Hour' of investigative opportunity. It is then that physical evidence is at its freshest (even fragile evidence may be recovered), when eyewitnesses' and victims' memories are at their sharpest, and suspects least prepared with explanations or excuses for what has happened.

We go into more detail in the pages that follow; first, though, we are going to describe a crime scene and summarise the things you should do and not do when you are the first law officer (**First Officer Attending** or FOA) entering a place where a crime has been reported or where it is suspected:

A Crime Scene

A crime scene can be:
The suspect (weapons, DNA, fingerprints, traces, body fluids, fibres, footprints)
The place (where the crime took place: a building, a vehicle, a structure, a site, a geographical location, a map reference)
The victim, *but do not describe the victim in this way* (may bear traces of an assault, or attack, or ordeal; of an assailant; may recall vividly, may know offender).

There are two priorities at a crime scene:
do preserve important evidence and
don't contaminate the scene.

Crime scene indicators

The scene may show evidence of:
unauthorised entry (broken windows, forced locks)
physical assault (blood spatter on walls, stains on carpets, handfuls of hair)
searches for money or things to steal (ransacked cupboards, clothing strewn about, opened drawers)
vandalism (graffiti on walls or mirrors, destruction of items)
seizure of a weapon (knives missing from racks, evidence of a bottle having been broken for use as a weapon)

> **a struggle, or fight** (overturned furniture, broken crockery and glass, damaged pictures, photographs, and so on)
>
> **anything taken away** (victim may identify (or you may see) things like open or emptied handbags, open and discarded cash or jewellery boxes, open safes, broken cabinets containing objects)
>
> **anything left behind** (such as items used to effect entry, discarded weapons, discharge from a firearm)

If you are the first on the scene, you need to build a picture of what has happened. A report of an abduction of a child or young person might produce evidence and physical traces of what occurred. You must be alert to possibilities of evidence recovery and aware of what kinds of evidence are important to establish which kinds of crime: such as empty containers and forced entry for burglary, blood from an assault, body fluids from a sex attack and so on. The views of witnesses and victims are important in any context to establish what went on and whether a crime has been committed. Suspects, even if absent from the scene, can be put in the frame by witnesses and victims.

It follows from this, again, that you must have an understanding of the investigative process, which includes an understanding and appreciation of forensic scientific evidence, where it might be found and what it might tell the investigators. A common response, in the aftermath of a sexual attack during which the victim might have fought off the attacker, is that the victim wants to wash. This is a normal response to a traumatic event, but there might be important physical evidence on, say, the victim's hands and face which should be recovered, so you would have to gently insist that things are left as they are until specialists arrive. Fortunately, many people (well versed in crime fiction) will understand this, but you should be prepared to explain how important it is that nothing is touched, rearranged or restored until it has been examined and, if it is evidence, photographed or recovered.

6.2 **Crime in Progress?**

We have so far been assuming that any offenders have left the crime scene, but it might be the case that you have to detain suspects (in which case the same principles about preserving evidence pertain as for the victim: don't allow a suspect to wash, to discard clothing or conceal anything). It might even happen that, if you arrived on the scene quietly and without lights and strobes (perhaps because a caller had reported a 'crime in progress'), that the crime itself, or another crime, *is still being committed* at the scene.

If you arrive at a location where you suspect a crime to be continuing, you must proceed with great caution, aware of the need to protect your own and your colleagues' safety, consistent with saving life and protecting anyone who is being or has been attacked. If the discharge of a firearm has been reported, for instance, and you happen to be closest to the scene and therefore arrive before any armed police can get there, you will need to be very careful indeed that you do not 'spook' an offender into firing at you or anyone else. As a priority, you need to get other people out of the line of fire, and establish a cordon to keep the public, yourself and your colleagues at a safe distance. Entering a strange building in pursuit of someone armed with a firearm is brave but foolhardy; it could also be fatal for you and your colleagues. The same applies to a building on fire, or a building or scene in the aftermath of an explosion.

We discuss later on what to do in establishing a cordon and outer perimeter around the crime scene; all those things can be done once you have ascertained that there is no further risk of injury to anyone in the vicinity of the crime scene. You and your colleagues must take immediate steps to isolate the largest practicable area around the 'seat' of the crime, so that evidence is preserved and contamination is kept to the barest minimum. If anyone points out the alleged offender or a suspect, that offender or suspect person must be detained and, ideally, isolated from others.

6.2.1 **Aggravating factors**

There might be aggravating factors which may make a crime scene even more important:

Aggravating or complicating factors at a crime scene

- The crime seems to be part of a significant series (such as the third reported attack on an elderly person, or the sixth example of a break-in on a lone female at home at night)
- The crime scene is in a place which is a 'hot spot' or where there is a local priority issue agreed with residents
- A weapon has been used, such as a firearm
- A weapon has been used but not recovered from the scene (so the assailant could strike again)
- The **victim** was in a position of trust (schoolteacher or nurse, for example)
- The **suspect** was in a position of trust (a solicitor or warden of a hostel, for example)
- The offence had a sexual motive
- The offence showed evidence of hate crime (such as the expression of racism or homophobia)
- A victim's injuries turn out to be worse than first thought (such as evidence of serious internal or tissue injury)
- A known serious offender has been detained or is identified as having taken part, particularly if being managed under Multi-Agency Public Protection Arrangements (MAPPA)
- The victim is a vulnerable child or adult.

6.2.2 **Summary**

Actions at a crime scene may be summarised in order like this:

- Your first and absolute duty is the preservation of life. Immediately get people away from any source of danger
- If that means you have to let an armed offender escape, then so be it, but note and report what will be needed to pursue any offender (description, build, clothing, apparent weapons, vehicle registration, type, appearance)
- If a crime has occurred, you need to know what it was, take steps to detect what has happened (or is still happening), and minimise any further offending
- You must give time and thought to identifying and dealing with victims, witnesses and suspects. You must be reassuring and gentle with victims, who may be traumatised (deeply upset and disturbed)
- You must **secure** and **preserve** all available evidence and
  - prevent any further crimes where possible
  - ensure that you, and others, **avoid contamination** of the crime scene
  - be alert to the offender's route into and away from the crime scene
  - consider and implement a cordon
  - consider whether there might be **aggravating factors**
  - if you are not sure whether or not you are dealing with a crime, err on the side of caution and assume that you are
  - retain **witnesses** and, when time permits, record details and anything material to the offence
  - keep your PNB up to date
  - keep Control informed, and
  - assume that you are in charge until someone with authority tells you otherwise (this is to avoid you going off shift without 'handing over' the case to another investigator or officer).

KEY POINT

Be in no doubt. Your actions at a crime scene may make the difference between a successful and an unsuccessful prosecution of an offender.

6.3 **Common Approach Paths (CAP)**

A cardinal rule to be observed at any crime scene is the establishment of a CAP. The purpose of this is to ensure that there is only one 'official' route into and out of the crime scene itself, so that the chance of accidental contamination of the scene by visitors is reduced to the minimum.

Even if you are gloved before you go into the crime scene, it is unlikely that you will also be gowned and booted in protective clothing—that tends to be the apparel of those who come after you. In other words, because you are a Special

Constable entering a crime scene not knowing what you will find, you may have to touch things (to move them out of the way so as to gain access to any injured parties, or to make closer inspection of a person or thing). There may be times when you have to move injured people—perhaps to get access to them for emergency life support or resuscitation—and thereby run the risk of contaminating the crime scene. **Your first duty, to preserve life, overrides any other consideration**, which is why the CAP is so important. If everyone who comes after you (paramedics, pathologist, Crime Scene Investigators (CSIs), Fire and Rescue Service personnel, sundry other Special Constables and police regulars, detectives, doctors, coroner's officers, press and others) all choose their own way in, any forensic evidence at the site is likely to be irretrievably compromised.

6.3.1 Establishing a CAP

Choose a logical route: preferably one which is direct and which can handle human traffic: hard-standing tarmac is preferable to grass or a muddy track (as well as avoiding the risk of introducing material from outside the crime scene to the inside). *If possible, choose a route that is unlikely to have been used by either the victim or the offender.*

Obstacles must be avoided, such as trees, vehicles, smashed lights, broken doors, overturned furniture and so on, since the positioning and condition of such items may furnish important indications of what happened in the crime. Do not tie tape to convenient objects—such as trees and lamp posts—which you would actually prefer to be *within* your crime scene.

A very important point: you *should not attempt to cover evidence, or close doors and windows at any major scenes*, but you can do so at a volume-crime scene, or at the scene of an assault, if the CSI is likely to be delayed getting there. Having said that, if rain, snow or wind is getting into the crime scene you should consider closing doors or windows: but you should make sure that you do not wipe prints or blood off the surfaces you touch, and:

- always wear protective (surgical-type) gloves
- always make a PNB entry
- always inform the CSI, and
- do **not** use 'Police do not cross' tape inside a premises except, say, a block of flats—tape is best employed in making a cordon **outside** the crime scene itself.

If there is a body or bodies at the scene, you are obliged to look persistently for signs of life and to take remedial action if you find any such signs, but if you cannot detect a pulse or breathing, and you judge that you cannot resuscitate the victim(s), you should not move the person(s) more than necessary.

If you observe footprints or bloodstains (inside or outside), placing a box over them until the CSI arrives is probably enough. This is vital if it is raining, as any temporary cover is better than none at all. Remember, though, to draw the CSI's attention to what you have done.

Think of the CAP as the most sensible route to the scene which does not gratuitously contaminate evidence, even if this means a detour. In some instances, it might be better to offer authorised visitors to the crime scene an exit from it by a different route, if a particularly narrow route (a cliff path, say, or a canal towpath) might mean those returning along it cause difficulties or delay for those newly arriving at the scene.

A final point to be made about the CAP is that it is important to exclude from the crime scene the morbidly curious, the casual onlooker and the journalist. Help will arrive to support you, but it takes time. In addition to creating the CAP itself, you might have to arrange a rendezvous point (RV) or vehicle parking area for those attending the crime scene. Extend the cordon around the crime scene as far out as is practicable, to keep sightseers and sensation-seekers at bay. The outer cordon can always be brought in later if need be, but if it is too restricted to begin with, important evidence might be overlooked or compromised, and people might be able to get too close to the crime scene for their own safety, or they may begin to hamper the investigation.

The simplest way to think of the crime scene is in concentric circles, as in Figure 6.1:

Figure 6.1 Schematic for routes into or out of a crime scene

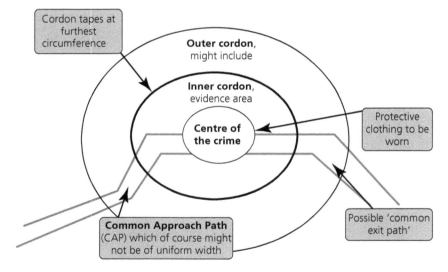

TEST BOX 26

Let's test your understanding of a crime scene with our next knowledge check:

1. What is important about the so-called '**Golden Hour**'?
2. Why might a **suspect** be a 'crime scene'?

3. What are the two main **priorities** at a crime scene?
4. Give four examples of **crime scene indicators**.
5. Give four examples of **aggravating factors** at a crime scene.
6. What is your overriding priority at a crime scene?
7. You must preserve and secure all evidence, and what else?
8. What should govern your choice of a CAP?

6.4 **Forensic Science in Police Investigations**

The investigation of crime scenes using forensic science cannot be assessed in isolation. We normally use the word 'forensic' quite loosely to mean 'scientific evidence' (that is, evidence supported, explained or detected using scientific methods); but the word really relates to law and legal evidence. Like any other evidence, 'forensic evidence' explains to the investigator what has happened—at least in part—and ultimately helps a court to determine whether or not the person accused of a crime committed it. Although it is an integral element in most police investigations (some would argue that it is vital to successful prosecutions), forensic work must be put into a larger context. For example, at a crime scene a CSI might recover excellent fingerprint samples or substantial DNA, but this work might be wasted unless the police officer in charge of the investigation can, at least, detect the crime or, at most, produce a successful case which leads to conviction of the offender. In other words, forensic investigation cannot, of itself, produce a criminal prosecution. It is the investigating police officer, Special or regular, who does that, in conjunction with all the other apparatus of criminal justice.

Police officers generally have a very sketchy or imperfect understanding of forensic science and therefore of its potential benefit in crime scene analysis and the investigation of evidence at the scene. In its report more than ten years ago (in 2002: *Under the Microscope Refocused*), HMIC deplored the general lack of understanding at all levels in policing, which meant that valuable opportunities were being missed, a point echoed by David Barclay (2009). What this means is that it is incumbent on all Special Constables to try to understand at least the outlines and potential for forensic science in aiding police investigations. We cannot hope to do the subject justice in this book, which is focused on the whole Special Constabulary remit, but there are good references in the Further Reading section at the end of this chapter. You do not need to be a scientist to understand forensic science but if you persist in finding it an opaque subject, talk to a friendly CSI and ask for a 'walk through, talk through', which most would be very happy to provide. A Special Constable with the necessary grasp of what to do at a crime scene and knowledge of how forensic science can aid an investigation is a boon to a CSI, so most will see a percentage in helping you.

6.4.1 **Types of forensic evidence**

Now we consider what kinds of evidence are produced by the application of science to a crime scene. Perhaps some of it will be familiar to you from films and fiction, but remember that this is **real**, as is your role in preserving any such evidence: there is an offender at the end of this chain.

6.4.1.1 **DNA**

DNA is an abbreviation for **deoxyribonucleic acid**, a chemical found in all the cells in our bodies which have a nucleus. The chemical carries information about us in the form of a chemical code, or 'language', which is passed on from one generation to the next. DNA determines our physical characteristics, such as hair and eye colour. Except for identical twins, each person's DNA is unique. Half of the DNA is inherited from our father and half from our mother.

DNA can be extracted from cells in the body that contain a nucleus, which include blood, semen, saliva, other 'bodily fluids' and hair samples. The technology, though it has advanced exponentially in the last five years, is not yet sophisticated enough to allow the examination of every single difference between people's DNA. The techniques currently used by specialist laboratories look at specific areas of 'nuclear' DNA, which vary in length between people, so that 'DNA profiling' analyses and measures these differences in length. **SGMplus** was the profiling technique originally used for samples to be entered on the National DNA Database (NDNAD), looking at 11 areas (ten plus a sex indicator) to give a discrimination profile of 1 in 1,000,000,000.

SGMplus held good for a number of years (and therefore we still see it in the printed literature) but it has been superseded by **Short Tandem Repeat** profiling (STR). This is the commonest current method of DNA analysis, and looks at specific 'short lengths' of the DNA that are repeated end-to-end within the DNA molecule. Different people will have different numbers of 'repeats', and hence different lengths of this repeated DNA. The STR profiling technique examines the lengths of the repeat units and converts the lengths into digital outputs, known as the 'DNA profile' (Coleman, 2003).

Low Copy Number (LCN): LCN DNA analysis is an expansion of the SGM-plus technique described in the previous paragraph. LCN is used when the amount of DNA present is very low and many copies of the DNA have to be made in order to obtain a profile. This allows profiles to be obtained from traces that are too small to be seen with the naked eye, or which might be very degraded. However, there is an ever-present danger that the result could be affected by contamination, simply because the amounts are so microscopic.

Mitochondrial samples: mitochondrial DNA, inherited from the maternal line only, is not found in the nucleus of a cell but in the body's mitochondria (the substance that makes up chromosomatic cells). The methodology for analysing this is different from STR analysis, and the results are far less powerful in discriminating between individuals (1 in 100 is typical), but it can be used to eliminate a suspect conclusively. The main use of mitochondrial DNA is in analysis of decomposed tissue, because it is resistant to ageing. It is also possible to use the technique to analyse samples such as faeces, bone and hair shafts, which cannot be analysed using STR methods. Mitochondrial DNA analysis is time-consuming and expensive, and is most used in complex or 'cold' crime cases.

The DNA sampling process: the process described here is that recommended for all police forces. A sample can be taken by a CSI at a crime scene (blood, tissue, cigarette ends, etc), which is then **bagged and tagged**, that is, identified and sealed. It is normal to take a number of samples, each of which is separately processed, so that there is back-up or 'reserve' sampling. The sample is then checked and despatched to a scientific laboratory for analysis. Whilst it is always preferable for a CSI to do this work, it might be that no CSI is immediately available to come to your crime scene or, in your judgement, a piece of evidence might degrade very quickly (bloodstains in rain, for example, or hairs in a breeze). In such cases, it is up to you to 'bag and tag' the item as best you can.

Your force may have its own policy on this because procedures vary considerably. The point is that the item is handled with gloved hands, it is placed in a bag (preferably of see-through plastic) or in a sturdy box if a needle or blade, and the whole container is sealed and signed: hence the 'bagged and tagged' label for this process. There are some other things you need to remember. Under the Code of Practice in the Criminal Procedure and Investigations Act 1996, a Special Constable *has a duty to record and retain material which may be relevant to the investigation*, so you are acting entirely properly when you 'bag and tag' the item.

Another sample might be taken from a suspect in custody. The sampling in a custody suite may be undertaken by any Special Constable or designated police staff, and usually consists of what is technically described as a '*non-intimate buccal scrape sample*', or 'mouth swab'. This involves the insertion of a small grooved plastic stick (like a cotton bud) which is rubbed against the inside of the suspect's cheek to loosen and collect skin cells which contain DNA. It is the least intrusive of the possible collection techniques, and may be undertaken by an 'amateur' (that is, a non-scientist), with care. The swab should then be placed in a plastic tube, which then should be sealed. The process is then repeated so that there are always two samples for each suspect.

The scientific laboratory uses an automated ('robotic') profiling system in five stages followed by an interpretation stage, which consists of techniques to separate and identify the DNA 'fragments', amplifying them into the specific areas noted earlier. A laser beam then converts the DNA fragments into mathematical data for interpretation. The interpretation stage uses specialist computer software which assigns numbers to the fragments of DNA. It is this combination of the sizes of fragments across the sites of interest which produces a unique string of numbers. The numbers are then loaded into the NDNAD and the result is fed back to the originating police force.

6.4.1.2 **Fingerprints**

Compared with the relatively recent developments in genetics, which followed the discovery of DNA, the science behind fingerprint identification is now over 100 years old, and has been tested on innumerable occasions in courts as well as in scientific laboratories across the world. Indeed, so venerable is the fingerprint system in the British criminal justice system that it is in danger of being slighted merely because it is so familiar as a forensic technique. You might have thought that there was little left in fingerprinting to discover, and that all criminals would habitually use gloves rather than run the risk of being identified through their 'dabs'. In reality, processes for fingerprinting are being developed all the time (digitising images and the growth of 'palm-print' technology, for example), and criminals remain peculiarly indifferent to the likelihood of being identified through their 'prints' at a crime scene.

Fingerprints may be taken in a number of ways. At a crime scene, they can be detected by 'dusting' reflective or polished surfaces, and 'lifting' the prints on to tape, or they can be detected and photographed through a series of chemical and physical treatments. Occasionally, prints can be obtained on an object taken from a crime scene which is then subjected to fluoroscopic techniques. In practice, photography is used only when the prints would otherwise be damaged by 'lifting'.

The process for taking prints from suspects in custody or at the scene of a crime is entirely electronic. This involves a suspect's fingers being pressed on to a glass plate or 'platen' where his/her 'prints' are scanned electronically. The resultant digital data are sent electronically to **IDENT-1**, a UK-wide automated analysis system which, in 2005, replaced the National Automated Fingerprint Identification System (NAFIS). IDENT-1, which includes palm-prints in its databases, can record, analyse and compare digital information and make 'matches' quite quickly.

The science of fingerprinting: the hand (palm), toes and fingers are covered with tiny ridges of skin called 'papillary ridges' (also known as 'friction ridges') which are separated by depressions called 'furrows'. The combinations of ridges and furrows (subclassified further into 'whorls', 'arches' and 'loops') on the soft pads of the fingertips and toes (and palms), are unique to each individual. No one human has a combination which is the same as any other, or at least, no match has ever been made between two humans. The characteristic 'print' remains the same throughout an individual's lifetime.

There are three types of fingerprint: **latent prints**, which are invisible, generally, to the naked eye, are made by transferring drops of perspiration and natural oils from the skin ridges to another surface; **visible prints**, which are made through the contact of the skin ridges with a coloured material (such as soot, blood or dust) prior to leaving the print on another surface; and **plastic prints**, which are the impressions of prints left on a 'malleable' surface, such as wet clay, fresh putty or soap. Plastic prints can be transferred, of course, to other surfaces, like visible prints, if quantities of the malleable substance adhere to the fingertips. This is why the average bathroom contains hundreds of fingerprints: the users of the bathroom are in perpetual contact with 'malleable' surfaces, from skin cream to shampoo.

The second and third classes of fingerprint are relatively easy to find; 'latent prints' are much more difficult to detect and require special techniques to make them both visible and 'liftable'. When it comes to the technique of comparing prints, the individuality of a fingerprint is determined by examination of its ridge characteristics, called **minutiae**. There are probably as many as 150 classifiable *minutiae* in any single fingerprint.

6.4.1.3 Ultra-violet photography

This is a forensic investigation technique which requires specialist training and equipment. The layers of human skin (the 'dermis') contain, in their base, a substance called melanin, a dark pigment which absorbs ultra-violet radiation from the sun. When the body sustains an injury, cells called melanocytes (containing melanin) migrate to the wound during the healing process. This leaves an area which is 'depigmented', or without colour, surrounded by a heavily pigmented area which delineates the shape of the object which produced the trauma. Whilst this may not be visible to the human eye, it can be photographed using ultra-violet light. This is of forensic use when considering injuries such as bite-marks, kicks (the imprint of a shoe), burns and other latent injury marks, but is of especial value in revealing long-term abuse injuries which are no longer apparent from normal physical examination.

6.4.1.4 Shoemarks

The footprint, beloved of detective fiction of a certain vintage, has been given a new lease of life since a 'shoemark' at the scene of a crime can be forensically matched in some instances, with the footwear of a suspect. In the event of a match, as with DNA and fingerprints, physical proof shows that the suspect was present at the crime scene (at some point), and therefore has an explanation to give. What has changed is the creation of a shoemark database, by means of which comparisons may be made with some accuracy, and thus there is a searchable repository to which Special Constables may have recourse. What happens normally is that CSIs will take photographs and 'lifts' of shoemarks at the scene of a crime.

6.4.2 Summary

So integral is forensic science to successful preparation of cases against accused persons that it is difficult to imagine a major case succeeding without some aspect of science placing an offender in a place at a time. Some 'cold' cases (and some miscarriages of justice) have been resolved through advances in DNA analysis, and through the matching of DNA with new samples, often long after the event. Forensic science is almost always objective, detached, factual and persuasive. Offenders, confronted with irrefutable evidence, often plead guilty—saving the courts and the Special Constabulary valuable time. There seems to be no limit to the ways in which all aspects of scientific research can be pressed into the service of justice—though specialist commentators have noted the occasionally sharp dislocation between the 'rules' of science and the rule of law.

TEST BOX 27

Now you should self-test what you know about police use of forensic science.

1. When and where did HMIC say that police officers 'have a very sketchy understanding' of forensic science in the service of criminal investigation?
2. What chemical is abbreviated to DNA?
3. Give two examples of where we can find DNA samples.
4. What replaced SGMplus and the profiling technique for DNA samples?
5. When might a Low Copy Number analysis be helpful?
6. From whom do people obtain mitochondrial DNA?
7. What use is mitochondrial DNA in criminal investigation?
8. How would you commonly take a non-invasive sample of DNA from a suspect?
9. What are 'papillary ridges'?
10. What are the three types of fingerprint?
11. What is useful about ultra-violet photography?
12. Why might shoemarks help your investigation?

6.5 Preserving Physical Evidence

Physical evidence may take many forms at a crime scene. Here are a few of them:

Crime scenes: physical evidence

Location where the crime(s) took place
Body or part of a body (the body itself is a crime scene within a larger context)
Any place where the body has lain or from where it has been moved
Anywhere there is a physical trace such as tyre marks, footprints, broken glass from a window or a bottle, location of an object that might have been a weapon
A victim (injured party) whose body, like a murder victim, could be a crime scene (bruises in domestic violence, broken bones, cuts or wounds)
Any witnesses
An attack site

Means of transporting a body or injured party (such as a car, van, quad bike and the like)

Clothing connected to victim or offender

Material on which victim may have been laid or in which wrapped

Access or escape routes for offender or victim

Premises connected to the victim or to a suspect (remember evidence might have been removed from the crime scene and placed or secreted elsewhere)

Articles or objects brought in or used by victim or offender

Be aware of the potential for multiple crime scenes.

(Adapted from Roycroft, 2007)

It is important for the Special Constable attending a crime scene to be aware that the scene itself may only be part of where the crime occurred. There may be secondary and tertiary sites. In kidnap cases, for example, the seizure part of the crime, the transportation of the victim, the holding of the victim and his/her subsequent release, or the collection of any ransom, may all be crime scenes, whilst the equipment used by the kidnappers, from vehicles to a secure holding area to communications equipment, may all be important sources of physical evidence.

A further dimension to the usefulness of physical evidence is that it can be used to corroborate (or deny) the statements of witnesses, victim(s) or offender(s). This will assist in the (not necessarily actual) reconstruction of the crime and the sequence of events involved. Eyewitnesses can be mistaken (as any experienced Special Constable will confirm), confused as to the logic of events or still in a state of shock. Those bank or building society staff who witness a violent armed robbery, for example, may take some time to be able to piece together a coherent account of what took place. If witnesses say that the robbers fired a sawn-off shotgun into the ceiling of the bank, and the CSI recovers a single spent round from a rifle in a wall, there might be difficulties in reconciling the two accounts of what took place. Physical evidence is not suggestible and cannot be influenced, even subliminally, as witnesses sometimes are.

The final point to make is that Special Constables must pay particular attention to the **continuity of evidence**. This sequence ensures the integrity of physical evidence recovered from a crime scene. As we have noted in other sections, the defence counsel team for an accused person will seek faults in the process by which the case against their client was assembled and conducted. Gaps in the continuity of evidence may be opportunities to suggest or allude to contamination of the evidence. Being able to account for every step of identifying, 'bagging and tagging' and then identifying and retaining physical evidence, is an essential part of modern police professionalism. Yet, every year, cases are lost because simple continuity of evidence rules were not observed.

6.6 **Contamination**

To avoid contamination at a crime scene:

- no one should enter a crime scene unless properly clothed and
- the movement and number of persons at a crime scene should be kept to the minimum.

(Adapted from Page, 2004)

This is pretty much an ideal prescription since Special Constables and others on patrol or answering an emergency call do not routinely carry protective clothing, though they should have surgical or protective gloves with them. Perhaps Special Constables should also routinely carry face masks, as these are small, light and easily pocketed. The point is nonetheless well made: the FOA at a crime scene should do **only what is necessary to save life and preserve the scene**: otherwise there could be contamination of existing evidence of the crime which as a consequence might be damaged or compromised beyond practical use. No one expects sterile laboratory conditions at a crime scene—they are messy, untidy, bespattered and dishevelled places—and only a defence lawyer could seriously expect there to be no contamination of evidence at all. However, that is not the same as letting people trample about regardless.

ACPO has been so concerned about the needless and avoidable contamination of crime scenes that its Crime Committee made the following point in written evidence to a House of Lords Select Committee on Science and Technology:

[Paragraph 24] Because of the enormous advances in the science of DNA within recent years, the risk of cross contamination at a crime scene has increased significantly. A stray hair, [a] sneeze, other body fluid or fingerprint, all potentially prejudice a crime scene by the cross-contamination of a DNA exhibit. Single cell analysis and vastly improved methods of collecting DNA from a crime scene exacerbate the risk.

(ACPO, 2000)

As a consequence of this concern, ACPO added a **Police Elimination Database** to the NDNAD so that front-line police staff can be eliminated from the crime scene, thereby reducing potential and actual contamination. It is now routine for new entrants to a police force, including all Special Constables and PCSOs, as well as new CSIs and regular officers, to have both their fingerprints and DNA recorded so that they can be eliminated from crime enquiries.

Contamination of a crime scene can occur, of course, before a Special Constable arrives. Consider a stabbing on a street in daylight. By the time a Special Constable has got to the scene, it is possible that anything up to 25 people will have passed by, some of whom might be public-spirited enough or sufficiently experienced to render first aid to the victim. Inevitably there will have been considerable contamination of the crime scene by the public, from the best of motives, and part of the follow-up work at any crime scene will be the interviewing of witnesses and, if necessary, taking their prints and DNA samples to eliminate them from the physical evidence recovered from the scene.

6.7 Locard's Principle of Exchange: 'Evidence That Does Not Forget'

At this point, we need to consider the importance of trace evidence to an investigation, and go back in time to examine the principle that 'every contact leaves a trace' (Locard).

6.7.1 Trace evidence

Max Houck defines trace evidence like this:

Definition of trace evidence

Trace evidence is a category of evidence that is characterised by the analysis of materials that, because of their size or texture, are easily transferred from one location to another.

(Houck, 2009)

It is testimony to the accuracy of forensic science that the nature of this transfer 'from one location to another' is still important in crime scene investigation, since Edmund Locard (1877–1966) advocated the application of scientific methods and logic to criminal investigation and first described the nature of criminal traces, which he observed in his science laboratory in Lyon, France, in the period around the First World War (1914–18).

Nearly a hundred years after Locard's birth, a major US commentator on forensic science, Paul Kirk, Professor of 'Criminalistics' at the University of California, Berkeley, wrote this:

> Wherever he steps, whatever he touches, whatever he leaves, even unconsciously, will serve as a silent witness against him. Not only his fingerprints or his footprints, but his hair, the fibers [US spelling] from his clothes, the glass he breaks, the tool mark he leaves, the paint he scratches, the blood or semen he deposits or collects. All of these and more, bear mute witness against him. This is evidence that does not forget. It is not confused by the excitement of the moment. It is not absent because human witnesses are. It is factual evidence. Physical evidence cannot be wrong, it cannot perjure itself, it cannot be wholly absent.
>
> (Quoted in Thornton and Kirk, 1974)

The principle of the exchange is that *when two things come into contact, information is exchanged by the transfer of trace material*. It occurs even if the results are not visible (Houck, 2009: 167). Ever since Locard's observation, forensic scientists and crime scene investigators have used this 'exchange principle':

Transfer of evidence

Pressure applied during contact (the greater the pressure, the more items are transferred)

The number of contacts (again, the greater the contact the more will transfer)

How easily the item transfers material (mud transfers more easily than concrete)

The form of the evidence (solid/particulate, liquid or gas/aerosol)

How much of the item is involved in the contact (1 sq cm transfers less than 1 sq m).

(Adapted from Houck, 2009: 167–8)

But it is not just the nature of the transfer that is important, it is the nature of the thing itself, where it is, and how long it will endure:

The persistence of evidence

The kind of evidence (hairs, glass, blood)

The location of the evidence (indoors or outdoors, protected or unprotected)

The environment around the evidence (raining, dry, permeable, impermeable—hard or soft surfaces)

Time from transfer to collection (generally, the shorter the time elapsed, the better the condition of the evidence)

Activity on or around the site of the evidence (the lower the amount of activity, the better the chance of collection and the lower the chance of contamination).

(Adapted from Houck, 2009: 169)

The final importance of trace evidence may be in indicating 'association in criminal activity' (Houck, 2009: 194). Although DNA analysis can often tell crime investigators 'who', it cannot tell 'what', where', 'when' or 'how'. Trace evidence can, but only if the FOA is alive to the possibilities of evidence recovery from the moment of his/her arrival at the crime scene.

TEST BOX 28

Now it is time for a knowledge check about what you have learned in these
sections about preserving evidence, contamination and Locard's Principle
of Exchange:

1. Suggest four sites at a crime scene where there will be **physical evidence**.
2. What is the 'continuity of evidence'?
3. What are the two principles to govern access to a crime scene?
4. As a result of concern about contamination, what did ACPO create as
   part of the National DNA Database (NDNAD)?
5. When and where did Edmund Locard formulate his Principle that 'every
   contact leaves a trace'?
6. What do Americans call forensic science?
7. Name two considerations about the transfer of evidence.

Further Reading

ACPO, Written submission on DNA evidence to House of Lords (2000, ACPO, available at <http://www.publications.parliament.uk/pa/ld199900/ldselect/ldsctech/115/115we05.htm; accessed 1 March 2010)

Barclay, D, 'Using Forensic Science in Major Crime Inquiries' in Fraser, J and Williams, R (eds.), *Handbook of Forensic Science* (2009, Cullompton: Willan Publishing), Ch 13

Broeders, A, 'Principles of Forensic Identification Science' in Newburn, T, Williamson, T and Wright, A, *Handbook of Criminal Investigation* (2007, Cullompton: Willan Publishing), Ch 12, particularly the subset 'All evidence is probabilistic', pp 316–18

Chisum, WJ and Turvey, B, 'Evidence Dynamics: Locard's Exchange Principle & Crime Reconstruction' (2000) 1(1) *Journal of Behavioral Profiling*, available at <http://www.profiling.org/journal/vol1_no1/jbp_toc_january2000_1-1_pub.html>; accessed 26 September 2009

Coleman, D, *DNA Best Practice Manual* (2003, London: ACPO)

Cooper, A and Mason, L, 'Forensic Resources and Criminal Investigations' in Fraser, J and Williams, R (eds.), *Handbook of Forensic Science* (2009, Cullompton: Willan Publishing), Ch 11

Fraser, J and Williams, R (eds.), *Handbook of Forensic Science* (2009, Cullompton: Willan Publishing)

HMIC, *Under the Microscope Refocused: A Revisit to the Thematic Inspection Report on Scientific and Technical Support* (2002, London: Home Office)

Houck, M, *Mute Witness: Trace Evidence Analysis* (2001, London: Academic Press)

——, 'Trace Evidence' in Fraser, J and Williams, R (eds.), *Handbook of Forensic Science* (2009, Cullompton: Willan Publishing), Ch 7, pp 166–95

Page, D, 'Scene of the Grime' (2004) 31(3) *Law Enforcement Technology* 108, 110, 112–113

Roycroft, M, 'What Solves Hard to Solve Murders' (2007) 3(1) *Journal of Homicide and Major Incident Investigation* 93

Thornton, J (ed.) and Kirk, P, *Crime Investigation*, 2nd edn. (1974, New York: Wiley & Sons)

Practical Operational Activities: Going to Court

7.1 **The Criminal Justice System**

It is often said that the police stand as the 'gateway' to the criminal justice system, since no one will enter the criminal justice process unless investigated and charged with an offence by the police or another law enforcement agency such as Revenue and Customs. It is now appropriate to consider what makes up the criminal justice system (CJS) in England and Wales. At its very simplest, the process looks like Figure 7.1:

Figure 7.1 Simplified criminal justice route

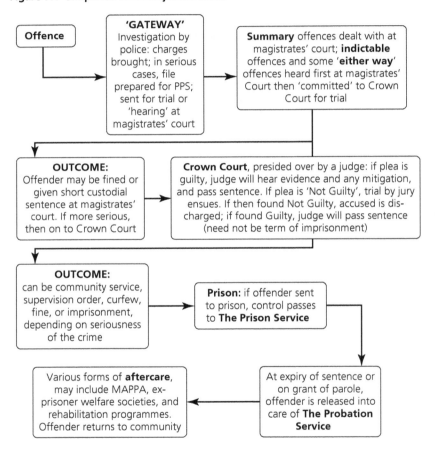

The experienced Special Constable will note that there are some gaps in the way we have depicted the criminal justice process in this diagram (such as habeas corpus, procedure in the event of a suspicious death, the role of the defence team and the time which elapses between indictment and hearing); but the basic system follows this route, or part of it, no matter what the court or crime. Offences in criminal law are classified in terms of their severity and their impact on people or communities. The following are the standard categories of offence:

Definition of offences

Summary: minor acts of disorder, road safety breaches, some forms of theft, possession of Class C drugs and so on; these are tried at the magistrates' court and are likely to attract a fine or community service order. It is still fairly unusual for magistrates to give a custodial sentence

'Either way': these are offences with a bigger impact than summary offences. For example, theft of a relatively small amount of money might be tried at a magistrates' court whilst a substantial theft might require trial at Crown Court. Depending on their seriousness, offences that can be tried 'either way' include fraud and burglary

Indictable only: these are the most serious offences, such as murder or rape, which can only be tried on indictment (a document accusing a named person of an offence) at a Crown Court before a judge

Indictable offences: a further 'greyish area' of offences, including arrest by someone other than a police officer. This group may include both 'either-way' and 'indictable-only' offences.

In this survey of the criminal justice system, it is helpful to consider briefly the kinds of court which examine actual or potential criminal charges. We examine the main criminal courts (except courts martial in the Armed Forces) in more detail in the sections which follow, but here is a summary:

Types of criminal court

Magistrates' court: an 'inferior' (lower) criminal court presided over by two or more 'lay' (unpaid) magistrates, the more experienced among whom will be titled Justices of the Peace (JP). Alternatively, courts may be served by a District Judge sitting alone (District Judges used to be called 'Stipendiary' (paid) Magistrates), and appointed from practising lawyers (barristers or solicitors)

Juvenile court: now more often called a Youth Court, it is a magistrates' court which has jurisdiction over crimes committed by young people aged under 18 years. This court is not normally open to the public

Coroner's court: a court convened to investigate deaths suspected of being unnatural or violent, and presided over by a coroner (who may be a medical practitioner or a barrister or solicitor 'with five years' standing'). If an *autopsy* (medical investigation of a corpse) does not show death by 'natural causes', the coroner may conduct an *inquest* (an enquiry), with a jury. An inquest is not a criminal trial, but if unlawful homicide is suspected, the coroner will adjourn (postpone) the inquest until the outcome of any criminal trial

Crown Court: a 'higher' court created by the Courts Act 1971 to take over the jurisdiction served by the old assizes and quarter sessions. The Crown Court has unlimited jurisdiction over all criminal cases tried on indictment, and also hears appeals from decisions in the magistrates' court.

Figure 7.2 The charge, conviction and appeals route

Police (or other agencies) charge a person with an offence and send the 'case papers' containing available evidence to the PPS

The **Public Prosecution Service (PPS)** (was the Crown Prosecution Service:) establishes from the evidence whether there is a case for the accused to answer (and whether there is a 'reasonable likelihood' of a conviction). If so (to both), the case will be sent to trial

First 'hearing' is at a **magistrates' court** with lay magistrates (JPs) or District Judge (ex-Stipendiary). Serious cases are referred to the Crown Court ('committal')

Crown Court: Judge (and jury if 'Not Guilty' plea) hears case and determines 'brought to justice' outcome, which can range from discharge to imprisonment

Court of Appeal (Criminal Division, under the Lord Chief Justice): panel of appellate judges hears appeal and makes ruling

The **Supreme Court,** created in July 2009 to replace the Law Lords of the House of Lords. This is effectively the last court of appeal in the UK (though technically there can be an appeal to the Crown or to the European Court of Justice—but both are very rare indeed). The judgment of the Supreme Court makes 'case law'; a verdict might be that the conviction is 'not safe'

There is a system for allocating cases between Crown Court centres, as follows:

First Tier: deals with both criminal and 'High Court' civil cases, served by *puisne* (pronounced 'pween' and meaning 'ordinary') judges, by *circuit* (experienced, including High Court) judges and *Recorders* (part-time judges).

Second Tier: deals only with criminal cases, but any of the three kinds of judge noted in First Tier may serve here.

Third Tier: only deals with criminal cases: served by circuit judges and Recorders only.

Finally in this section, we need to present an overview of the whole process of criminal justice in England and Wales (Scotland and Northern Ireland have different laws and processes). The nature of appeal needs to be considered, since it often plays a large part in the outcome of criminal cases. Defence teams that are not satisfied with the verdict against a client by a jury or judge in a Crown Court may appeal against the sentence (or verdict), and carry the appeal forward—if there are substantial legal grounds—as far as the Supreme Court (which replaced the 'Court of Law Lords' in 2009). There are a number of intermediate steps. Again, the simplest and most direct way of showing this is by means of a schematic, starting with the actions of the police following an offence and the arrest of the alleged offender, as shown in Figure 7.2.

7.2 **Magistrates' Courts**

Magistrates hear criminal cases, administer oaths of public office (such as a Special Constable's attestation) and sign search warrants. They have a limited jurisdiction in some civil matters, such as debt and 'family proceedings' (divorce, adoption and so on). The Courts Act 2003 gives magistrates national legal jurisdiction, but in practice all magistrates are assigned to a specific 'local justice area', usually reasonably close to where the magistrates themselves live.

Magistrates' courts are presided over either by:

Lay (unpaid) **magistrates**, trained in the administration of justice, questions of law, practice and procedure, and in sentencing in line with legislation. They sit in 'panels', usually of three, one of whom—usually the most experienced—acts as the Chair, and who addresses the court and the accused.

Magistrates appointed as **JPs** are advised on matters of law by a *Justices' Clerk*, who is always a qualified lawyer.

Or by a **District Judge**, who is a paid, professional lawyer trained to administer the law both in magistrates' courts and in some Crown Courts. District Judges sit alone and tend to be used in complex or difficult cases.

Magistrates' powers to hear and pass sentence are derived from the Magistrates' Courts Act 1980 but JPs have been around since the 14th century and the relationship between JPs (the magistracy) and the police—particularly the Special or Parish Constable—is the oldest continuous local law-enforcement relationship in British legal history (dating from 1361). Like Special

229

Constables, lay magistrates (JPs) are volunteers, drawn from the local communities, and often they have a very good knowledge of local situations and problems.

DISCUSSION POINTS

Is it better to have amateurs or paid professionals judging a community's offences?

Which of magistrates and District Judges are more likely to understand why offences are committed?

The principle that guides which court hears what case is that the place where either the alleged offence was committed, or the person charged with the offence lives or has his/her 'principal place of business', is within the court's **jurisdiction**. Magistrates' courts can only hear trials and pass sentence on adults for offences for which *the maximum penalty is six months in prison*. Accused people under the age of 18 are normally tried at a **Youth Court**, unless being tried with an adult. The likelihood of you attending a Youth Court is low, and so we shall not look at its work in any detail, referring you instead to Crawford and Newburn (2003).

The offences for which a magistrates' court passes sentence are called **summary offences**, and technically a magistrates' court sits as *a court of summary jurisdiction*—that is, a criminal court that tries without a jury, in which JPs decide all questions of law (assisted, as we noted earlier, by a Clerk to the Justices). The District Judge has the same powers and remit, though of course s/he sits alone and makes his/her own decisions. Summary offences constitute 95 per cent of all offences tried at court: it follows that very few of the total number of offences are tried at Crown Courts; but these, of course, are the more serious ones.

A crime may be classified as '**triable either way**' which usually depends on the severity of the offence or, for example, the amount involved in a theft. If an offence is classed as 'summary' then a magistrates' court will hear it. Such offences include burglary, fraud, theft and some instances of sexual assault. If an offence does not fall entirely within the 'summary' limitations, a magistrates' court will decide, on a preliminary hearing of the case with the outline evidence, whether the case should be *tried on indictment*: that is, at a Crown Court. An example might be in causing criminal damage: if the amount involved in the offence is £5,000 or less, it would probably be heard at a magistrates' court and tried summarily. If the amount is above £5,000, magistrates might decide to remit the case to the Crown Court (this is called 'referral'). Any *aggravating factor*, such as the use of violence or if the offence endangered life, means the case is more likely to go to the Crown Court for trial.

Straightforward **indictable offences**, such as murder and assault occasioning grievous bodily harm (GBH), are formally heard first at magistrates' courts, which may decide on questions of **bail**, or **remand in custody**, prior to committing the case to the Crown Court. All criminal cases in England and Wales, therefore, come first before magistrates' courts, whatever the severity or enormity of the crime. This is as true of mass acts of terrorism as it is of individual crimes of violence.

Task

Give examples of two offences under common law and two under statute law.

TEST BOX 29

Now it's time for a knowledge check on what you have learned to this point:

1. In what sense can the police be called the 'gateway' to the criminal justice system?
2. What plea necessitates a jury trial?
3. Name three possible outcomes from the criminal justice process.
4. What 'lay' persons might preside at an 'inferior' court?
5. What do we now call a 'stipendiary magistrate'?
6. What does a coroner's court do?
7. What are 'puisne' judges in a Crown Court?
8. What is tried at the *third tier*?
9. When was the Supreme Court created?
10. What legislation gives magistrates their powers?
11. Who advises lay magistrates and JPs on points of law?
12. What offences can magistrates try?

7.3 **Crown Court**

As we noted earlier, Crown Courts are where serious criminal offences are tried. Each county or metropolitan district now has one or two, numbers having been reduced considerably in the last five years. You will attend Crown Courts rarely, but when you do, it will be for serious crimes.

7.3.1 **Layout of a typical Crown Court**

A typical Crown Court, hearing serious or complex criminal cases, will have most of the following physical features, though not necessarily in the layout given here. We present this outline (Figure 7.3) as the most typical of Crown Court designs:

Figure 7.3 Schematic layout of a typical Crown Court

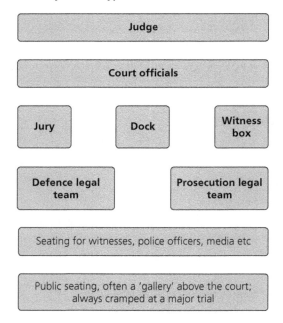

It can be seen from this outline that there are set 'spaces' in a courtroom for the various participants, and in a diagram, everything can look neat and orderly. In fact, courtrooms can be crowded, noisy places where people are often much closer to each other than our typical layout might suggest. For example, the jury 'box' is often close enough to both the witness box and the dock for members of the jury to 'read' the expressions of the accused and of witnesses, to see complexions, perspiration and hand movements quite clearly. This proximity can sometimes be oppressive, nowhere more so than when victims have to give evidence close to the person alleged to have carried out the offence(s).

7.3.2 **The role of the judge**

The judge presides in a Crown Court, listening to all the evidence, and s/he will summarise the evidence for and against the accused, for the jury. The judge passes sentence in findings of guilt (or guilty pleas, which earn a 30 per cent reduction in penalty, or prison sentence) and is responsible for keeping order in the courtroom, which includes curtailing the excesses of lawyers for either side, such as when they ask witnesses leading questions. Judges will have been appointed following long experience of the legal profession, in which they could have been a defence lawyer, a lawyer in the Public Prosecution Service or both; and most have practised as barristers rather than solicitors, though one or two serving judges were not 'called to the Bar' (to practise as barristers). Judges begin as Recorders (some of whom are part time) before going on to become *puisne* or ordinary judges, becoming circuit judges as they gain experience. The usual pinnacle of a judge's career is to become a High Court judge, specialising in particular areas of the law, but some go further, to appointment as a judge in the Court of Appeal, usually entailing ennoblement to the House of Lords, or even as a Lord Justice in appointment to the Supreme Court.

For all the majesty of their office, and the sometimes gloomy splendour which surrounds them, Crown Court judges are not unchallenged. Defence teams can appeal against a judge's sentence if they see it as too severe, or think that the jury was 'misdirected' by the judge, and judges' decisions can be overturned by the Court of Appeal, or the Supreme Court. This has some dangers, since sentences can also now be appealed (by the Attorney General on behalf of the Public Prosecution Service) as too lenient. Some recent cases, in which judges' sentences were indeed perceived as too lenient (one in a prominent rape case, and another in the trial of a paedophile), resulted, after appeal, in increased prison terms for the offenders. The media may be seen to play a part in orchestrating calls for tougher sentences, particularly for 'dramatic' crimes such as child murder or abuse.

7.3.3 The Public Prosecution Service (PPS)

Until comparatively recently (1986), the police would retain a solicitor or sometimes themselves present the 'prosecution case' at a magistrates' court. Now, both at magistrates' courts and Crown Courts, the prosecution case is presented by lawyers retained by the government's PPS. Increasingly, the PPS's own lawyers are presenting cases at both courts, if qualified to do so.

The PPS was the Crown Prosecution Service (CPS) until 2009. The Prosecution of Offences Act 1985 established the CPS to prosecute criminal offences which had been investigated previously by the police forces of England and Wales, as well as by a number of specialist law-enforcement agencies, such as Customs and Excise, as it then was (now an investigative arm in The National Crime Agency, NCA). In simplified form, the context of the PPS in the criminal justice system looks like Figure 7.4 (overleaf).

The primary role of the PPS is, by examination of the police 'case files' of evidence, interview, and investigation following an offence, to determine whether the case made should proceed to criminal prosecution or, in some instances, to pursue a non-court option (such as official 'conditional caution').

Figure 7.4 The PPS structure and other legal partnerships

In late July 2009, the DPP announced that the CPS would merge with the Revenue and Customs Prosecution Office to create a single **Public Prosecution Service** for the police, the UK Border Agency, HM Revenue and Customs and SOCA. Keir Starmer, the DPP, noted that:

> Most fundamentally, we need to recognize that we have developed a criminal justice *system*, when what we need is a criminal justice *service*. A system can all too easily become process-driven. A service is about standards and should focus on protecting the public by dealing efficiently and effectively with criminal conduct while respecting the human rights of all concerned.

(Starmer, 2009; emphases in original)

These are laudable aims, but merely incorporating other agencies' prosecution services into one larger 'Public Prosecution Service' will not of itself alter the structure of criminal justice in England and Wales. Far more profound changes would be needed to change the CJ *system* into a CJ *service*, as any victim of crime will tell you. The annual British Crime Survey (BCS), which analyses how victims feel about crime, often records how alien and disorientating they find the CJS. It will also take some time, we think, for 'PPS' to replace 'CPS' in the police lexicon. The changes to the criminal justice system, suggested by Mr Starmer, will take a minimum of five years to implement, even supposing that there is widespread agreement to what he has proposed.

There is a two-part test which the PPS applies to all cases constructed by the police—deriving from the *Code for Crown* [Public] *Prosecutors* which the DPP issued as guidance:

PPS—The two-part test

Evidence: is there a realistic prospect of conviction before the courts (that is, a conviction is more likely than not)?

Public interest: is it in the public interest to proceed with this case, if the crime happened a long time ago, or if it is fairly minimal but the public feel uneasy about it (such as criminal damage); or (if there is no likely prospect of conviction) should the costs of a trial be incurred?

There are times when some seasoned Special Constables will tell you that the PPS is too timid, or is lacking in a sense of justice, or even that it is risk-averse, in deciding not to pursue a case to prosecution. But the PPS bases its judgements on its experience of having taken Special Constabulary evidence to court and then have cases fail the test of 'guilt beyond all reasonable doubt', so it is not surprising that the PPS prefers a watertight, well-evidenced case where the chances are that a presumption of guilt will be made by a jury or bench. Increasingly, the PPS helps to guide the police investigation, discussing what evidence is necessary and what interviews have to be carried out.

7.3.4 **The legal defence team**

Under the 'adversarial' structure of the law in England and Wales, every person accused of an offence is entitled to **legal representation**, in the same way that, in law, every person is entitled to know what the offence is of which s/he has been accused, and entitled to be **tried openly** (unless there are convincing grounds for parts of a trial to be *in camera*, that is, in secret: such as trials for espionage or treason). The cornerstone of all of this fairness and openness is the legal defence team.

It might be that the 'team' consists of one person, a solicitor, appearing in a magistrates' court to plead in mitigation for his/her 'client' facing a driving ban; or it might be a full-blown team consisting of a senior barrister who is also a Queen's Counsel (QC), one or more junior barristers, one or more legal clerks and one or more solicitors; who might appear in support of the accused person at a major criminal trial. The principle is the same for both: the legal defence team appears for the accused and is, or should be, allowed access to all material relating to the case against the accused, including evidence which is not part of the prosecution case, such as extraneous CCTV footage.

The role of the legal defence team is to have access to all the evidence, to be present in support of the alleged offender at any formal (recorded) police interviews and to challenge the prosecution case. The legal team may be retained at the expense of the accused or might be paid for from public funds (**legal aid**) if the accused cannot afford his/her own lawyer. Funds for legal aid have been affected by the economic recession, and the level at which it is available has been reduced (that is, more people must pay for their representation). Unless lawyers appear *pro bono* (that is, unpaid; from *pro bono publico*, Latin, meaning 'for the public good') it is likely that, progressively, fewer people will be able to afford legal representation, since lawyers' fees are already high.

Whether this will mean an increase in miscarriages of justice is not yet certain, but this may be a reasonable presumption. In the interests of justice, as well as professionalism, this means that any case for prosecution prepared or evidenced by a Special Constable for the PPS must be well researched, impeccably presented and include all available evidence.

KEY POINT

Remember it is not for the Special Constable to prove guilt: you are there to help the court to ascertain the truth of what happened. Only a court can find a person guilty of an offence.

TEST BOX 30

At this point, you should self-test what you have learned about the structure of the courts and the major players in them.

1. What does a judge do at a Crown Court?
2. What office is the DPP?
3. What is the 'two-part' test?
4. What is the 'burden of proof' in criminal prosecutions?
5. What is the name for the system that opposes prosecution and defence in a trial?
6. What Latin phrase is used to describe defence lawyers who appear for little or no fee?
7. Who can find an offender guilty?

7.4 The Nature of Evidence

Going to court and giving evidence is a serious business, which you must approach in a professional and prepared manner.

7.4.1 The law of evidence

When you go to court as a Special Constable to give evidence, it is important that you understand precisely what kinds of evidence you are presenting for the court to consider. First, there is **direct evidence:** this *establishes a particular fact in issue*. For example, the existence of an iron bar used in an assault could be produced in court ('real' evidence, see later in this section), together with a statement from someone who saw that bar (or a bar) in the possession of the accused. A witness might be called as well to testify directly to this assertion.

Second, there is **circumstantial evidence:** circumstantial evidence is *evidence of a fact which may be inferred or supposed*. For example, if a person in a shopping mall was beaten about the head with an iron bar and the accused had been seen carrying such a bar *at the time and in the immediate area*, the **circumstances** suggest that the accused might have been the assailant.

Circumstantial evidence on its own is not usually enough to convict 'beyond reasonable doubt', but it often corroborates or supports the hypothesis that X committed the crime. This points to a clear use of circumstantial evidence: *to prompt the inference that a suspect in a crime has at least the means or opportunity to have committed the crime*.

Whilst there might be both direct and circumstantial evidence in a case presented to a court, most evidence is 'oral' (spoken). **Oral evidence** consists of statements made in court by witnesses concerning *matters of which they have direct knowledge*, such as something they touched, smelled, saw, heard or tasted. Examples include hearing a shot, smelling alcohol, feeling a hand on your leg, seeing someone leave a house, tasting something unexpected in a drink, and may be supported or augmented by **documentary evidence**. This consists of *information obtained by production of a document* (or a copy, authenticated for the court) *as evidence of matter contained in it*. A 'document' may be writing, typing, printing, a map, a drawing, a sketch, a photograph, a disc, a tape, a video, a still image on a mobile phone, a moving image on a mobile phone, a digitised 'picture' from any electronic means of record and any film 'or the like'.

A further category is '**real**' or '**objective**' **evidence**, which consists *in the production of an object or thing for the court to see* and inspect. An example might be that a Special Constable produces in court a list of stolen items (this would be oral and documentary evidence), but also produces one of the stolen items for inspection: this would be 'real' evidence, which exists in all dimensions.

There is a further and final distinction to be made. First, **original evidence** consists in *that which is produced 'first-hand'*, without any intermediary (such as a statement) or interpretation (such as 'decoding' digital images). Examples would include *direct testimony* ('he shouted at me to lie down') and *direct experience* ('she threw the glass at me from a metre away'). This is distinct from a category of evidence often regarded as more uncertain or ambiguous: **hearsay evidence**, which consists in *'second-hand' evidence, of what someone else actually or implicitly said* (verbally, in writing, or by conduct, such as nodding or shaking the head). A Special Constable's pocket notebook (PNB) containing a statement in which an accused person admitted guilt to a crime, is actually hearsay evidence, though it would be admitted in a court. Not all hearsay is so reliable: recording in a PNB that Ms X said that Dr Y told her that Mr Z had stolen Mrs C's watch, is not very convincing and could be ambiguous.

Hearsay evidence usually requires corroborative or supporting evidence to be believable; but exceptions are made for deathbed confessions and the like.

These explanations have been collated and adapted from English and Card (2009), Jefferson (2007) and Martin and Turner (2004).

KEY POINT—CHARGING STANDARDS

A final point is about 'charging standards'. The PPS offers guidance concerning cases of offences against the person through the use of what are commonly known as 'charging standards'. These standards are designed to assist prosecutors in selecting the most appropriate charge. The decision to charge is based upon the severity of the injury sustained by the victim. However, the guidance is quite clear that the standards should never be used to make any investigatory decision, such as making an arrest.

The PPS charging standards can be found at <http://www.cps.gov.uk/legal/l_to_o/ offences_against_the_person/#P48_1458>; accessed 28 October 2012

7.5 *Actus Reus* and *Mens Rea*

The Latin phrase *actus reus* can be translated as 'a guilty act'. The *mens rea* is the second part of the 'equation'—the 'guilty mind' which accompanies the 'guilty act'—the act must be done knowing it to be against the law. This is why, in English and Welsh law (and most other legal systems), a child under the age of ten years cannot be convicted of a crime, since the law presumes that the child cannot yet tell the difference between right and wrong and therefore cannot have a 'guilty mind'.

The two parts do not exist separately: the *mens rea* qualifies the *actus reus* (Jefferson, 2007: 43), so in a rape the offender must recklessly intend sexual intercourse or oral sex, *and* know that the victim does not consent. Thus, all the elements here—'offender', 'victim', 'sexual intercourse or oral sex' and 'consent'—are the *actus reus*. The rapist's 'reckless intent' to commit the offence is the *mens rea* (Jefferson, 2007: 43–4). The 'equation' between the two 'elements' can be expressed like this (Figure 7.5):

Figure 7.5 *Actus reus* and *mens rea*

| *actus reus* (physical element) | + | *mens rea* ('guilt' element) | = | crime or offence |

Actus reus is not entirely definable as an act, because sometimes the *omission of action or the failure to do something* may result in a crime—such as letting someone starve to death or failing to report a road accident. In one case (*DPP v Santana-Bermudez* [2003] EWHC 2908 (Admin)), the accused did not tell a police officer intending to search him that he had a hypodermic needle in a pocket. This omission amounted to *actus reus* (and the charge of assault causing actual bodily harm or ABH) when the officer was injured by the needle (Martin and Turner, 2004: 10).

7.6 **Bad Character Evidence**

On a similar basis, the rule used to be that a court could not consider the accused's character, but the Criminal Justice Act 2003 abolished that exemption. The Act provides that evidence of the accused's bad character is admissible in criminal proceedings subject to the following conditions:

Evidence of bad character is admissible only if:

- all parties agree to its being admissible
- 'it is evidence adduced by the accused...or is given in answer to a question asked by [him/her] during cross-examination ...'
- it is important explanatory evidence
- it is relevant to an important matter in issue between the accused and the prosecution
- 'it has substantial probative [evidential] value in relation to...[an] issue between the accused and a co-accused'
- it is evidence to correct a false impression given by the accused or
- the accused has made an attack on another person's character.

(Summarised from English and Card, 2009: 249)

TEST BOX 31

This is a brief knowledge check to make sure you understand the nature of giving evidence:

1. Name three categories of evidence.
2. What characterises oral evidence?
3. Distinguish between *actus reus* and *mens rea*.
4. What is 'bad character' evidence?

7.7 **Going to Court**

If you are called to appear in court (the technical term is '*summonsed*') to give evidence in a case, you need to be prepared properly and professionally for the experience. That said, following Lord Justice Auld's reforms in 2001 by which many offences were removed from magistrates' courts and punished with a fixed penalty notice (FPN) instead, whereas previously many Special Constables attended court as a matter almost of routine, these days *Special Constables are much less likely to go to court*. However, when they do, the offences will tend to greater seriousness than in the past. The corollary is that, as a Special Constable, you are far more likely to issue a FPN. This has annoyed the magistracy a little, because they see their role being undermined by instant fines on the streets instead of the steady process of law, added to which more than 50 per cent of fines remain unpaid—so defaulters end up in court anyway.

The advent of the 'virtual court' may well make a physical appearance in court a fairly unusual event altogether, but for the rest of this section, we are going to assume that you are a Special Constable who has to appear in a physical court and give evidence, on oath, in the witness box. It does not signify whether your evidence is given at a magistrates' court, a Youth Court, a coroner's court or the Crown Court; the processes are common to all places. Only the trappings and the nature or process of cross-examination (challenges to your evidence) will vary. In a magistrates' court, it might be a District Judge or a defence 'duty' solicitor who asks you to explain some point or to clarify your actions, whilst in a Crown Court this may done by the barrister 'lead' for the defendant's defence team.

7.7.1 **Making an impression**

In these days of relaxed dress codes and relaxed manners, it sometimes causes concern when Special Constables are told to look smart for court. But, if you think about it, courts are formal places with a serious purpose and it is insulting to everyone there if you do not make an effort to look well presented and smart. This has two distinct purposes, to do with making the right impression. First, *it shows respect to the court*. You would not (we presume) turn up to a job interview wearing your gym kit or nightwear, because that is not the place for such clothing. The same applies to appearing in court. You are a Special Constable and should be in uniform and looking the business. This leads to the second point: *you will be judged on your appearance*. However compelling your evidence is, and however clearly recorded and articulated, however modulated your voice and arrestingly brilliant your brain, most people will make judgements about you by looking at you.

7.7.2 **In the building**

When you get to court (and we assume that you will have attended one before to familiarise yourself during your training, if not regularly since) you wait to be called into the courtroom. There might be a considerable wait, the claims for speeded-up criminal justice processes notwithstanding, and you may not speak to other witnesses while you wait your turn. There may be a reserved place for witnesses, or you might have to mill about with everyone else, also waiting to be called. Hanging about for an hour beyond the time given on your formal notice to attend court is about par. *Always be prepared for delay*, postponement or recess because others have not turned up, or because the defence or prosecution wants a delay for some reason. When finally called by name (usually by a court usher, distinguishable in black clothing or black robes), you enter the court and go to the witness box.

7.7.3 **Taking the oath**

The first thing that you will be asked to do is to take the oath or make an affirmation. All this means is that *you promise to tell the truth*. The *oath* is for people who have a religious faith or belief system, and is invariably accompanied by some symbol or expression of that faith or belief. For Muslims, for example, it is the Holy Koran; for Hindus it is the Holy Gita, for Christians it is the Holy Bible (sometimes the New Testament only), whilst for Jews it may be the Scroll or Torah, or the Holy Bible (Old Testament only), and Sikhs swear by the Guru Nanak. Some faiths require a ritual or symbolic purification, such as washing the mouth or the lighting of a candle, whilst others require an image or picture to be present when they take the oath. All non-believers, some Quakers, Buddhists, Jehovah's Witnesses, Mormons and others will make an *affirmation*, the wording for which is '*I do solemnly, sincerely and truly declare and affirm ...*'

All will promise, by whatever they cherish most as their faith or their reason, to *tell the truth, the whole truth and nothing but the truth*. It is a solemn moment in a solemn undertaking, and reminds everyone that evidence is not to be given or taken lightly. The law is very clear: there are heavy penalties for committing perjury (telling lies on oath), as well as showing 'contempt of court' or 'perverting the course of justice'.

7.8 **Giving Evidence**

Now comes the moment when you actually give your evidence. Make sure that you have your PNB and that you ask permission to consult it to refresh your memory for a fact or time.

7.8.1 **Not an expert**

The first thing to establish is that you are not an 'expert witness'. The term is much misused and usually refers to someone with specialist knowledge, like a forensic scientist or a pathologist, who is experienced in giving evidence in court. But defence teams often challenge expert testimony with experts of their own, directly exploiting the propensity of experts to disagree and, in some cases, to be mistaken in their conclusions (such as, famously, those judgements made by Professor Sir Roy Meadow, which led to wrongful imprisonment; see Batt, 2004).

You are a witness like everyone else in the case and you have no special status or privileges, though it is likely that your evidence will be given some weight because you are a police officer. As far as any defence counsel is concerned, this may also mean that you are fair game for a blunt onslaught, where your professionalism can be impugned and your objectivity challenged. That is more likely in a Crown Court as a tactic, but it is not unknown in a magistrates' court, particularly when a defence solicitor wants to attack the prosecution case and cast doubt on police procedures. Some solicitors make a good living from challenging police processes in magistrates' courts, particularly in trials for dangerous or reckless driving, where the letter of the law appears to matter less than the *minutiae* of process.

If there is a defence solicitor present in the magistrates' court, the Special Constable might be questioned about his/her PNB which, of course, forms part of the evidence. The solicitor might ask the officer when the record in the PNB was made. It may have been made at the time (*contemporaneous*) and this will be proven by subsequent entries which post-date the entry on the incident. Alternatively, the PNB could have been written up or additional notes made after the excitement had subsided and the offender was in the cells. The point we should like to make here is that this small delay is perfectly acceptable, but **the PNB really does need to be written up before going off duty**. Any further delay would look slapdash and unprofessional and, if completion had been the following day or the day after, the worth of the evidence itself might be called into question by a defence solicitor.

7.8.2 Giving evidence at Crown Court

We remind you that only about 5 per cent of criminal cases go to the Crown Court, as we have seen previously, but those cases will be the serious ones. The first thing that will happen in a Crown Court is that the charge against the accused will be read out and the accused is asked to plead Guilty or Not Guilty.

If the accused pleads Guilty, the jury will not be required and matters will proceed swiftly to sentencing. The Special Constable's evidence now becomes pivotal to the prosecution case. Rather than make a statement, as in the magistrates' court, the officer's evidence is now brought out by the prosecuting counsel through a series of questions. The same needs exist for accuracy and calm professionalism, and the questioning will seek to make the case against the accused.

> **KEY POINT**
>
> Note that the Special Constable must be careful not to give an opinion, but to present evidence which s/he experienced directly, either by what s/he saw, smelled, heard or felt, or had taken in evidence, and also what, if anything, the accused had said in a post-arrest statement.

The defence rises to cross-examine when the witness has finished giving evidence. Remember what the defence role is: accused people are presumed *innocent until proven guilty*, and the defence team will try to show that its client did not commit the offence with which s/he is charged. Or, if the charge is irrefutable, the attempt will be to mitigate the charge, either by suggesting that the assault was in self-defence or that the accused was in fear of his/her life and that is why s/he lashed out. A secondary tactic would be to try to shake or cast in doubt the reliability of witness testimony. This is done by trying to spot anomalies, inconsistencies or contradictions in the evidence by provoking the witness or by confusing and bewildering the witness. It's important to realise that these are tactics to suggest innocence or mitigation of the accused, just as the prosecution uses tactics to reinforce the accused's guilt. You will often be told that such ploys are business, there's nothing personal in it. Yet that is hard to believe if someone has deliberately suggested that you are hard of hearing, short-sighted, incompetent, not much cop, a control freak, an officious busybody or just someone hiding his/her inadequacy behind a uniform.

Police officers have tactics themselves to deal with this approach to their evidence. Some count silently to three before replying to the question. Some do not respond unless a specific question is asked. Others play each question with a 'dead bat', saying as little as possible. All try to remain calm and refuse to rise to the dangled bait. They try not to lose their tempers or fall into the trap of trying to justify themselves. Be careful though—any attempt by you to score off the defence counsel may harm your professional image, or look like contempt of court—and you might not succeed anyway. We're sorry, but insults are a one-way traffic in a courtroom, and that's towards you, not from you.

The defence will try, if it suits their strategy, to provoke you, make you lose your temper or make you out to be a fool, in order to discredit your evidence or to throw doubt on your actions. But it can have the reverse effect. If the Special Constable stays calm, rational and in control, it is the defence that can look increasingly desperate and devoid of purpose and direction. The jury will be impressed by your evidence, as well as your demeanour, if you deal calmly with histrionic questioning. It is all about impressions: your steady response to hostile questions actually reinforces your credibility as a witness.

Many Special Constables with experience of going to court will describe the tactics used variously to disrupt, dismay or discomfit an officer's testimony. The golden rule is *never to lose your temper*; always to remain calm and controlled, professional and detached, whatever the provocation. After all, it's what you do all the time on the job, isn't it?

TEST BOX 32

Here is the final knowledge check for you to be sure that you have understood what is involved in going to court:

1. Who revised much of the criminal justice system to speed up the process and replace some hearings with fixed penalties?
2. What is 'cross-examination'?
3. What is the alternative to giving evidence on oath?
4. What is the difference in giving police evidence, respectively, at magistrates' courts and Crown Courts?
5. What tactics can defeat questions designed to belittle you or question your evidence?

Further Reading

Auld, Lord Justice, *A Review of the Criminal Courts of England and Wales* (2001, London: TSO)

Batt, J, *Stolen Innocence, A Mother's Fight For Justice, The Authorised Story of Sally Clark* (2004, London: Ebury Press)

Crawford, A and Newburn, T, *Youth Offending and Restorative Justice: Implementing Reform in Youth Justice* (2003, Cullompton: Willan Publishing)

Doak, J and McGourlay, C, *Criminal Evidence in Context* (2009, Abingdon: Routledge-Cavendish)

English, J and Card, R, *Police Law*, 11th edn. (2009, Oxford: Oxford University Press), esp Ch 7, 'The Law of Evidence'

Fitzpatrick, B, Menzies, C and Hunter, R, *Going to Court* (2006, Oxford: Oxford University Press)

Martin, J and Turner, C, *Criminal Law*, 2nd edn. (2004, London: Hodder Arnold)

Starmer, K, *The Public Prosecution Service: Setting the Standard* (2009, London: CPS)

Tapper, C, *Cross and Tapper on Evidence*, 11th edn. (2007, Oxford: Oxford University Press)

Answers to Tests

The following, in numerical order, are our answers to the 'knowledge checks' that we have set you throughout the book.

Test Box 1

1. The partnership between the police and the public (Working Group on the Special Constable, 1995–96).
2. The Special Constable, the employer and the police force.
3. Any four from: Roads/Highways (VOSA and HATO), private and commercial security staff, the Special Constabulary, Community Partners such as PACT or CCTV, PCSOs, regular police officers, Police Staff and PSVs, Neighbourhood Watch, Rural and Parish Wardens, other CSAs and Parking Attendants.
4. Choose any three from: administrative help, mystery shoppers (checking public service from the police and others), puppy walkers, maintaining gardens, staffing satellite front counters, organising public meetings, data input, washing police cars, emergency exercise role players, search and rescue, role-playing for training and assisting at events.
5. All PCSOs in England and Wales have a suite of standard powers, but individual Chief Constables have the discretion to add to these if appropriate.
6. Community Safety Accreditation Scheme: normally applied by Chief Constables to people who assist with community safety.
7. People without police powers acting in a subordinate role to the police could become 'nosy vigilantes'. Training is important, as is educating the public in what CSAS appointees do.
8. A uniformed police inspector.
9. Forty-three, not including CNC, British Transport Police or MOD police.
10. They can be accepted only if they have indefinite leave to enter or remain in the United Kingdom; like every other applicant, they will have to be vetted and any convictions or cautions assessed.

Test Box 2

1. To 'conduct local intelligence-based patrols and…crime prevention initiatives'.
2. Any three from: assist regular officers, help at police major incidents, conduct foot patrols, assist at the scene of accidents, enforce road safety initiatives, conduct house-to-house enquiries, provide security at major events, present evidence in court, tackle anti-social behaviour, tackle alcohol-related incidents, educate young people about crime prevention.

3. The truncheon (the side baton and other variants all appeared more or less at the same time. The generic self-defence weapon for 150 years was the wooden truncheon, itself preceded by the stave.
4. Baseball caps.
5. Airwave.
6. Knife, glass, blade, slash, spike and other 'sharp instrument' attacks.
7. Load vest is adjustable webbing mesh with pockets which is worn over body armour.
8. The duty belt.
9. Personal Protection Equipment.
10. Section 5 of the Firearms Act 1968.

Test Box 3

1. Knowledge, Understanding, Skills, Attitudes, Behaviours.
2. Between 12 and 16 weeks (including one weekday evening and one weekend day).
3. Written material you should study in advance of a training session.
4. Board blast, case studies, demonstration, small-group work, individual study, lectures, electronic ('e') learning, presentations, role-play and practical sessions.
5. This one! The knowledge check.
6. New police officers attend a formal ceremony in which they take the oath of 'the office of constable' in front of a magistrate: it is the 'swearing in' of a 'warranted' police officer.
7. During training, every three months; later it is likely to slip to twice yearly (but it shouldn't).
8. Your Professional Development Profile (which of course you remembered...) shows your supervisor your progress towards Independent Patrol and other learning needs and competences.
9. The Special Constable training sessions run on a weekday evening are a chance for you to catch up with administration, meet fellow officers, learn information from supervisory officers and for them to advise you of changes in process, law or policy, including an intelligence briefing.
10. National Occupational Standards: those for patrol officers indicate basic competencies (including the five personal qualities standards) See 3.3 for more detail on NOS.

Test Box 4

1. Initial Learning for the Special Constabulary.
2. Induction; Legislation, Policies and Guidelines (LPG); and Operational.
3. SI 2008 No 2864.

4. Ethical standards in public life, first articulated by Lord Nolan's Committee in 1995.
5. Nick Hardwick, then Chair of the Independent Police Complaints Commission (IPCC), in 2008.
6. Proportional, Legal, Authorised, Necessary.
7. Not doing what you should in public office.
8. Thinking critically about what you have experienced.
9. Learning is cyclical and endless: what happened? How can I improve? Action next time.
10. Continual evaluation of hazards and risks in a developing critical situation.
11. Cardio-pulmonary resuscitation (restoring heart beat).

Test Box 5

1. Neighbourhood is primarily place; community is a combination of things which people have in common.
2. Work, profession, skills, professional associations, interests, demography, education/learning, faith/belief, identity and ethnicity, shared past experiences, shared internet 'clubs', shared hobbies and recreations, sports, common problems, impairment, politics, clubs and pubs, gender.
3. Reduce crime and anti-social behaviour, make neighbourhoods safer, protect public and raise confidence in the police, improving people's lives so that they are less likely to offend or re-offend.
4. Community Safety Partnership.
5. Police, Police and Crime Commissioner, Local Authority, Fire and Rescue Service and primary health care trust.
6. Partners And Communities Together.
7. Time-consuming to arrange public meetings, not all people like public meetings, apathy, partners in PACT not attending, costs, public zealots who hijack the agenda, low-level offending, how representative are those who attend?
8. Increase risk, increase effort, reduce reward, reduce provocation, remove excuses.
9. 'An attempt to capture the central features of the policed environment to which the law-abiding public responds' (Fielding *et al*, 2002).
10. Litter, dog-fouling, nuisance noise, signs of criminal damage, congregating youths, graffiti, abandoned cars.
11. Expression, content, effect, control signal.
12. Martin Innes when at the University of Surrey with Surrey Police.

Test Box 6

1. They are 'alternative offences'; it's one or the other. The defences are: self-defence, reasonable force and consent.

2. No, it can include psychiatric injury.
3. *It is an offence for any person to assault, resist or wilfully obstruct a police officer, or any person assisting a constable in the lawful execution of his/her duty.* See s 89 of the Police Act 1996.
4. S/he must be 'in the lawful execution of his/her duties and exercising his/her powers with authorisation'. In other words, it is not enough for the officer simply to be 'on duty'.
5. Triable summarily and the penalty would be a fine.
6. Section 38 of the Offences Against the Person Act 1861.
7. The level of injury sustained and the sentence that the court is likely to pass.

Test Box 7

1. Rowdy, unruly, boisterous, loud, raucous or unrestrained conduct.
2. **Abuse** (from which we get *abusive*) is the use of language to insult or degrade someone. **Harassment** is behaviour which makes someone feel annoyed, persecuted, irritated or aggravated. Remember these are precise meanings in law, and you need to know them.
3. Section 3(1).
4. Intent is shown by making someone believe that immediate unlawful violence will be used against him/her, or provoked by the offender's actions, words or behaviour, including the use of written material or signage.
5. There are three defences: that the offender believed that no one could see or hear him/her in public, that inside a dwelling s/he had no reason to believe that anyone could hear or see him/her and that the conduct was reasonable and did not cause anyone to be harassed, alarmed or distressed.

Test Box 8

1. When a person 'dishonestly appropriates property belonging to another with the intention of permanently depriving the other of it' (s 1, Theft Act 1968).
2. (a) Believing a lawful right to take the item, (b) would have had owner's consent if the owner had known and (c) the owner could not be discovered by taking reasonable steps.
3. Money, personal property, real property, legal control by a trustee, things in [an] action, plants or fungi growing wild, wild creatures, tangible property.
4. The offence of robbery.
5. Using a firearm, an offensive weapon or an explosive.
6. See s 12(1) of the Theft Act 1968, a conveyance is something which is constructed or adapted to carry someone whether by land, air or water.
7. A fine.

Test Box 9

1. Destroying or damaging property, threats to cause criminal damage, having articles with intent to destroy or damage property.
2. Having permission, his/her or another's property is in need of protection.
3. Intention to destroy or damage can be communicated in any way, including email, text message, letter, phone call or fax.
4. Triable either way; but if the value of the property damaged or destroyed is less than £5,000, the offence is tried summarily. The penalty is six months' imprisonment and/or a fine not exceeding the statutory maximum if tried summarily, and ten years' imprisonment on indictment.

Test Box 10

1. At night, in clubs and other parts of the night-time economy.
2. A street name for heroin.
3. Stimulation; alertness, sounds and colours are more intense, can feel great love for the people around them, nonsensical chatter, sometimes feelings of anxiety, panic attacks and confusion, physical overheating.
4. Tetrahydrocannabinol, or THC.
5. Small mirrors, razors, straws, small squares of paper or plastic clingfilm.
6. Arrogance, overconfidence, aggression.
7. Space to cope with sudden aggression, access to personal protection equipment, watch out for discarding items or equipment, wear gloves, take care when handling needles or sharps.

Test Box 11

1. Police And Criminal Evidence Act 1984.
2. Gives you the power to stop, search and detain on reasonable grounds.
3. They safeguard the rights of the suspect.
4. No. You must have **reasonable grounds** to stop, search or detain someone. Stereotyping is not part of those grounds.
5. Within a dwelling; PACE is for use in public places; it does not give you powers inside someone's residence.
6. Offensive weapons, bladed or pointed articles, prohibited fireworks, things that might be used for criminal purposes.
7. **G**rounds for suspicion, **O**bject of search, **W**arrant card (yours), **I**dentity (yours), **S**tation (where you are based), **E**ntitlement (of person searched to copy of your search record), **L**egal power, **Y**ou (suspect) are detained so that you can be searched.
8. The person's cooperation, the relevance of the search, only jacket, outer coat or gloves can be removed in public, restrictions of where you can search (hair

but not hats), don't have to be in uniform, detention must be reasonable and kept to a minimum.

9. Make a record of the search, either then or soon afterwards. In normal circumstances you would provide the person searched with a copy of your search record.

Test Box 12

1. Kitchen knife, scissors, a craft knife, a chisel, a pocket-knife, a spear, a dagger, a scalpel or any other article which has been given a cutting edge or blade.
2. Any kind of article with a point, for example a needle, geometry compasses, a bradawl.
3. Lawful authority such as soldiers with bayonets on ceremonial duty, use at work (wood chisels), religious reasons, ceremonial or national costume.
4. Any article made, adapted or intended for causing injury; s 1(4) of the Prevention of Crime Act 1953.
5. It is an offence, when not at one's place of abode to have with him/her any article for use...with any burglary or theft; s 25 of the Theft Act 1968.

Test Box 13

1. Section 12 of the Licensing Act 1872.
2. *Rendered incapable through alcohol*, but courts will decide on the fact. You can give as your opinion in court that someone was drunk.
3. Physical unsteadiness, glazed eyes, slurred speech, smelling of 'intoxicating liquor'.
4. Not defined in law, but it is *unruly or offensive behaviour* exacerbated (made worse) by drink. It is an offence for a drunk person to display 'unruly or offensive behaviour' in any highway, public place or licensed premises.

Test Box 14

1. Spontaneous incidents, pre-planned incidents involving the use or threat of firearms.
2. Normally a (duty 'Gold') chief officer, but 'Gold' can be a chief superintendent in some forces.
3. When someone possesses a firearm, or is so dangerous that armed presence is required, or in an operation responding to a threat assessment (such as criminals suspected of transporting weapons) and to deal with a dangerous animal or to end its suffering.
4. Identify offender, secure the location and precisely locate the incident.
5. '[A] lethal-barrelled weapon...from which any shot, bullet or other missile can be discharged.'

Test Box 15

1. Someone is about to commit or is committing an offence and there are 'reasonable grounds' for believing that an arrest is necessary.
2. Section 24(5) of the PACE Act 1984 and Code G, para 2.9.
3. '*[A] conclusion that one or more people reach in agreement as a result of personal experience or understanding*', though you should note that in normal circumstances, it is for a court to decide if an action was, or was not, reasonable.
4. No; whatever their rank or position. Responsibility for arrest lies solely with the arresting officer: note the case law attending this.
5. Prevent a crime being committed, to prevent injury to self or another, to avoid physical injury, to prevent loss of or damage to property, to prevent an offence against public decency and to prevent unlawful obstruction of the highway, to protect a child or other vulnerable person, to allow the prompt investigation of an offence and to stop the person disappearing.
6. Section 3(1) of the Criminal Law Act 1967 and s 117 of the PACE Act 1984.
7. Caution the person arrested, and record in your PNB the circumstances, the reasons for arrest, that you gave the caution and anything said by the person at the time of the arrest.
8. Section 32(1) of the PACE Act 1984.
9. Because PACE Code C, para 11.1A says that any questioning of a suspect constitutes an interview, and interviews should be carried out in a suitable place (not the back of a police car); though if a suspect makes a voluntary comment or statement you should record it in your PNB.
10. Code C, para 2.1A.
11. If it is necessary to remove an article which the detainee would not be allowed to keep.
12. It must be carried out by an officer of the same sex in an area away from other people, in a safe place with at least two other persons present and 'with regard to sensitivity' (PACE Act 1984, Code C, Annex A10).
13. To have someone informed, to consult a solicitor in private and to consult the PACE Act 1984 Codes of Conduct.

Test Box 16

1. Start and finish of each duty; contemporaneous account of incidents and events, shows when you consulted another officer, may help your recall in court, should be written in clear, non-exclusionary language.
2. Carry it at all times on duty, record evidence, get new PNBs from your supervisor, PNB often has useful information, refer to it in court, it is police property, use for diagrams as well as text, use only the PNB not scraps of paper and don't lose it.
3. NO ELBOWS(S) - look it up in 4.14.3.

Test Box 17

1. Computer Misuse Act 1990.
2. Fairly and lawfully, for a lawful purpose, adequate and relevant to purpose and kept no longer than necessary.
3. Information about people, vehicles and property.
4. Name, Age, Sex, Colour and Height.
5. Alpha Mike Echo X-ray.
6. An arrest warrant and a warrant of commitment.
7. Sections 163 and 4 of the Road Traffic Act 1988.
8. Anyone you are pursuing or anyone liable to be detained, or a child absent from care.
9. • Without seeking the permission of the occupant (otherwise this might be self-defeating)
   • to save someone from him/herself as well as from a third party
   • without having to give an occupant a reason for using the power of entry if it is impossible, impracticable or undesirable to do so
   • only to the extent that was reasonably required to satisfy the objective for using the power of entry.

Test Box 18

1. By summons, by warrant, by arrest without a warrant.
2. Details, date, time, location of the offence; full name, date of birth and address (including postcode) of suspect, driving licence number and national insurance number.
3. Cautions given and compliance with PACE, any direct questions and replies following the caution, visual evidence, explaining the offence to the suspect and saying that you are reporting for the offence, giving a 'now' caution and inviting endorsement of the PNB account.

Test Box 19

1. The form, number 11 in the Manual of Guidance, used to make a statement by a member of a police force.
2. Always give the number of pages, sign and date the declaration; keep a copy.
3. Time, day, date, location, SC status, any others present.
4. What the person actually said (verbatim).
5. What you saw, smelled, touched, tasted or heard; the evidence of your senses.
6. Striking through with one line.
7. Because there could be consequences for you if these personal details are disclosed to the accused or publicly.

Test Box 20

1. It is neither a criminal offence nor part of statute law: it is common law.
2. *'A breach of the peace is committed whenever harm is done, or is likely to be done to a person, or, in his presence to his property, or, whenever a person is in fear of being harmed through an assault, affray, riot or other disturbance.'* Remember that a key ingredient is ***harm***.
3. Any of **Pursue, Prevent, Protect, Prepare**.
4. Any of **Low, Moderate, Substantial, Severe, Critical** (in ascending order).
5. Where and when property was found, detailed description of the property, details of the finder, location of property if retained by the finder (except drugs, which must always be seized).
6. Freedom of judgement and action, authority to decide and choose, selecting the best course of action, having considered all the facts and all the alternatives available.
7. PACE Act 1984, Code C, para 10.
8. Not under arrest, free to leave.
9. Anything which could be used in evidence against the suspect, such as admission of guilt; anything relating to the offence itself, such as identifying those involved.

Test Box 21

1. Victims, witnesses and suspects, for low-level offences.
2. They must be carried out under caution and in accordance with the PACE Act 1984, Code C (including para 10.1).
3. What you do might affect positively or adversely what follows; this equates with your actions as 'first officer attending' an incident. Your calm, authoritative approach and competence in execution of your duties can mean the difference between a successful prosecution and a failure in court.
4. That officers, as well as they can, should test what they are told against what they know.
5. Professionalising the Investigative Process.
6. 'Who, what, where, when, why and how' questions which are not suited to simple 'yes' or 'no' replies.
7. When you suggest the answer in the question, such as 'you think that Barry McCormack did this, don't you?' Leading a witness, victim or a suspect is not good practice.

Test Box 22

1. If you have reason to believe the driver is under the influence of drink or drugs, if there has been a 'moving offence' or if the vehicle is involved in an accident.

2. Sections 4 and 5 of the Road Traffic Act 1988.

3. Is the person the most recent driver? How long ago did this person drive? Where was s/he is relation to the vehicle? Does s/he have the car keys? The purpose of the questions is to establish who may have committed the offence: it can be more than one person.

4. The evidential test is blood, breath or urine; taken by a qualified medical practitioner at a police station.

5. Breath = 35 micrograms per 100 millilitres of alcohol; blood = 80 milligrams per 100 millilitres; urine = 107 milligrams per 100 millilitres.

6. They add up to 8.

7. 'Roadside tests' under ss 6A 6B and 6C of the Road Traffic Act 1988; they are only for drivers of vehicles.

8. Breath, impairment and drugs tests.

9. 'I suspect that you are driving a motor vehicle on a road under the influence of alcohol. I require you to provide a specimen of breath for a breath test here. Failure to do so may make you liable to arrest and prosecution.'

10. You don't; a qualified medical practitioner takes a blood sample.

Test Box 23

1. '[A]n unintended occurrence which has an adverse physical result'; but we now call them road traffic 'collisions', remember?

2. Location, vehicle, damage and injury.

3. Horse, cattle, ass, mule, pig, sheep, goat, or dog.

4. His/her name and address, the vehicle owner's name and address if different, and identifying particulars of the vehicle, such as the registration number.

5. Section 170(4) of the Road Traffic Act 1988.

Test Box 24

1. The first is a non-endorsable, the second is an endorsable, fixed penalty notice.

2. Stop the driver of a mechanically powered vehicle or person on a pedal cycle; failure to stop is an offence.

3. 17 years; the category F vehicles are tractors and the like.

4. The type of licence held—provisional or full; name and address of the holder, date of birth of the holder, date of issue and expiry, a driver number, photograph of the licence holder and his/her facsimile signature, together with a list of categories of vehicle the holder can drive and any endorsements.

5. Third party insurance.

6. Taxis, ambulances and passenger vehicles with more than eight seats.

7. Vehicle Defect Rectification Scheme.

8. A 'bald' tyre is when part of the original tread has been worn below the minimum tread depth for the vehicle class.

9. Direction and hazard warning lights.
10. When you cannot see for more than 100 metres or 328 feet.

Test Box 25

1. Section 28 of the Crime and Disorder Act 1998; aggravated means 'made more serious'.
2. Assaults, criminal damage, public order offences and harassment.
3. Demonstration of hostility is based on the victim's membership or presumed membership of a racial or religious group.
4. Six months' imprisonment and/or a fine.
5. Fear or provocation of violence, intentional harassment, alarm or distress, causing the same; s 31(1)(a), (b) and (c).

Test Box 26

1. It is when evidence is at its freshest and (probably) most plentiful. It is also when recollections (victims, witnesses) are sharpest—but not necessarily most detailed—and it is when suspects are least prepared with excuses or explanations. Preserving the scene is vital to allow recovery of evidence.
2. Because from the suspect, evidence may be retrieved that indicates or proves presence at a crime, such as DNA, fingerprints, traces, body fluids, fibres and footprints.
3. Preserve evidence and avoid contamination.
4. May include unauthorised entry, physical assault, searches, vandalism, seizure of a weapon, a struggle or fight, anything taken away and anything left behind.
5. May include crime as part of a series, in a hot spot, a weapon has been used, a weapon used but not recovered, the victim or suspect was in a position of trust, the offence was sexually motivated, it may have been hate crime, the victim was more badly hurt than was first thought (internal injury), the suspect is a known serious offender, the victim was a child or a vulnerable adult.
6. Your first and absolute duty is to preserve life, and this overrides everything else.
7. Prevent further crimes if you can, avoid contamination, ascertain the offender's route in and out of the crime scene, secure a CAP, cordon the outer area, think about any aggravating factors, assume that it is a crime scene until it can be proven that it is not, retain witnesses and record details in your PNB, inform Control, assume that you are in charge until told you are not.
8. Avoiding contamination of the crime scene, not duplicating the offender's route in and out, avoid obstacles, don't close doors or windows unless you must, think about one way in and one way out if practical.

Test Box 27

1. 2002, in *Under the Microscope Revisited*.
2. Deoxyribonucleic acid.
3. Hair, blood, semen, saliva and urine.
4. Short Tandem Repeat profiling, or STRs.
5. When the amount of DNA present is very small—but there is always a danger of contamination at the microscopic level.
6. From their mothers, it is inherited only from the maternal line.
7. It can eliminate a suspect and, because it is resistant to ageing, it can be recovered from 'cold' cases.
8. Using a 'buccal scrape sample' or 'mouth swab' painlessly to obtain cells from inside a suspect's mouth.
9. Tiny friction ridges on palm, fingers and toes.
10. Latent, visible and plastic.
11. It can reveal bruising which is no longer visible in ordinary light; this is particularly useful in detecting long-term abuse.
12. In the event of match between suspect and print at a crime scene, it proves presence, which a suspect will have to explain.

Test Box 28

1. The location itself, a body or part of a body, anywhere the body has rested, or been moved, a physical trace, a victim whose body may have evidence (bruising, cuts), an attack site, any witnesses, means of transporting a body or materials, clothing of victim or offender, material used to wrap or secure the victim/body, routes in and out, premises, articles brought in or used.
2. A sequence ensuring 'the integrity of physical evidence recovered from a crime scene'.
3. No one should enter unless properly clothed, people present should be the fewest possible.
4. A Police Elimination Database, so that front-line officers could be eliminated from any crime scene and thus reduce potential contamination or confusion.
5. At the time of the First World War (1914–18) in Lyon, France.
6. 'Criminalistics'.
7. Pressure during contact, number of contacts, how easily the item transfers, the form or nature of the evidence and how much of the item is involved.

Test Box 29

1. Because the police, through arrest and charge of offenders, initiate the criminal justice process.

2. Not Guilty; at Crown Court.
3. Community service, supervision order, curfew, fine or imprisonment—depending on the seriousness of the crime. Another outcome could be a finding of not guilty, or, in a magistrates' court, summary outcomes such as cautions or being 'bound over to keep the peace'.
4. Unpaid magistrates or JPs in a magistrate's court.
5. A District Judge—always a paid professional lawyer.
6. 'Unnatural' or violent deaths are subject to an 'inquest' (enquiry) under a coroner (doctor or lawyer).
7. 'Ordinary' judges (not experienced 'circuit' judges).
8. Criminal cases only, presided over by circuit judges or Recorders.
9. July 2009, replacing the Law Lords.
10. The Magistrates' Courts Act 1980.
11. The Clerk to the Justices, a professional lawyer.
12. 'Summary' offences and those at the lower end of 'either way'. A magistrates' court hears and passes sentence on offences that would carry a six months' prison sentence as the maximum penalty. Magistrates and District Judges also refer cases on indictment, to the Crown Court.

Test Box 30

1. Hears the evidence for and against the accused, rules on admissibility of evidence, keeps order in the courtroom, summarises evidence for the jury and passes sentence on findings of guilt.
2. The Director of Public Prosecutions.
3. Realistic prospect of conviction, public interest in the case.
4. 'Guilt beyond all reasonable doubt'.
5. The 'adversarial system'—as opposed to the system elsewhere in Europe, where questioning of suspects and witnesses is led by a judge, called the 'inquisitorial' system.
6. Pro bono publico; for the public good. Very occasionally, prominent lawyers will do this to enhance their public profiles.
7. Only the courts. The role of the police is to ascertain the truth of what happened.

Test Box 31

1. Direct, circumstantial, oral, documentary and 'real' evidence ('first hand' or 'hearsay').
2. What the witness 'touched, saw, smelled, heard or tasted': the evidence of the senses.
3. *Actus reus* is the 'guilty act', while *mens rea* is the 'guilty mind' in any criminal event.

4. That the accused has failings which are relevant to the current criminal charge, such as a previous history of violence. The tests for admitting 'bad character' evidence are stringent.

Test Box 32

1. Lord Justice Auld in 2001.
2. Challenge to or questioning of evidence or testimony by a witness or suspect.
3. Making an affirmation.
4. In a magistrates' court a police officer may make a statement; in a Crown Court, police evidence is given through questions and answers.
5. Remaining calm and steady, answering courteously but firmly, sticking to the facts and not giving opinions, refusing to justify actions, counting to three or playing the questions with a 'dead bat' without being provoked to anger.

Further Reading

[NB: Place of publication is London, unless otherwise indicated. The date of a publication followed by 'a' or 'b' denotes that the author or originator of the publication produced two or more publications in the same year.]

ACPO, *Citizen Focus Hallmarks Summary* (2008, NPIA) available at <http://cfnp.npia. police.uk/files/cf_hallmarks_summary.pdf>; accessed 14 November 2012

——/NPIA, *Practice Advice on Professionalising the Business of Neighbourhood Policing* (2006, Wyboston: National Centre for Policing Excellence, part of NPIA), available at <http://cfnp.npia.police.uk/files/np_neighbourhoodpolicin.pdf>; accessed 14 November 2012

——,——, *Police Health and Safety: A Management Benchmarking Standard* (2007, Association of Chief Police Officers)

Alderson, J, *Policing Freedom* (1979, Plymouth: McDonald and Evans)

——, *Law and Order* (1984, Hamish Hamilton)

——and Stead, P (eds.), *The Police We Deserve* (1973, Wolfe Publishing)

Alexander, J, *Investigation into Premature Wastage of Special Constables* (2000, Home Office Police and Reducing Crime Unit)

Almandras, S, 'Special Constables', Standard Note SNHA/1154 (31 October 2008, House of Commons Library)

Anon, 'Making Specials Count', *Police Professional*, No 102, 13 March, pp 18–21

Audit Commission, *Hearts and Minds: Commissioning from the Voluntary Sector* (2007, Audit Commission)

Baggott, M and Wallace, M, *Neighbourhood Policing Progress Report* (May 2006, Home Office)

Barclay, D, 'Using Forensic Science in Major Crime Inquiries' in Fraser, J and Williams, R (eds.), *Handbook of Forensic Science* (2009, Cullompton: Willan Publishing), Ch 13

Barron, T, *The Special Constable's Manual* (1994, Police Review Publishing); a 1999 reprint may be more available: (1999, York: New Police Bookshop)

Beaufort-Moore, D, *Crime Scene Management,* Blackstone's Practical Policing (2009, Oxford: Oxford University Press)

Blackledge, R (ed.), *Forensic Analysis on the Cutting Edge: New Methods for Trace Evidence Analysis* (2007, Hoboken, NJ: John Wiley & Sons)

Bland, N and Read, T, 'Policing Anti-Social Behaviour', Police Research Series Paper 123 (2003, Home Office)

Brand, S and Price, R, *The Economic and Social Costs of Crime*, Home Office Research Study 217 (2005, Home Office)

Brogden, M and Nijhar, P, *Community Policing: National and International Models and Approaches* (2005, Cullompton: Willan Publishing)

Caless, B, 'Numties in Yellow Jackets' (2007) 1(2) *Policing: A Journal of Policy and Practice* 187–95

——(ed.), with Bryant, R, Spruce, B and Underwood, R, *Blackstone's Police Community Support Officer's Handbook*, 2nd edn. (2010, Oxford: Oxford University Press)

Calligan, S, *Taking Statements*, 6th edn. (2007, Goole: The New Police Bookshop)

Casey, L, 'Engaging Communities in Fighting Crime', *Cabinet Office Crime and Communities Review* (2008), available at <http://webarchive.nationalarchives.gov.uk/+/http://www.cabinetoffice.gov.uk/newsroom/news_releases/2008/080618_fighting_crime.aspx>; accessed 19 November 2012

Clarke, C, 'Hot Products: Understanding, Anticipating and Reducing Demand for Stolen Goods', Police Research Series Paper 112 (1999, Home Office)

Cohen, L and Felson, M (1979), 'Social Change and Crime Rate Trends: A Routine Activity Approach', reprinted in Part XI, 'Environmental Criminology' in Cullen, F and Agnew, R (eds.), *Criminological Theory: Past to Present, Essential Readings* (2007, Oxford: Oxford University Press)

Coleman, D, *DNA Best Practice Manual* (2003, ACPO)

Crawford, A and Lister, S, *Extended Police Family: Visible Patrols in Residential Areas* (2004, York: Joseph Rowntree Foundation)

Crowe, T, *Crime Prevention Through Environmental Design*, 2nd edn. (2000, Elsevier Butterworth-Heinemann)

Crown Prosecution Service, *Prosecution Team Manual of Guidance*, 2004 edn., available at <http://www.cps.gov.uk/legal/d_to_g/disclosure_manual/index.html>; accessed 29 November 2012

Davis Smith, J and Rankin, M, *Attracting Employer Support for the Special Constabulary*, Home Office Policing and Reducing Crime Unit Occasional Paper (1999, Home Office)

Dean, J, 'Role of Special Constables: A Case Study' (1997) 70(1) *Police Journal*, January, 45–8

Edwards, C, *Changing Police Theories for 21st Century Societies* (2005, Leichhardt, New South Wales: The Federation Press), particularly Ch 14 'Control of Policing', and the sections 'Police and Privatisation', pp 311–13, and 'Private Security as Private Police', pp 314–16

Elliot, C and Quinn, F, *English Legal System*, 7th edn. (2006, Harlow: Pearson Longman), especially Ch 20 'Sentencing'

Emsley, C, *The English Police: A Political and Social History*, 2nd edn. (1996, Longman)

English, J and Card, R, *Police Law*, 11th edn. (2009, Oxford: Oxford University Press), especially Ch 7 'The Law of Evidence'

Fahy, P *et al* (Strategy Working Group members), *National Strategy for the Special Constabulary* (2007, Working Group on Strategy, NPIA Conference, 3 December)

Felson, M and Clarke, R, 'Opportunity Makes the Thief: Practical Theory for Crime Prevention', Police Research Series Paper 98 (1998, Home Office)

Fielding, N, *Community Policing* (1995, reprinted 2002, Oxford: Clarendon Press)

——, 'Getting the Best out of Community Policing', The Police Foundation, Paper 3 (May 2009)

——, Innes, M and Fielding, J, *Reassurance Policing & the Visual Environmental Audit in Surrey Police: A Report* (2002, Guildford: University of Surrey)

Fitzpatrick, B, Menzies, C and Hunter, R, *Going to Court*, Blackstone's Practical Policing (2006, Oxford: Oxford University Press)

Flanagan, Sir R, *Modernising the Police Service: A Thematic Inspection of Workforce Modernisation: The Role, Management and Deployment of Police Staff in the Police Service of*

England and Wales (2004, Her Majesty's Inspectorate of Constabulary (HMIC), Home Office)

Forrest, S, Myhill, A and Tilley, N, 'Practical Lessons for Involving the Community in Crime and Disorder Problem-Solving', Home Office Development and Practice Report 43 (2005, Home Office)

Fraser, J and Williams, R (eds.), *Handbook of Forensic Science* (2009, Cullompton: Willan Publishing)

Gaston, K and Alexander, J, 'Effective Organisation and Management of Public Sector Volunteer Workers: Police Special Constables' (2001) 14(1) *The International Journal of Public Sector Management* 59–74

Gibson, B, *The Magistrates' Court* (2009, Waterside Press)

——and Cavadino, P, *The Criminal Justice System; An Introduction* (2008, Waterside Press)

Gilbertson, D, 'Plastic Policemen: Introduction of Community Support Officers', *Police Review*, 21 February 2003, pp 28–9

Gill, M and Mawby, RI, *A Special Constable: A Study of the Police Reserve* (1990, Aldershot: Avebury/Gower)

Hadfield, P, *Bar Wars: Contesting the Night in Contemporary British Cities* (2006, Oxford: Oxford University Press)

Hansard, ACPO (Crime Committee), *Written Evidence to the House of Lords Select Committee on Science and Technology* (2000) available at <http://www.publications. parliament.uk/pa/ld199900/ldselect/ldsctech/115/115we05.htm>; accessed 1 March 2010

Harfield, C (ed.), *Blackstone's Police Operational Handbook: Practice and Procedure,* (2009, Oxford: Oxford University Press)

HMIC, *Under the Microscope Refocused: A Revisit to the Thematic Inspection Report on Scientific and Technical Support* (2002, Home Office)

——, *Serving Neighbourhoods & Individuals: A Thematic Report on Neighbourhood Policing and Developing Citizen Focus Policing* (2008), available at <http://www.hmic.gov.uk/ SiteCollectionDocuments/Thematics/THM_20081101.pdf>; accessed 12 November 2009

Home Office, Circular 60/1990 (revised 19/2000)

——, *Report of the Working Group on the Special Constabulary in England and Wales, 1995–1996* (1997, Home Office Communications Directorate)

——, White Paper, *Building Communities, Beating Crime* (2004), available at <http:// webarchive.nationalarchives.gov.uk/20080603033722/police.homeoffice.gov.uk/ publications/police-reform/wp04_complete.pdf>; accessed 19 November 2012

——, *Community Policing: The Neighbourhood Policing Programme* (2005)

——, *Citizen Focus: Good Practice Guide* (2006a)

——, *British Crime Survey: Measuring Crime for 25 Years* (2006b), report available at <http://www.homeoffice.gov.uk/rds/pdfs07/bcs25.pdf>; accessed 11 October 2009

——, *Citizen Focus: A Practical Guide to Improving Police Follow-Up with Victims and Witnesses* (2007), available at <http://cfnp.npia.police.uk/files/cf_victimsandwitnesses. pdf>; accessed 19 November 2012

——Green Paper, *From the Neighbourhood to the National: Policing our Communities Together*, Cm 7448 (2008, TSO), available at <http://www.official-documents.gov. uk/document/cm74/7448/7448.pdf>; accessed 19 November 2012

Houck, M, *Mute Witness: Trace Evidence Analysis* (2001, Academic Press)

——, 'Trace Evidence' in Fraser, J and Williams, R (eds.), *Handbook of Forensic Science* (2009, Cullompton: Willan Publishing), Ch 7, pp 166–95

——and Maxfield, M, *Surveying Crime in the Twenty-First Century* (2007, Cullompton: Willan Publishing)

Innes, M, Fielding, N and Langan, S, *Signal Crimes and Control Signs: Towards an Evidence-Based Conceptual Framework for Reassurance Policing, A report for Surrey Police* (2002, Guildford: University of Surrey)

Kolb, D, *Experiential Learning: Experience as a Source of Learning and Development* (1984, Englewood Cliffs, NJ: Prentice Hall)

Mulchandani, R and Sigurdsson, J, 'Police Service Strength: England and Wales', Home Office Statistical Bulletin 13/09 (2009, Home Office)

Newburn, T, Williamson, T and Wright, A, *A Handbook of Criminal Investigation* (2007, Cullompton: Willan Publishing)

Nolan, Lord, *First Report of the Committee on Standards in Public Life*, Cm 2850-I (1995, TSO)

O'Connor, D, *Closing the Gap: A Review of the Fitness for Purpose of the Current Structure of Policing in England and Wales*, HM Inspectorate of Constabulary (September 2005, Home Office)

Phillips, Sir D, Caless, B and Bryant, R, 'Intelligence and its Application to Contemporary Policing' (2007) 1(4) *Policing: A Journal of Policy and Practice* 438–46

Police (Conduct) Regulations, Statutory Instrument 2008 No 2864, available at <http://www.legislation.gov.uk/uksi/2008/2864/contents/made>; accessed 19 November 2012

Reiner, R, *The Blue-Coated Worker* (1978, Cambridge: Cambridge University Press)

——, *The Politics of the Police* (1985, Brighton: Wheatsheaf Press), and 3rd edn. (2000, Oxford: Oxford University Press)

——, *Chief Constables, Bosses, Bobbies or Bureaucrats?* (1991, Oxford: Oxford University Press)

Seth, R, *The Specials* (1961, Victor Gollancz)

Skills for Justice, *A Guide to the Development of Education and Training Using the National Occupational Standards* (2006, Sheffield: Skills for Justice)

Smith, J and Rankin, M, 'Attracting Employer Support for the Special Constabulary', Home Office Police and Reducing Crime Unit Report No 141 (1999, Home Office), available at <http://www.homeoffice.gov.uk/rds/pdfs2/ah141.pdf>; accessed 1 December 2008

Starmer, K, *The Public Prosecution Service: Setting the Standard* (2009, CPS)

Thames Valley Police, 'Katesgrove Environmental Visual Audit' (2009), available at <http://www.thamesvalley.police.uk/yournh-tvp-pol-area-read-newsitem?id=90173>; accessed 9 November 2009

White, P (ed.), *Crime Scene to Court: The Essentials of Forensic Science* (2004, Cambridge: Royal Society of Chemistry)

Williams, A, 'Special Volunteers: Perceptions of an Area Special Constabulary', unpublished MSc thesis, 1999, University of Middlesex (Bramshill ref: 3FW WIL O/S, C14675)

Wilson, A, 'Is Business Missing a Trick in its Support for the Voluntary Sector?', Leadership development across the sectors (2009, Corporate Citizenship), available at <http://www.corporate-citizenship.com/>; accessed 28 May 2009

Wilson, D, Ashton, J and Sharp, D, *What Everyone in Britain Should Know About the Police* (2001, Oxford: Blackstone Press)

Wright, A, *Policing: An Introduction to Concepts and Practice* (2002, Cullompton: Willan Publishing)

Index